Volumes of A HISTORY OF PHILOSOPHY now available in Image Books:

A History of Philosophy

VOLUME VII

Modern Philosophy

PART II

Schopenhauer to Nietzsche

by Frederick Copleston, S. J.

IMAGE BOOKS
A Division of Doubleday & Company, Inc.
Garden City, New York

Image Books Edition
by special arrangement with The Newman Press
Image Books Edition published September 1965

DE LICENTIA SUPERIORUM ORDINIS:
John Coventry, S.J., *Praep. Prov. Angliae*

NIHIL OBSTAT:
T. Gornall, S.J., *Censor Deputatus*

IMPRIMATUR:
✠ Franciscus, *Archiepiscopus Birmingamiensis*

Birmingamiae, die 26a Junii 1962

CONTENTS

tology; N. Hartmann – The metaphysics of Being;
Heidegger, the Thomists – Concluding reflections.

THE REACTION AGAINST METAPHYSICAL IDEALISM

Chapter Twelve

EARLIER OPPONENTS AND CRITICS

Fries and his disciples – The realism of Herbart – Beneke and psychology as the fundamental science – The logic of Bolzano – Weisse and I. H. Fichte as critics of Hegel.

1. The development of idealism at the hands of Fichte, Schelling and Hegel was regarded as a great mistake by Jakob Friedrich Fries (1773–1843). In his view the proper and profitable task for philosophy was to carry on the work of Kant without turning the Kantian philosophy into a system of metaphysics. True, Fries himself made use of the word 'metaphysics', and in 1824 he published a *System of Metaphysics (System der Metaphysik)*. But this word meant for him a critique of human knowledge, not a science of the Absolute. To this extent, therefore, he walked in the footsteps of Kant. Yet at the same time he turned Kant's transcendental critique of knowledge into a psychological investigation, a process of psychological self-observation. Although, therefore, Fries starts with Kant and tries to correct and develop his position, the fact that this correction takes the form of psychologizing the Kantian critique results in a certain measure of affinity with the attitude of Locke. For according to Fries we must investigate the nature and laws and scope of knowledge before we can tackle problems about the object of knowledge. And the method of pursuing this investigation is empirical observation.

Fries did not by any means confine his activities to the theory of knowledge. In 1803 he published a *Philosophical Theory of Right (Philosophische Rechtslehre)* and in 1818 an *Ethics (Ethik)*. His political ideas were liberal, and in 1819 he was deprived of his chair at Jena. Some years later, however, he was nominated to a chair of mathematics and physics in the same university. He had already published some works on natural philosophy and physics, and he tried to unite the mathematical physics of Newton with the Kantian philosophy as he interpreted it.

In 1832 Fries published a *Handbook of the Philosophy of Religion and of Philosophical Aesthetics* (*Handbuch der Religionsphilosophie und der philosophischen Aesthetik*). As a boy he had been educated in the traditions of pietism, and he maintained to the end an insistence on religious feeling and interior piety. On the one hand we have mathematical and scientific knowledge; on the other hand we have the presage of religious and aesthetic feeling, its witness to the Being which lies behind the sphere of phenomena. Practical or moral faith relates us to noumenal reality, but religious and aesthetic feeling gives us a further assurance that the reality behind phenomena is that which moral faith conceives it to be. Fries thus added to Kant's doctrine of practical faith an insistence on the value of religious emotion.

Fries was not without influence. Prominent among his disciples was E. F. Apelt (1812–59), who defended his master's psychological interpretation of Kant and insisted on the need for a close union between philosophy and science.[1] And it is worth mentioning that the celebrated philosopher of religion Rudolf Otto (1869–1937) was influenced by Fries's insistence on the fundamental importance of feeling in religion, though it would be quite incorrect to call Otto a disciple of Fries.

In the early part of the present century the so-called Neo-Friesian School was founded by Leonard Nelson (1882–1927).

2. Among the contemporary opponents of post-Kantian idealism the name of Fries is much less widely known than that of Johann Friedrich Herbart (1776–1841). In 1809 Herbart was nominated to the chair at Königsberg which had once been held by Kant, and he occupied it until 1833 when he went to Göttingen. While in Switzerland (1797–1800) he had known Pestalozzi, and he took a great interest in and wrote on educational subjects. Among his main philosophical works are his *Introduction to Philosophy* (*Einleitung in die Philosophie*, 1813), *Psychology as a Science* (*Psychologie als Wissenschaft*, 1824–5) and *General Metaphysics* (*Allgemeine Metaphysik*, 1828–9).

Herbart once remarked that he was a Kantian of the year 1828. He meant, of course, that though he paid tribute to the work of the great thinker whose chair he then occupied, a good deal of water had flowed under the bridge in the meantime, and that he did not simply accept the Kantian system as it came from the hands of the master. Indeed, Herbart cannot be called a Kantian in any ordinary sense. To be sure, he rejected post-Kantian idealism. But to regard post-Kantian idealism as a perversion of the thought of Kant is not necessarily the same as to be a Kantian. And in some respects Herbart's affinities are with the pre-Kantian philosophers rather than with Kant himself.

When considered under one aspect at least, Herbart's account of philosophy has an extremely modern flavour. For he describes philosophy as the elaboration (*Bearbeitung*) of concepts. An obvious objection to this description is that no indication is given of the peculiar subject-matter of philosophy. Any science might be described in this way. But it is Herbart's contention that philosophy does not possess a peculiar subject-matter of its own alongside the subject-matters of the various particular sciences. Or, more accurately, we cannot say from the start that philosophy has a particular field of reality as its peculiar subject-matter. We must first describe it as the activity of elaborating and clarifying concepts.

It is in the course of this activity that the different branches of philosophy arise. For example, if we concern ourselves with working out the theory of distinct concepts and their combination and the principles of the clarification of concepts, we are engaged in logic. If, however, we apply logical principles to the clarification of concepts furnished by experience, we are engaged in metaphysics.

In Herbart's opinion this work of clarification is essential. For when the fundamental concepts derived from experience are submitted to logical analysis, they show themselves to be riddled with contradictions. Take, for example, the concept of a thing. If it can properly be called a thing, it must be one, a unity. But if we try to describe it, it is resolved into a plurality of qualities. It is one and many, one and not-one, at the same time. We are thus faced with a contradiction, and we cannot rest content with it. It is not, however, a question of simply rejecting the concept derived from experience. For if we sever the link between thought and experience, we cut ourselves off from reality. What is required is a clarification and elaboration of the concept in such a way that the contradiction disappears.

Herbart assumes, therefore, that the principle of non-contradiction is fundamental. He will have nothing to do with the dialectical logic of Hegel which in his opinion blurs this principle. Reality must be without contradiction. That is to say, it must be of such a kind that a true world-view or account of the world would be a harmonious system of mutually consistent and intrinsically non-contradictory concepts. Raw experience, so to speak, does not present us with such a world-view. It belongs to philosophy to construct it by clarifying, modifying and rendering consistent the concepts derived from experience and used in the sciences.

A better way of expressing Herbart's point of view would be to say that reality is of such a kind that a complete account of it would take the form of a comprehensive system of mutually consistent non-contradictory propositions. It is indeed arguable that Hegel himself had a similar ideal of truth, and that he should not be interpreted as having denied the principle of non-contradiction. After all, Herbart too allows contradictions to emerge from our ordinary ways of regarding things and then tries to resolve them. But Hegel speaks as though contradictions were a feature of the process of reality itself, of the life of the Absolute, whereas for Herbart contradictions emerge only from our inadequate ways of conceiving reality: they are not a feature of reality itself. Hence Herbart's view bears more resemblance to that of F. H. Bradley than it does to that of Hegel. And in point of fact Bradley was considerably influenced by Herbart.[2]

Now, let us assume that our ordinary view of things contains or gives rise to contradictions. We regard a rose as one thing and a lump of sugar as another thing. Each seems to be a unity. But when we try to describe them, each dissolves into a plurality of qualities. The rose is red, fragrant and soft; the sugar is white, sweet and hard. In each case we attribute the qualities to a uniting substance or thing. But what is it? If we try to say anything about it, the unity dissolves once more into a plurality. Or, if we say that it underlies the qualities, it seems to be a different thing. We can no longer say that the rose *is* red, fragrant and soft.

According to Herbart, the solution of this problem lies in postulating a plurality of simple and unchangeable entities or substances which he calls 'reals' (*Realen*). They enter into different relations with one another, and phenomenal qualities and changes correspond to these relations. For instance, the lump of sugar, which appears to us as a unit, is composed of a plurality of unextended and changeless entities. And the various phenomenal qualities of the sugar correspond to the relations in which these entities stand to one another, while the phenomenal changes in the sugar correspond to the changing relations between the entities. We are thus able to harmonize unity and multiplicity, constancy and change.

After having proposed, therefore, a view of philosophy which has been recently fashionable in this country, namely that philosophy consists in the clarification of concepts or in conceptual analysis, Herbart goes on to raise a problem to which Bradley subsequently gave a good deal of attention in *Appearance and Reality*. But whereas Bradley, in accordance with the spirit of post-Kantian idealism, finds the solution in terms of a One which 'appears' as a multiplicity of things, Herbart has recourse to a pluralistic metaphysics which calls to mind the atoms of Democritus and the monads of Leibniz. His 'reals' are indeed different from Democritus's atoms in that they are said to possess qualities, though these, being metaphenomenal, are unknowable. Further, though each 'real' is simply and essentially unchanging, they do not seem to be, like Leibniz's monads, 'windowless'. For each 'real' is said to preserve its self-identity in the face of disturbances (*Störungen*) from other such entities, so that there appears to be some reciprocal influence. At the same time Herbart's theory obviously has affinity with pre-Kantian metaphysics.

The theory of disturbances, each of which calls forth a self-preservative reaction on the part of the disturbed entity, gives rise to some difficulty. For it is not easy to reconcile it with the idea that space, time and causal interaction are phenomenal. To be sure, Herbart assumes that phenomenal occurrences are grounded on and explicable by the behaviour of the 'reals'. And the world of the 'reals' is not taken to be the static reality of Parmenides. But it seems arguable that so far as the postulated relations between 'reals' are thought at all, they are inevitably brought into the phenomenal sphere. For they can hardly be thought except in terms of relations which are said to be phenomenal.

In any case it is on this metaphysical basis that Herbart constructs his psychology. The soul is a simple and unextended substance or 'real'. It is not, however, to be identified with the pure subject or ego of consciousness. The soul, considered simply as such, is not conscious at all. Nor is it furnished with any Kantian apparatus of *a priori* forms and categories. All psychical activities are secondary and derived. That is to say, the soul strives to preserve itself in face of disturbances occasioned by other 'reals', and the self-preservative reactions are expressed in sensations and ideas. And mental life is constituted by the relations and interactions between sensations and ideas. The idea of distinct faculties can be thrown overboard. For instance, an idea which meets with hindrance can be called a desire, while an idea which is accompanied by a supposition of success can be called a volition. There is no need to postulate appetitive and volitional faculties. The relevant psychical phenomena can be explained in terms of ideas which are themselves explicable in terms of stimuli directly or indirectly caused by the soul's self-preservative reactions to disturbances.

An interesting feature of Herbart's psychology is his theory of the subconscious. Ideas may be associated with one another, but they may also be mutually opposed. In this case a state of tension is set up, and some idea or ideas are forced below the level of consciousness. They then turn into impulses, though they can return to consciousness as ideas. We may also note Herbart's insistence not only that on the conscious level consciousness of objects other than the self precedes self-consciousness but also that self-consciousness is always empirical self-consciousness, consciousness of the me-object. There are ego-ideas, but there is no such thing as pure self-consciousness.

Though, however, Herbart's theory of the subconscious is not without historical importance, the salient feature of his psychology is perhaps his attempt to make it a science by mathematicizing it. Thus he assumes that ideas have varying degrees of intensity, and that the relations between them can be expressed in mathematical formulas. When, for example, an idea has been inhibited and forced below the level of consciousness, its return to consciousness will involve the return, according to a mathematically determinable sequence, of associated ideas. And if we possessed sufficient empirical evidence, we could predict the cause of such events. In principle at any rate psychology is capable of being turned into an exact science, the statics and dynamics of the mental life of presentations.

Psychology, therefore, like metaphysics, is concerned with the real. Aesthetics and ethics are concerned with values. The more fundamental of these two is aesthetics. For the ethical judgment is a subdivision of the aesthetic judgment, the judgment of taste which expresses approval or disapproval. But this is not to say that the ethical judgment has no objective reference. For approval and disapproval are grounded in certain relations, and in the case of ethics these are relations of the will, of which Herbart discovers five. In the first place experience shows that we express approval of the relation in which the will is in agreement with a person's inner conviction. That is to say, we express approval in accordance with the ideal of inner freedom.[3] Secondly our approval is given to a relation of harmony between the different tendencies or strivings of the individual will. And our approval is then elicited in accordance with the ideal of perfection. Thirdly we approve the relation in which one will takes as its object the satisfaction of another will. And here it is the ideal of benevolence which informs our judgment. Fourthly approval or disapproval is elicited in accordance with the idea of justice. We disapprove a relation of conflict or disharmony between several wills, while we approve a relation in which each will allows the others to limit it. Fifthly we disapprove a relation in which deliberate good and evil acts are unrecompensed. Here the idea of retribution is operative.

It is in the light of this theory of values that Herbart criticizes the Kantian ethics. We cannot take the categorical imperative as an ultimate moral fact. For we can always ask whence the practical reason or will derives its authority. Behind a command and obedience to it there must be something which warrants respect for the command. And this is found in the recognition of values, the morally beautiful and pleasing.

We cannot enter here into Herbart's educational theory. But it is worth noting that it involves a combination of his ethics with his psychology. Ethics, with its theory of values, provides the end or aim of education, namely character-development. The goal of the moral life is the perfect conformity of the will with moral ideals or values. And this is virtue. But to estimate how this aim is to be pedagogically attained we have to take account of psychology and utilize its laws and principles. The main end of education is moral, but the educator has to build upon the two masses of presentations derived from experience of the world and from social intercourse and environment. The first basis has to be developed into knowledge, the second into benevolence towards and sympathy with others.

Herbart's philosophy clearly lacked the romantic appeal of the great idealist systems. In one sense it was out of date. That is to say, it looked back behind Kant, and its author was out of sympathy with the contemporary prevailing movement in Germany. But in another sense it was very much up to date. For it demanded a closer integration of philosophy and science and looked forward to some of the systems which followed the collapse of idealism and demanded precisely this integration. The most significant features of Herbart's philosophy were probably his psychology and his educational theory. In the second field he helped to provide a theoretical background for the practical ideas of Pestalozzi. In the field of psychology he exercised a stimulative influence. But in view of his idea of psychology as the mechanics of the mental life of sensations and ideas it is as well to remind oneself that he was no materialist. Matter was for him phenomenal. Further, he accepted a form of the argument from design, pointing to a divine supersensible Being.

3. The importance of psychology was even more strongly emphasized by Friedrich Eduard Beneke (1798–1854). Beneke was considerably influenced by the writings of Herbart,

but he was certainly not a disciple. He was also influenced by Fries, but above all he derived inspiration from British thought and had a high regard for Locke. He was quite out of sympathy with the dominant idealist philosophy and encountered great difficulties in his academic career. In the end he appears to have committed suicide, an event which elicited some remarks in thoroughly bad taste from Arthur Schopenhauer.

In Beneke's view psychology is the fundamental science and the basis of philosophy. It should not be grounded, as with Herbart, on metaphysics. On the contrary, it is or ought to be grounded on interior experience which reveals to us the fundamental psychical processes. Mathematics is no help and is not required. Beneke was indeed influenced by the associationist psychology, but he did not share Herbart's notion of turning psychology into an exact science by mathematicizing it. He looked rather to the introspective method of the English empiricists.

As for the soul, it is, as Locke rightly claimed, devoid of innate ideas. There are also, as Herbart saw, no distinct faculties in the traditional sense. But we can discover a number of predispositions or impulses which can be called faculties if we wish to do so. And the unity of the self results from the harmonization of these impulses. Further, pedagogy and ethics, which are both applied psychology, show how the impulses and predispositions are to be developed and harmonized in view of a hierarchy of goods or values determined by a consideration of actions and their effects.

Beneke's philosophy is doubtless very small beer compared with the grandiose systems of German idealism. At the same time we can see perhaps in the emphasis which he lays upon impulses as the fundamental elements in the psychical life and in his tendency to stress the practical rather than the theoretical some affinity with the shift towards voluntarism which was given large-scale expression in the metaphysical system of Schopenhauer, the very man who made caustic remarks about Beneke's suicide. For the matter of that, Fichte had already emphasized the fundamental role of impulse and drive.

4. Chronological reasons justify the inclusion in this chap-

ter of some brief reference to Bernhard Bolzano (1781–1848), even if his rediscovery as a forerunner in certain respects of modern logical developments tends to make one think of him as a more recent writer than he actually was.

Bolzano was born in Prague of an Italian father and German mother. In 1805 he was ordained priest and soon afterwards he was appointed to the chair of philosophy of religion in the University of Prague. But at the end of 1819 he was deprived of his post, not, as has sometimes been stated, by his ecclesiastical superiors, but by order of the Emperor in Vienna. The imperial decree made special mention of Bolzano's objectionable doctrines on war, social rank and civic disobedience. In point of fact Bolzano had told the students that war would one day be regarded with the same abhorrence as duelling, that social differences would in time be reduced to proper limits, and that obedience to the civil power was limited by the moral conscience and by the norms of the legitimate exercise of sovereignty. And though these views may have been objectionable in the eyes of the Holy Roman Emperor, they were far from being theologically heretical. Indeed, the ecclesiastical authorities at Prague, when instructed by Vienna to investigate the case of Bolzano, declared that he was an orthodox Catholic. However, Bolzano had to abandon teaching and he devoted himself to a life of study and writing, though he had some difficulties about publication, at any rate in the Austrian dominions.

In 1827 Bolzano published anonymously a work, commonly called *Athanasia*, on the grounds of belief in the immortality of the soul. His chief work, *Theory of Science: an Essay towards a Detailed and for the most part New Exposition of Logic (Wissenschaftslehre: Versuch einer ausführlichen und grösstenteils neuen Darstellung der Logik)* appeared in four volumes in 1837. The *Paradoxes of the Infinite (Paradoxen des Unendlichen)* was published posthumously in 1851. In addition he wrote a considerable number of papers on logical, mathematical, physical, aesthetic and political themes, many of them for the Bohemian Society of the Sciences of which he was an active member.

In a short account which he wrote of his intellectual development Bolzano remarked that at no time had he felt inclined to recognize any given philosophical system as the one true philosophy. Referring to Kant, whose first *Critique* he had begun to study in his eighteenth year, he admitted that he found much to approve of in the critical philosophy. At the same time he found much to disagree with and much that was lacking. For example, while he welcomed the distinction between analytic and synthetic propositions, he could not agree with Kant's explanation of the distinction. Nor could he accept the view of mathematical propositions as synthetic propositions based on *a priori* intuitions. For he had himself succeeded in deducing some geometrical truths by analysis of concepts. Mathematics, he thought, is purely conceptual in character, and it should be constructed by a rigorous process of analysis.

This insistence on conceptual analysis and on logical rigour was indeed characteristic of Bolzano. Not only did he find fault with leading philosophers for failing to define their terms,[4] for slovenly conceptual analysis and for lack of consistency in their use of terms, but he also made it clear that in his opinion nobody could be a good philosopher unless he was a good mathematician. Obviously, he was not disposed to regard with a particularly kindly eye the goings-on of the metaphysical idealists.

Further, the tendency of Bolzano's mind was to depsychologize logic, to formalize it and to set it free from any intrinsic connection with the subject or ego or productive imagination or any other subjective factor. And this tendency shows itself in his theory of the proposition in itself (*der Satz an sich*). A proposition in itself is defined as 'a statement that something is or is not, irrespective of whether this statement is true or false, irrespective of whether anyone has ever formulated it in words, and even irrespective of whether it has ever been present in any mind as a thought'.[5] The idea of propositions in themselves may give rise to some difficulties; but it is clear that for Bolzano the primary element in a proposition is its objective content or meaning. Its being thought or posited by a subject is a secondary factor, irrelevant to the objective meaning.

Bolzano also speaks of the presentation in itself (*die Vorstellung an sich*). This is described as whatever can be a component part in a proposition but which does not by itself constitute a proposition. Hence no presentation or concept can be in itself true or false. For truth and falsity are predicated only of propositions, not of their component parts taken singly. But the meaning or content of a presentation in itself can be analysed; and this can be done without reference to any subject. Logically speaking, the subject is irrelevant. For example, if idea X is conceived by A, B and C, there are three ideas from the psychological point of view but only one from the point of view of the logical analyst who is interested simply in the content of the concept. It seems to me disputable whether the range of meaning of a concept can be analysed in abstraction from the propositions in which it is employed. For meaning is determined by use. But in any case Bolzano's concern with de-psychologizing logic is clear enough.

In the third place Bolzano speaks of the judgment in itself (*das Urteil an sich*). Every judgment expresses and affirms a proposition.

Now, if there are propositions in themselves, there must also be truths in themselves (*Wahrheiten an sich*), namely those propositions which are in fact true. Their truth does not, however, depend in any way on their being expressed and affirmed in judgments by thinking subjects. And this holds good not only of finite subjects but also of God. Truths in themselves are not true because God posits them; God thinks them because they are true. Bolzano does not mean that it is false to say that God makes true factual propositions about the world to be true in the sense that God is creator and thus responsible for there being a world at all. He is looking at the matter from the logician's point of view and maintaining that the truth of a proposition does not depend on its being thought by a subject, whether finite or infinite. The truth of a mathematical proposition, for example, depends on the meanings of the terms, not on whether it is thought by a mathematician, human or divine.

As a philosopher, Bolzano rejected Kant's condemnation of metaphysics and maintained that important truths about God and about the spirituality and immortality of the soul could be proved. In his general metaphysical outlook he was influenced by Leibniz. Bolzano did not indeed accept Leibniz's theory of 'windowless' monads; but he shared his conviction that every substance is an active being, its activity being expressed in some form of representation or, as Leibniz puts it, perception. But Bolzano's significance does not lie in his metaphysics but in his work as logician and mathematician. It was his status as a mathematician which first met with recognition, but in modern times tribute has been paid to him as a logician, notably by Edmund Husserl.

5. In the foregoing sections of this chapter we have been concerned with thinkers who stood apart from the movement of post-Kantian metaphysical idealism and followed other lines of thought. We can now consider briefly two philosophers who belonged to the idealist movement but who both developed a critical attitude towards absolute idealism.

(a) Christian Hermann Weisse (1801–66), who was a professor in the University of Leipzig, stood at one time fairly close to Hegel, though he considered that Hegel had exaggerated the role of logic, particularly by trying (according to Weisse's interpretation) to deduce reality from the abstract forms of Being. We require the idea of a personal creative God to make the system tenable.

In his development of a speculative theism Weisse was stimulated by the later religious philosophy of Schelling. And in the *Philosophical Problem of Today* (*Das philosophische Problem der Gegenwart*, 1842) he maintained that Hegel had developed in his logic the negative side of philosophy. The Hegelian dialectic provides us with the idea of the possible Godhead. The logical Absolute is not the real God, but it is the necessary logical foundation of his reality. Hegel, of course, might have agreed. For the logical Idea as such was not for him the existing divine Being. But what Weisse was concerned to defend was the idea of a personal and free God, whose existence cannot be deduced from the absolute Idea, though it presupposes the validity of the Idea. That is to say, the divine Being, if there is one, must be self-thinking Thought, a personal and self-conscious Being. But that there is such a Being must be shown in some other way than by *a priori* logical deduction. Further, Weisse tried to show that God cannot be *a* Person, and that we must accept the Christian doctrine of the Trinity.

(*b*) Weisse's criticism of Hegel seemed to be only half-hearted in the eyes of Immanuel Hermann Fichte (1796–1879), son of the famous idealist. The younger Fichte laid emphasis on the individual human personality, and he was strongly opposed to what he regarded as Hegel's tendency to merge the individual in the universal. In Hegelianism as he interpreted it the human person was presented as being no more than a transitory moment in the life of universal Spirit, whereas in his own view the development of personality was the end of creation and man was assured of personal immortality.

The thought of the younger Fichte passed through several stages, from a period when the influence of his father and of Kant was strong to his later concentration on a philosophical anthropology, accompanied by a marked interest in the preconscious aspects of man and in parapsychological phenomena. But the general framework of his philosophy was provided by a speculative theism in which he tried to combine idealist themes with theism and with an emphasis on the human personality. In his *Speculative Theology or General Doctrine of Religion* (*Die spekulative Theologie oder allgemeine Religionslehre*, 1846), which forms the third volume of his trilogy on speculative theism, God is represented as the supreme personal unity of the ideal and the real. The ideal aspect of God is his infinite self-consciousness, while the real aspect is formed by the monads which are the eternal thoughts of God. Creation signifies the act of endowing these monads with free will, with a life of their own. And the development of the human personality is a development of self-consciousness on a basis of preconscious or subconscious levels.

Obviously I. H. Fichte was strongly influenced by the idealist movement. One would hardly expect anything else. But he laid great emphasis on the personal nature of God and on the value and immortality of the human person. And it was in the name of this personalistic idealism that he attacked the Hegelian system in which, he was convinced, finite personality was offered up in sacrifice to the all-devouring Absolute.

Chapter Thirteen

SCHOPENHAUER (1)

*Life and writings — Schopenhauer's doctorate dissertation —
The world as Idea — The biological function of concepts and
the possibility of metaphysics — The world as the manifestation of the Will to live — Metaphysical pessimism — Some critical comments.*

1. A philosophy's ability to strike our imaginations by presenting an original and dramatic picture of the universe is
obviously not an infallible criterion of its truth. But it certainly adds greatly to its interest. It is not, however, a quality
which is conspicuously present in any of the philosophies
considered in the last chapter. Herbart, it is true, produced
a general system. But if one had to single out the dramatic
visions of the world provided by nineteenth-century philosophers, it would hardly occur to anyone to mention Herbart.
Hegel, yes; Marx, yes; Nietzsche, yes; but not, I think, Herbart. And still less the sober logician and mathematician
Bolzano. In 1819, however, when Herbart was professor at
Königsberg and Hegel had recently moved from Heidelberg
to Berlin, there appeared the main work of Arthur Schopenhauer, which, though it excited little notice at the time, expressed an interpretation of the world and of human life that
was both striking in itself and opposed in certain important
respects to the interpretations offered by the great idealists.
There are indeed certain family likenesses between the system of Schopenhauer and those of the idealists. But its author, who never minced words, professed an utter contempt
for Fichte, Schelling and Hegel, especially the last named,
and regarded himself as their great opponent and the pur-
veyor of the real truth to mankind.

Arthur Schopenhauer was born at Danzig on February
22nd, 1788. His father, a wealthy merchant, hoped that his
son would follow in his footsteps, and he allowed the boy to

spend the years 1803–4 in visiting England, France and other countries on the understanding that at the conclusion of the tour he would take up work in a business house. The young Schopenhauer fulfilled his promise, but he had no relish for a business career and on his father's death in 1803 he obtained his mother's consent to his continuing his studies. In 1809 he entered the University of Göttingen to study medicine, but he changed to philosophy in his second year at the university. As he put it, life is a problem and he had decided to spend his time reflecting on it.

From Göttingen, where he became an admirer of Plato, Schopenhauer went in 1811 to Berlin to listen to the lectures of Fichte and Schleiermacher. The former's obscurity was repugnant to him, while the latter's assertion that nobody could be a real philosopher without being religious elicited the sarcastic comment that nobody who is religious takes to philosophy, as he has no need of it.

Schopenhauer regarded himself as a cosmopolitan, and at no time was he a German nationalist. Having, as he subsequently said, a detestation for all military affairs he prudently left Berlin when Prussia rose against Napoleon and devoted himself in peaceful retirement to the preparation of a dissertation *On the Fourfold Root of the Principle of Sufficient Reason* (*Ueber die vierfache Wurzel des Satzes vom zureichenden Grunde*) which won for him the doctorate at Jena and was published in 1813. Goethe congratulated the author, and in return Schopenhauer wrote his essay *On Vision and Colours* (*Ueber das Sehen und die Farben*, 1816) in which he more or less supported Goethe against Newton. But apart from the flattering reception accorded it by the great poet the *Fourfold Root* was practically unnoticed and unsold. The author, however, continued to look on it as an indispensable introduction to his philosophy, and something will be said about it in the next section.

From May 1814 until September 1818 Schopenhauer was living at Dresden. And it was there that he composed his main philosophical work, *The World as Will and Idea* (*Die Welt als Wille und Vorstellung*). Having consigned the manuscript to the publishers Schopenhauer left for an art tour of Italy. The work appeared early in 1819, and the author had the consolation of finding that some philosophers, such as Herbart and Beneke, took notice of it. But this consolation was offset by the very small sale of a book which its author believed to contain the secret of the universe.

Encouraged, however, by the fact that his *magnum opus* had not passed entirely unnoticed and eager to expound the truth about the world by word of mouth as well as in writing, Schopenhauer betook himself to Berlin and started lecturing there in 1820. Though he held no university chair, he did not hesitate to choose for his lectures the hour at which Hegel was accustomed to lecture. The enterprise was a complete failure, and Schopenhauer left off lecturing after one semester. His doctrine was scarcely representative of the dominant *Zeitgeist* or spirit of the time.

After some wanderings Schopenhauer settled at Frankfurt on the Main in 1833. He read widely in European literature, consulted scientific books and journals, being quick to notice points which would serve as illustrations or empirical confirmation of his philosophical theories, visited the theatre and continued writing. In 1836 he published *On the Will in Nature* (*Ueber den Willen in der Natur*), and in 1839 he won a prize from the Scientific Society of Drontheim in Norway for an essay on freedom. He failed, however, to obtain a similar prize from the Royal Danish Academy of the Sciences for an essay on the foundations of ethics. One of the reasons given for the refusal of the prize was the writer's disrespectful references to leading philosophers. Schopenhauer had a great admiration for Kant, but he had the habit of referring to thinkers such as Fichte, Schelling and Hegel in terms which were, to put it mildly, unconventional, however amusing his expressions may be to later generations. The two essays were published together in 1841 under the title *The Two Fundamental Problems of Ethics* (*Die beiden Grundprobleme der Ethik*).

In 1844 Schopenhauer published a second edition of *The World as Will and Idea* with fifty supplementary chapters. In the preface to this edition he took the opportunity of making quite clear his views about German university professors of philosophy, just in case his attitude might not have been sufficiently indicated already. In 1851 he published a successful collection of essays entitled *Parerga and Paralipomena*, dealing with a wide variety of topics. Finally, in 1859 he published a third and augmented edition of his *magnum opus*.

After the failure of the Revolution of 1848, a revolution for which Schopenhauer had no sympathy at all, people were more ready to pay attention to a philosophy which emphasized the evil in the world and the vanity of life and preached a turning away from life to aesthetic contemplation and asceticism. And in the last decade of his life Schopenhauer became a famous man. Visitors came to see him from all sides and were entertained by his brilliant conversational powers. And though the German professors had not forgotten his sarcasm and abuse, lectures were delivered on his system in several universities, a sure sign that he had at last arrived. He died in September 1860.

Schopenhauer possessed a great breadth of culture, and he could write extremely well. A man of strong character and will, he was never afraid to express his opinions; and he had a gift of wit. He also possessed a considerable fund of practical sense and business acumen. But he was egoistic, vain, quarrelsome and, on occasion, even boorish; and he can hardly be said to have been remarkable for gifts of the heart. His relations with women were not exactly what one expects from a man who discoursed with eloquence on ethical, ascetical and mystical matters; and his literary executors suppressed some of his remarks about the female sex. Further, his theoretical sensitivity to the sufferings of humanity was not accompanied by any very practical efforts to alleviate it. But, as he sagely remarked, it is no more necessary for a philosopher to be a saint than for a saint to be a philosopher. And while as a man he can scarcely be considered as one of the most lovable of philosophers, his outstanding gifts as a writer are, I think, unquestionable.

2. In his doctorate dissertation Schopenhauer writes under the strong influence of Kant. The world of experience is the phenomenal world: it is object for a subject. And as such it is the world of our mental presentations (*Vorstellungen*). But no object is ever presented to us in a state of complete isolation and detachment. That is to say, all our presentations are

related to or connected with other presentations in regular ways. And knowledge or science is precisely knowledge of these regular relations. 'Science, that is to say, signifies a *system* of objects known',[1] not a mere aggregate of presentations. And there must be a sufficient reason for this relatedness or correctedness. Thus the general principle which governs our knowledge of objects or phenomena is the principle of sufficient reason.

As a preliminary enunciation of the principle of sufficient reason Schopenhauer chooses 'the Wolffian formulation as the most general: *Nihil est sine ratione cur potius sit quam non sit*. Nothing is without a reason [*Grund*, ground] why it is.'[2] But he goes on to discover four main types or classes of objects and four main types of relatedness or connection. And he draws the conclusion that there are four fundamental forms of the principle of sufficient reason and that the principle in its general enunciation is an abstraction from them. Hence the title of the dissertation, *On the Fourfold Root of the Principle of Sufficient Reason*.

The first class of objects or presentations is that of our intuitive, empirical and complete[3] presentations. This may not sound very enlightening; but in the language of ordinary realism the objects in question are the physical objects which are causally related in space and time and which form the subject-matter of natural sciences such as physics and chemistry. According to Schopenhauer, this spatial, temporal and causal relatedness is to be ascribed to an activity of the mind which organizes the matter of phenomena, elementary sensations, according to the *a priori* forms of sensibility, namely space and time, and the pure form of causality which is the only category of the understanding. He thus follows Kant, though the Kantian categories of the understanding are reduced to one. And our knowledge of these presentations, of phenomena or, in realist language, of physical objects, is said to be governed by 'the principle of sufficient reason of becoming, *principium rationis sufficientis fiendi*'.[4]

The second class of objects consists of abstract concepts, and the relevant form of relatedness is the judgment. But a judgment does not express knowledge unless it is true. And 'truth is the relation of a judgment to something different from it, which can be called its ground'.[5] The ground or sufficient reason can be of different types. For instance, a judgment can have as its ground another judgment; and when we consider the rules of implication and inference in a formal way, we are in the province of logic.[6] But in any case the judgment, the synthesis of concepts, is governed by 'the principle of sufficient reason of knowing, *principium rationis sufficientis cognoscendi*'.[7]

The third class of objects comprises 'the *a priori* intuitions of the forms of outer and inner sense, space and time'.[8] Space and time are of such a nature that each part is related in a certain way to another. And 'the law according to which the parts of space and time . . . determine one another I call the principle of sufficient reason of being, *principium rationis sufficientis essendi*'.[9] In time, for example, this is the law of irreversible succession; and 'on this connection of the parts of time rests all counting'.[10] Arithmetic, in other words, rests on the law governing the relations between the parts of time, while geometry rests on the law governing the respective positions of the parts of space. We can say, therefore, that Schopenhauer's third class of objects are mathematical objects, and that the relevant form of the principle of sufficient reason or ground, which governs our knowledge of geometrical and arithmetical relations, is the law, or rather laws, according to which the parts of space and time are respectively related to one another.

The fourth class of objects contains only one member, namely 'the subject of willing considered as object for the knowing subject'.[11] That is to say, the object is the self as source or subject of volition. And the principle governing our knowledge of the relation between this subject and its volitions or acts of will is 'the principle of the ground (or sufficient reason) of acting, *principium rationis sufficientis agendi*; more briefly, the *law of motivation*'.[12] The implication of this is character-determinism. A man acts for motives, and the motives for which he acts have their ground or sufficient reason in his character. We understand the relation between a man's deliberate actions and himself as subject of volition where we see these actions as issuing from the character of the subject. But this subject will be considered later.

Schopenhauer's terminology is based on that of Wolff. But his general position is based on Kant's. The world is phenomenal, object for a subject. And it is the sphere of necessity. True, Schopenhauer recognizes different types of necessity. In the sphere of volition, for example, moral necessity rules, which is to be distinguished both from physical and from logical necessity. But within the sphere of presentations as a whole, the relations between them are governed by certain laws, described as distinct roots of the principle of sufficient reason.

It is to be noted, however, that the principle of sufficient reason applies only within the phenomenal sphere, the sphere of objects for a subject. It does not apply to the noumenon, metaphenomenal reality, whatever this may be. Nor can it be legitimately applied to the phenomenal world considered as a totality. For it governs relations *between* phenomena. Hence no cosmological argument for God's existence can be valid, if it is an argument from the world as a whole to God as cause or as sufficient ground of phenomena. And here again Schopenhauer is in substantial agreement with Kant, though he certainly does not follow Kant in proposing belief in God as a matter of practical or moral faith.

3. The doctorate dissertation which we have just briefly considered appears arid and unexciting in comparison with Schopenhauer's great work *The World as Will and Idea*. Yet Schopenhauer was justified in regarding the former as an introduction to the latter. For his *magnum opus* begins with the statement that 'the world is my idea'.[13] That is to say, the whole visible world or, as Schopenhauer describes it, the sum total of experience is object for a subject: its reality consists in its appearing to or being perceived by a subject. As Berkeley said, the *esse* of sensible things is *percipi*.

The following point should be noticed. The German word translated here by 'idea' is *Vorstellung*. And in the section on Schopenhauer's doctorate dissertation I translated this word by 'presentation', which is preferable to 'idea'. But the title *The World as Will and Idea* has become so familiar that it seems pedantic to insist on a change. At the same time it is important to understand that Schopenhauer distinguishes between intuitive presentations (*intuitive Vorstellungen*) and abstract presentations (*abstrakte Vorstellungen*) or concepts. And when Schopenhauer says that the world is my idea, he is referring to intuitive presentations. He does not mean, for example, that a tree is identical with my abstract concept of a tree. He means that the tree as perceived by me exists only in relation to me as a percipient subject. Its reality is exhausted, so to speak, in its perceptibility. It is simply what I perceive or can perceive it to be.

Schopenhauer's position can be clarified in this way. Abstract concepts are possessed only by man: intuitive presentations are common to man and animals, at least to the higher animals. There is a phenomenal world not only for man but also for animals. For the conditions of its possibility are present also in the latter, these conditions being the *a priori* forms of sensibility, namely space and time, and the category of the understanding, namely causality. In Schopenhauer's view understanding (*Verstand*) is found also in animals. And the *principium rationis sufficientis fiendi* operates, for instance, in a dog, for which there exists a world of causally related things. But animals do not possess reason (*Vernunft*), the faculty of abstract concepts. A dog perceives things in space and time, and it can perceive concrete causal relations. But it does not follow that a dog can reflect abstractly about space, time or causality. To put the matter in another way, the statement that the visible world is object for a percipient subject applies as well to a dog as to a man. But it does not follow from this that a dog can know that the statement is true.

It should be added that according to Schopenhauer it was an important discovery of Kant that space and time, as the *a priori* conditions of the visible world, can be intuited in themselves. Hence they can be included in the range of our intuitive presentations which comprise 'the whole visible world, or the whole of experience, together with the conditions of its possibility'.[14] But it does not follow that a dog can intuit space and time in themselves and work out pure mathematics, though there is for it a spatio-temporal world.

Now, if the world is my idea, my body also must be my idea. For it is a visible thing. But we must go further than this. If it is true that the world exists only as object for a subject, it is also true that the percipient subject is correlative with the object. 'For me [Schopenhauer] matter and intelligence are inseparable correlates, existing only for one another, and therefore only relatively . . . the two together constitute *the world as idea*, which is just Kant's *appearance*, and consequently something secondary.'[15] The world as idea or presentation thus comprises both perceiver and perceived. This totality is, as Kant said, empirically real but transcendentally ideal.

For Kant Schopenhauer had a profound respect, and he claimed to be Kant's true successor. But his theory of the phenomenal character of empirical reality was powerfully reinforced by, though not derived from, another factor. Shortly after the publication of his doctorate dissertation in 1813 Schopenhauer met at Weimar an Oriental scholar, F. Mayer, who introduced him to Indian philosophical literature. And he retained an interest in Oriental philosophy up to the end of his life. As an old man he meditated on the text of the Upanishads. It is not surprising, therefore, if he associated his theory of the world as idea or presentation with the Indian doctrine of Maya. Individual subjects and objects are all appearance, Maya.

Now, if the world is phenomenal, the question arises, what is the noumenon? What is the reality which lies behind the veil of Maya? And Schopenhauer's discussion of the nature of this reality and of its self-manifestation forms the really interesting part of his system. For the theory of the world as idea, though it is in Schopenhauer's opinion an indispensable part of his philosophy, is obviously a development of Kant's position, whereas his theory of the world as will is original[16] and contains the expression of his characteristic interpretation of human life. Before, however, we approach this topic, something must be said about his theory of the practical function of concepts, which possesses an intrinsic interest of its own.

4. As we have seen, besides intuitive presentations man possesses also abstract concepts which are formed by reason and presuppose experience, whether directly or indirectly. But why do we form them? What is their function? Schopenhauer's answer is that their primary function is practical. 'The great utility of concepts consists in the fact that by

means of them the original material of knowledge is easier to handle, survey and order.'[17] In comparison with intuitive presentations, with immediate perceptive knowledge, abstract concepts are in a sense poor. For they omit a great deal, the differences, for example, between individual members of a class. But they are required if communication is to be possible and if experimental knowledge is to be retained and handed on. 'The greatest value of rational or abstract knowledge lies in its communicability and in the possibility of retaining it permanently. It is chiefly on this account that it is so inestimably important for practice.'[18] Schopenhauer also mentions the ethical importance of concepts and abstract reasoning. A moral man guides his conduct by principles. And principles require concepts.

But Schopenhauer is not concerned simply with pointing out examples of the practical value of concepts. He is also at pains to show how this practical value is connected with his general theory of cognition. Knowledge is the servant of the will. Or, to omit metaphysics for the present, knowledge is in the first instance the instrument of satisfying physical needs, the servant of the body. In animals needs are less complicated than in man, and they are more easily satisfied. Perception is sufficient, especially as Nature has provided animals with their own means of attack and defence, such as the claws of the lion and the sting of the wasp. But with the further development of the organism, in particular of the brain, there is a corresponding development of needs and wants. And a higher type of knowledge is required to satisfy them. In man reason appears, which enables him to discover new ways of satisfying his needs, to invent tools, and so on.[19]

Reason, therefore, has a primarily biological function. If one may so speak, Nature intends it as an instrument for satisfying the needs of a more highly complicated and developed organism than that of the animal. But the needs in question are physical needs. Reason is primarily concerned with nourishment and propagation, with the bodily needs of the individual and species. And it follows from this that reason is unfitted for penetrating through the veil of phenomena to the underlying reality, the noumenon. The concept is a practical instrument: it stands for a number of things belonging to the same class and enables us to deal easily and economically with a vast amount of material. But it is not adapted for going beyond phenomena to any underlying essence or thing-in-itself.

In this case, we may well ask, how can metaphysics be possible? Schopenhauer answers that though the intellect is by nature the servant of the will, it is capable in man of developing to such an extent that it can achieve objectivity. That is to say, though man's mind is in the first instance an instrument for satisfying his bodily needs, it can develop a kind of surplus energy which sets it free, at least temporarily, from the service of desire. Man then becomes a disinterested spectator: he can adopt a contemplative attitude, as in aesthetic contemplation and in philosophy.

Clearly, this claim on behalf of the human mind does not by itself dispose of the difficulty which arises out of Schopenhauer's account of the concept. For systematic and communicable philosophy must be expressed in concepts. And if the concept is fitted for dealing only with phenomena, metaphysics appears to be ruled out. But Schopenhauer replies that metaphysical philosophy is possible provided that there is a fundamental intuition on the level of perceptive knowledge, which gives us direct insight into the nature of the reality underlying phenomena, an insight which philosophy endeavours to express in conceptual form. Philosophy, therefore, involves an interplay between intuition and conceptual reasoning. 'To enrich the concept from intuition is the constant concern of poetry and philosophy.'[20] Concepts do not provide us with new knowledge: intuition is fundamental. But intuition must be raised to the conceptual level if it is to become philosophy.

Schopenhauer is in a rather difficult position. He does not wish to postulate as the basis of philosophy an exceptional intuition which would be something entirely different from perception on the one hand and abstract reasoning on the other. Hence the intuition of which he is speaking must be on the level of perceptive knowledge. But perception is concerned with individual objects, and so with phenomena. For individuality belongs to the phenomenal sphere. He is forced, therefore, to try to show that even on the level of perception there can be an intuitive awareness of the noumenon, an awareness which forms the basis for philosophical mediation.

Leaving the nature of this intuition for consideration in the next section, we can pause to note how in some respects Schopenhauer anticipates certain Bergsonian positions. For Bergson emphasized the practical function of intelligence and the inability of the concept to grasp the reality of life. And he went on to base philosophy on intuition and to depict the philosopher's task as being partly that of endeavouring to mediate this intuition, so far as this is possible, on the conceptual level. Hence for Bergson as for Schopenhauer philosophy involves the interplay of intuition and discursive or conceptual reasoning. I do not mean to imply that Bergson actually took his ideas from Schopenhauer. For I am not aware of any real evidence to show that he did. The notion that if philosopher X holds views which are similar to his predecessor Y, the former must necessarily have borrowed from or been influenced by the latter, is absurd. But the fact remains that though Bergson, when he became aware of the similarity, distinguished between his idea of intuition and that of the German philosopher, there is an obvious analogy between their positions. In other words, the same current or line of thought which found expression in the philosophy of Schopenhauer, when considered under the aspects in question, reappeared in the thought of Bergson. To put the matter in another way, there is some continuity, though there is also difference, between the system of Schopenhauer and the philosophy of Life of which the thought of Bergson is a notable example.

5. Kant maintained that the thing-in-itself, the correlative of the phenomenon, is unknowable. Schopenhauer, however, tells us what it is. It is Will. 'Thing-in-itself signifies that which exists independently of our perception, in short that which properly is. For Democritus this was formed matter. It was the same at bottom for Locke. For Kant it was $=X$. For me it is Will.'[21] And this is one single Will. For multiplicity can exist only in the spatio-temporal world, the sphere of phenomena. There cannot be more than one metaphenomenal reality or thing-in-itself. In other words, the inside of the world, so to speak, is one reality, whereas the outside,

the appearance of this reality, is the empirical world which consists of finite things.

How does Schopenhauer arrive at the conviction that the thing-in-itself is Will? To find the key to reality I must look within myself. For in inner consciousness or inwardly directed perception lies 'the single narrow door to the truth'.[22] Through this inner consciousness I am aware that the bodily action which is said to follow or result from volition is not something different from volition but one and the same. That is to say, the bodily action is simply the objectified will: it is the will become idea or presentation. Indeed, the whole body is nothing but objectified will, will as a presentation to consciousness. According to Schopenhauer anyone can understand this if he enters into himself. And once he has this fundamental intuition, he has the key to reality. He has only to extend his discovery to the world at large.

This Schopenhauer proceeds to do. He sees the manifestation of the one individual Will in the impulse by which the magnet turns to the north pole, in the phenomena of attraction and repulsion, in gravitation, in animal instinct, in human desire and so on. Wherever he looks, whether in the inorganic or in the organic sphere, he discovers empirical confirmation of his thesis that phenomena constitute the appearance of the one metaphysical Will.

The natural question to ask is this? If the thing-in-itself is manifested in such diverse phenomena as the universal forces of Nature, such as gravity, and human volition, why call it 'Will'? Would not 'Force' or 'Energy' be a more appropriate term, especially as the so-called Will, when considered in itself, is said to be 'without knowledge and merely a blind incessant impulse',[23] 'an endless striving'?[24] For the term 'Will', which implies rationality, seems to be hardly suitable for describing a blind impulse or striving.

Schopenhauer, however, defends his linguistic usage by maintaining that we ought to take our descriptive term from what is best known to us. We are immediately conscious of our own volition. And it is more appropriate to describe the less well known in terms of the better known than the other way round.

Besides being described as blind impulse, endless striving,

eternal becoming and so on, the metaphysical Will is characterized as the Will to live. Indeed, to say 'the Will' and to say 'the Will to live' are for Schopenhauer one and the same thing. As, therefore, empirical reality is the objectification or appearance of the metaphysical Will, it necessarily manifests the Will to live. And Schopenhauer has no difficulty in multiplying examples of this manifestation. We have only to look at Nature's concern for the maintenance of the species. Birds, for instance, build nests for the young which they do not yet know. Insects deposit their eggs where the larva may find nourishment. The whole series of phenomena of animal instinct manifests the omnipresence of the Will to live. If we look at the untiring activity of bees and ants and ask what it all leads to, what is attained by it, we can only answer 'the satisfaction of hunger and the sexual instinct',[25] the means, in other words, of maintaining the species in life. And if we look at man with his industry and trade, with his inventions and technology, we must admit that all this striving serves in the first instance only to sustain and to bring a certain amount of additional comfort to ephemeral individuals in their brief span of existence, and through them to contribute to the maintenance of the species.

All this fits in with what was said in the last section about Schopenhauer's theory of the biological function of reason as existing primarily to satisfy physical needs. We noticed indeed that the human intellect is capable of developing in such a way that it can free itself, at least temporarily, from the slavery of the Will. And we shall see later that Schopenhauer by no means confines the possible range of human activities to eating, drinking and copulation, the means of maintaining the life of the individual and of the species. But the primary function of reason manifests the character of the Will as the Will to live.

6. Now, if the Will is an endless striving, a blind urge or impulse which knows no cessation, it cannot find satisfaction or reach a state of tranquillity. It is always striving and never attaining. And this essential feature of the metaphysical Will is reflected in its self-objectification, above all in human life. Man seeks satisfaction, happiness, but he cannot attain it. What we call happiness or enjoyment is simply a temporary

cessation of desire. And desire, as the expression of a need or want, is a form of pain. Happiness, therefore, is 'the deliverance from a pain, from a want';[26] it is 'really and essentially always only *negative* and never positive'.[27] It soon turns to boredom, and the striving after satisfaction reasserts itself. It is boredom which makes beings who love one another so little as men do seek one another's company. And great intellectual powers simply increase the capacity for suffering and deepen the individual's isolation.

Each individual thing, as an objectification of the one Will to live, strives to assert its own existence at the expense of other things. Hence the world is the field of conflict, a conflict which manifests the nature of the Will as at variance with itself, as a tortured Will. And Schopenhauer finds illustrations of this conflict even in the inorganic sphere. But it is naturally to the organic and human spheres that he chiefly turns for empirical confirmation of his thesis. He dwells, for example, on the ways in which animals of one species prey on those of another. And when he comes to man, he really lets himself go. 'The chief source of the most serious evils which afflict man is man himself: *homo homini lupus*. Whoever keeps this last fact clearly in view sees the world as a hell which surpasses that of Dante through the fact that one man must be the devil of another.'[28] War and cruelty are, of course, grist for Schopenhauer's mill. And the man who showed no sympathy with the Revolution of 1848 speaks in the sharpest terms of industrial exploitation, slavery and such like social abuses.

We may note that it is the egoism, rapacity and hardness and cruelty of men which are for Schopenhauer the real justification of the State. So far from being a divine manifestation, the State is simply the creation of enlightened egoism which tries to make the world a little more tolerable than it would otherwise be.

Schopenhauer's pessimism is thus metaphysical in the sense that it is presented as a consequence of the nature of the metaphysical Will. The philosopher is not simply engaged in drawing attention to the empirical fact that there is much evil and suffering in the world. He is also indicating what he believes to be the cause of this empirical fact. The thing-in-itself being what it is, phenomenal reality must be marked with the black features which we actually observe. We can, of course, do something to alleviate suffering. This also is an empirical fact. But it is no good thinking that we can change the fundamental character of the world or of human life. If war, for instance, were abolished and if all men's material needs were met, the result would presumably be, on Schopenhauer's premises, a condition of intolerable boredom which would be succeeded by the return of conflict. In any case the prevalence of suffering and evil in the world is ultimately due to the nature of the thing-in-itself. And Schopenhauer is not slow to castigate what he regards as the facile optimism of Leibniz and the way in which the German idealists, especially Hegel, slur over the dark side of human existence or, when they admit it, justify it as 'rational'.

7. Needless to say, Schopenhauer thought that his theory of the phenomenal character of empirical reality fitted in well with his theory of the Will. That is to say, he thought that having once accepted Kant's general thesis of the phenomenal character of the world he could then go on, without inconsistency, to reveal the nature of the thing-in-itself. But this is questionable.

Take, for example, Schopenhauer's approach to the Will through inner consciousness. As Herbart remarked, on Schopenhauer's principles the Will, as viewed in inner perception, must be subject to the form of time: it is known in its successive acts. And these are phenomenal. We cannot arrive at the Will as a metaphenomenal reality. For in so far as we are conscious of it, it is phenomenal. True, we can talk about the metaphysical Will. But in so far as it is thought and spoken about, it must be, it seems, object for a subject, and so phenomenal.

Schopenhauer does indeed admit that we cannot know the metaphysical Will in itself, and that it may have attributes which are unknown by us and indeed incomprehensible to us. But he insists that it is known, even if only partially, in its manifestation or objectification, and that our own volition is for us its most distinct manifestation. In this case, however, the metaphysical Will seems to disintegrate, as it were, into phenomena, as far as our knowledge is concerned. And the conclusion seems to follow that we cannot know the thing-in-itself. To put the matter in another way, Schopenhauer does not wish to base his philosophy on a privileged and exceptional intuition of ultimate reality, but rather on our intuitive perception of our own volition. Yet this intuitive perception seems, on his own premises, to belong to the phenomenal sphere which includes the whole range of the subject-object relationship. In fine, once given the doctrine of *The World as Idea*, the first book of Schopenhauer's *magnum opus*, it is difficult to see how any access to the thing-in-itself is possible. Kant would presumably say that it was impossible.

This line of objection is, I think, justified. But it would, of course, be possible to cut Schopenhauer's philosophy adrift from its Kantian moorings and present it as a kind of hypothesis. The philosopher, let us suppose, was temperamentally inclined to see in a clear light and to emphasize the dark aspects of the world and of human life and history. So far from being secondary features, they seemed to him to constitute the world's most significant and positive aspects. And he considered that analysis of the concepts of happiness and of suffering confirmed this initial vision. On this basis he erected the explanatory hypothesis of the blind and endlessly striving impulse or force which he called the Will. And he could then look round to discover fresh empirical confirmation of his hypothesis in the inorganic, organic and specifically human spheres. Further, the hypothesis enabled him to make some general predictions about human life and history in the future.

It is obviously not my intention to suggest that Schopenhauer would have been willing to surrender his theory of the World as Idea. On the contrary, he laid emphasis on it. Nor is it my intention to suggest that Schopenhauer's picture of the world would be acceptable if it were presented as the lines just indicated above. His analysis of happiness as 'negative', to mention but one point of criticism, seems to me quite untenable. My point is rather that Schopenhauer's philosophy expresses a 'vision' of the world which draws attention to certain aspects of it. And this vision can perhaps be made clearer if his philosophy is expressed in the form of an hypothesis based on an exclusive attention to the aspects in question. To be sure, it is a one-sided vision or picture of the world. But precisely because of its one-sidedness and exaggeration it serves as an effective counter-balance or antithesis to a system such as that of Hegel in which attention is so focused on the triumphant march of Reason through history that the evil and suffering in the world are obscured from view by high-sounding phrases.

Chapter Fourteen

SCHOPENHAUER (2)

Aesthetic contemplation as a temporary escape from the slavery of the Will – The particular fine arts – Virtue and renunciation: the way of salvation – Schopenhauer and metaphysical idealism – The general influence of Schopenhauer – Notes on Eduard von Hartmann's development of Schopenhauer's philosophy.

1. The root of all evil for Schopenhauer is the slavery of the Will, subservience to the Will to live. But his claim has already been mentioned that the human mind has the capacity for developing beyond the extent required for the satisfaction of physical needs. It can develop, as it were, a surplus of energy over and above the energy required to fulfil its primary biological and practical function. Man is thus able to escape from the futile life of desire and striving, of egoistic self-assertion and conflict.

Schopenhauer describes two ways of escape from the slavery of the Will, the one temporary, an oasis in the desert, the other more lasting. The first is the way of aesthetic contemplation, the way of art; the second is the path of asceticism, the way of salvation. In this section we are concerned with the first, the way of escape through art.

In aesthetic contemplation man becomes the disinterested observer. Needless to say, this does not mean that aesthetic contemplation is uninteresting. If, for example, I regard a beautiful object as an object of desire or as a stimulant to desire, my point of view is not that of aesthetic contemplation: I am an 'interested' spectator. In point of fact I am the servant or instrument of the Will. But it is possible for me to regard the beautiful object neither as itself an object of desire nor as a stimulant to desire but simply and solely for its aesthetic significance. I am then a disinterested, but not an uninterested, spectator. And I am freed, temporarily at least, from the slavery of the Will.

This theory of temporary escape through aesthetic contemplation, whether of natural objects or of works of art, is linked by Schopenhauer with a metaphysical theory of what he calls Platonic Ideas. The Will is said to objectify itself immediately in Ideas which stand to individual natural things as archetypes to copies. They are 'the determinate species or the original unchanging forms and properties of all natural bodies, both inorganic and organic, and also the universal forces which reveal themselves according to natural laws'.[1] There are thus Ideas of natural forces such as gravity, and there are Ideas of species. But there are no Ideas of genuses. For while there are natural species, there are, according to Schopenhauer, no natural genuses.

The Ideas of species must not be confused with the immanent forms of things. The individual members of a species or natural class are said to be 'the empirical correlative of the Idea'.[2] And the Idea is an eternal archetype. It is for this reason, of course, that Schopenhauer identifies his Ideas with the Platonic Forms or Ideas.

How a blind Will or endless striving can reasonably be said to objectify itself immediately in Platonic Ideas, is something which I do not profess to understand. It seems to me that Schopenhauer, sharing the belief of Schelling and Hegel, in spite of his abuse of them, in the metaphysical significance of art and aesthetic intuition, and seeing that aesthetic contemplation offers a temporary escape from the slavery of desire, turns to a philosopher whom he greatly admires, namely Plato, and borrows from him a theory of Ideas which has no clear connection with the description of the Will as a blind, self-tortured impulse or striving. However, it is unnecessary to labour this aspect of the matter. The point is that the artistic genius is capable of apprehending the Ideas and of giving expression to them in works of art. And in aesthetic contemplation the beholder is participating in this apprehension of the Ideas. He thus rises above the temporal and changing and contemplates the eternal and unchanging. His attitude is contemplative, not appetitive. Appetite is stilled during aesthetic experience.

Schopenhauer's exaltation of the role of artistic genius represents a point of affinity with the romantic spirit. He does not, however, speak very clearly about the nature of artistic genius or about the relation between the genius and the ordinary man. Sometimes he seems to imply that genius means not only the ability to apprehend the Ideas but also the ability to express them in works of art. At other times he seems to imply that genius is simply the faculty of intuiting the Ideas, and that the ability to give external expression to them is a matter of technique which can be acquired by training and practice. The first way of speaking fits in best with what is presumably our normal conviction, namely that artistic genius involves the capacity for creative production. If a man lacked this capacity, we would not normally speak of him as an artistic genius or, for the matter of that, as an artist at all. The second way of speaking implies that everyone who is capable of aesthetic appreciation and contemplation participates in genius to some extent. But one might go on to claim with Benedetto Croce that aesthetic intuition involves interior expression, in the sense of imaginative recreation, as distinct from external expression. In this case both the creative artist and the man who contemplates and appreciates the work of art would 'express', though only the first would express externally. However, though it may be possible to bring together the two ways of speaking in some such manner, I think that for Schopenhauer artistic genius really involves both the faculty of intuiting the Ideas and the faculty of giving creative expression to this intuition, though this is aided by technical training. In this case the man who is not capable of producing works of art himself could still share in genius to the extent of intuiting the Ideas in and through their external expression.

The important point, however, in the present context is that in aesthetic contemplation a man transcends the original subjection of knowledge to the Will, to desire. He becomes the 'pure will-less subject of knowledge, who no longer traces relations in accordance with the principle of sufficient reason, but rests and is lost in fixed contemplation of the object presented to him, apart from its connection with any other object'.[3] If the object of contemplation is simply significant form, the Idea as concretely presented to perception, we are concerned with the beautiful. If, however, a man perceives the object of contemplation as having a hostile relation to his body, as menacing, that is to say, the objectification of the Will in the form of the human body by its power of greatness, he is contemplating the sublime. That is, he is contemplating the sublime provided that, while recognizing the menacing character of the object, he persists in objective contemplation and does not allow himself to be overwhelmed by the self-regarding emotion of fear. For instance, a man in a small boat at sea during a terrible storm is contemplating the sublime if he fixes his attention on the grandeur of the scene and the power of the elements.[4] But whether a man is contemplating the beautiful or the sublime, he is temporarily freed from the servitude of the Will. His mind enjoys a rest, as it were, from being an instrument for the satisfaction of desire and adopts a purely objective and disinterested point of view.

2. Both Schelling and Hegel arranged the particular fine arts in ascending series. And Schopenhauer too engages in this pastime. His standard of classification and arrangement is the series of grades of the Will's objectification. For example, architecture is said to express some low-grade Ideas such as gravity, cohesion, rigidity and hardness, the universal qualities of stone. Moreover, in expressing the tension between gravity and rigidity architecture expresses indirectly the conflict of the Will. Artistic hydraulics exhibits the Ideas of fluid matter in, for instance, fountains and artificial waterfalls, while artistic horticulture or landscape-gardening exhibits the Ideas of the higher grades of vegetative life. Historical painting and sculpture express the Idea of man, though sculpture is concerned principally with beauty and grace while painting is chiefly concerned with the expression of character and passion. Poetry is capable of representing Ideas of all grades. For its immediate material is concepts, though the poet tries by his use of epithets to bring down the abstract concept to the level of perception and thus to stimulate the imagination and enable the reader or hearer to apprehend the Idea in the perceptible object.[5] But though poetry is capable of representing all grades of Ideas, its chief object

is the representation of man as expressing himself through a series of actions and through the accompanying thoughts and emotions.

At the time there was controversy among writers on aesthetics about the range of the concept of fine art. But it would hardly be profitable to enter into a discussion about the propriety or impropriety of describing artistic hydraulics and landscape-gardening as fine arts. Nor need we discuss an arrangement of the arts which depends on correlating them with a questionable metaphysical system. Instead we can notice the two following points.

First, as one would expect, the supreme poetical art is for Schopenhauer tragedy. For in tragedy we witness the real character of human life transmuted into art and expressed in dramatic form, 'the unspeakable pain, the wail of humanity, the triumph of evil, the mocking mastery of chance and the irretrievable fall of the just and innocent'.[6]

Secondly, the highest of all arts is not tragedy but music. For music does not exhibit an Idea or Ideas, the immediate objectification of the Will: it exhibits the Will itself, the inner nature of the thing-in-itself.[7] In listening to music, therefore, a man receives a direct revelation, though not in conceptual form, of the reality which underlies phenomena. And he intuits this reality, revealed in the form of art, in an objective and disinterested manner, not as one caught in the grip of the Will's tyranny. Further, if it were possible to express accurately in concepts all that music expresses without concepts, we should have the true philosophy.

3. Aesthetic contemplation affords no more than a temporary or transient escape from the slavery of the Will. But Schopenhauer offers a lasting release through renunciation of the Will to live. Indeed, moral progress must take this form if morality is possible at all. For the Will to live, manifesting itself in egoism, self-assertion, hatred and conflict, is for Schopenhauer the source of evil. 'There really resides in the heart of each of us a wild beast which only waits the opportunity to rage and rave in order to injure others, and which, if they do not prevent it, would like to destroy them.'[8] This wild beast, this radical evil, is the direct expression of the Will to live. Hence morality, if it is possible, must involve

denial of the Will. And as man is an objectification of the Will, denial will mean self-denial, asceticism and mortification.

Schopenhauer does indeed say that in his philosophy the world possesses a moral significance. But what he means by this at first sight astonishing statement is this. Existence, life, is itself a crime: it is our original sin. And it is inevitably expiated by suffering and death. Hence we can say that justice reigns and, adapting Hegel's famous statement, that 'the world itself is the world's court of judgment'.[9] In this sense, therefore, the world possesses a moral significance. 'If we could lay all the misery of the world in one scale of the balance and all the guilt of the world in the other, the needle would certainly point to the centre.'[10] Schopenhauer speaks as though it were the Will itself which is guilty and the Will itself which pays the penalty. For it objectifies itself and suffers in its objectification. And this way of speaking may seem to be extravagant. For the sufferings of men must be phenomenal on Schopenhauer's premises: they can hardly affect the thing-in-itself. Passing over this point, however, we can draw from the statement that existence or life is itself a crime the conclusion that morality, if it is possible, must take the form of denial of the Will to live, of a turning away from life.

Given these premises, it may well appear to follow that the highest moral act will be suicide. But Schopenhauer argues that suicide expresses a surrender to the Will rather than a denial of it. For the man who commits suicide does so to escape certain evils. And if he could escape from them without killing himself, he would do so. Hence suicide is, paradoxically, the expression of a concealed will to live. Consequently, denial and renunciation must take some form other than suicide.

But is morality possible within the framework of Schopenhauer's philosophy? The individual human being is an objectification of the one individual Will, and his actions are determined. Schopenhauer draws a distinction between the intelligible and empirical characters. The metaphysical Will objectifies itself in the individual will, and this individual will, when considered in itself and anteriorly to its acts, is the intelligible or noumenal character. The individual will as manifested through its successive acts is the empirical character. Now, consciousness has for its object the particular acts of the will. And these appear successively. A man thus comes to know his character only gradually and imperfectly: in principle he is in the same position as an outsider. He does not foresee his future acts of will but is conscious only of acts already posited. He therefore seems to himself to be free. And this feeling of freedom is quite natural. Yet the empirical act is really the unfolding of the intelligible or noumenal character. The former is the consequence of the latter and determined by it. As Spinoza said, the feeling or persuasion of freedom is really the effect of ignorance of the determining causes of one's actions.

At first sight, therefore, there would seem to be little point in indicating how people ought to act if they wish to escape from the slavery of desire and restless striving. For their actions are determined by their character. And these characters are objectifications of the Will, which is the Will to live and manifests itself precisely in desire and restless striving.

Schopenhauer argues, however, that character-determinism does not exclude changes in conduct. Let us suppose, for example, that I am accustomed to act in the way most calculated to bring me financial gain. One day somebody persuades me that treasure in heaven is more valuable and lasting than treasure on earth. And my new conviction leads to a change in conduct. Instead of trying to avail myself of an opportunity to enrich myself at the expense of Tom Jones I leave the opportunity of financial gain to him. My friends, if I have any, may say that my character has changed. But in point of fact I am the same sort of man that I was before. The actions which I now perform are different from my past actions, but my character has not changed. For I act for the same sort of motive, namely personal gain, though I have changed my view about what constitutes the most gainful line of conduct. In other words, my intelligible character determines what sort of motives move me to act; and the motive remains the same whether I am amassing riches on earth or renouncing them for celestial wealth.

Taken by itself, indeed, this example does not help us to understand how a denial of the Will to live can be possible. For it illustrates the permanence of egoism rather than the emergence of radical self-denial. And though it may be useful as indicating a plausible way of reconciling with the theory of character-determinism the empirical facts which appear to show the possibility of changes in character, it does not explain how the Will to live can turn back on itself, in and through its objectification, and deny itself. But we can pass over this point for the moment. It is sufficient to note that the idea of changing one's point of view plays an important role in Schopenhauer's philosophy as it does in that of Spinoza. For Schopenhauer envisages a progressive seeing through, as it were, the veil of Maya, the phenomenal world of individuality and multiplicity. This is possible because of the intellect's capacity to develop beyond the extent required for the fulfilment of its primary practical functions. And the degrees of moral advance correspond with the degrees of penetration of the veil of Maya.

Individuality is phenomenal. The noumenon is one: a plurality of individuals exists only for the phenomenal subject. And a man may, in the first instance, penetrate the illusion of individuality to the extent that he sets others on the same level as himself and does them no injury. We then have the just man, as distinct from the man who is so enmeshed in the veil of Maya that he asserts himself to the exclusion of others.

But it is possible to go further. A man may penetrate the veil of Maya to the extent of seeing that all individuals are really one. For they are all phenomena of the one undivided Will. We then have the ethical level of sympathy. We have goodness or virtue which is characterized by a disinterested love of others. True goodness is not, as Kant thought, a matter of obeying the categorical imperative for the sake of duty alone. True goodness is love, *agape* or *caritas* in distinction from *eros*, which is self-directed. And love is sympathy. 'All true and pure love is sympathy (*Mitleid*), and all love which is not sympathy is selfishness (*Selbstsucht*). *Eros* is selfishness; *agape* is sympathy.'[11] Schopenhauer combined his enthusiasm for the Hindu philosophy of Maya with a great admiration for the Buddha. And he had perhaps more sympathy with the Buddhist ethic than with more dynamic western concepts of altruism.

We can, however, go further still. For in and through man the Will can attain such a clear knowledge of itself that it turns from itself in horror and denies itself. The human will then ceases to become attached to anything, and the man pursues the path of asceticism and holiness. Schopenhauer proceeds, therefore, to extol voluntary chastity, poverty and self-mortification and holds out the prospect of a complete deliverance at death from the servitude of the Will.

It was remarked above that it is difficult to understand how the Will's denial of itself is possible. And Schopenhauer recognizes the difficulty. That the Will, manifested or objectified in the phenomenon, should deny itself and renounce what the phenomenon expresses, namely the Will to live, is, Schopenhauer frankly admits, a case of self-contradiction. But, contradiction or not, this radical act of self-denial can take place, even though it happens only in exceptional or rare cases. The Will in itself is free. For it is not subject to the principle of sufficient reason. And in the case of total self-denial, total self-renunciation, the essential freedom of the Will, the thing-in-itself, is made manifest in the phenomenon. In other words, Schopenhauer admits an exception to the principle of determinism. The free metaphysical Will 'by abolishing the nature which lies at the foundation of the phenomenon, while the phenomenon itself continues to exist in time, brings about a contradiction of the phenomenon with itself'.[12] That is to say, the saint does not kill himself; he continues to exist in time. But he totally renounces the reality which lies at the foundation of himself as a phenomenon and can be said to 'abolish it', namely the Will. This is a contradiction, but it is a contradiction which manifests the truth that the Will transcends the principle of sufficient reason.

What, we may ask, is the final end of virtue and holiness? Obviously, the man who denies the Will treats the world as nothing. For it is simply the appearance of the Will, which he denies. And in this sense at least it is true to say that when the Will turns and denies itself, 'our world with all its suns and milky ways is—nothing'.[13] But what happens a death? Does it mean total extinction or not?

'Before us', says Schopenhauer, 'there is indeed only noth ingness.'[14] And if, as seems to be the case, there can be nc question on his premisses of personal immortality, there i a sense in which this must obviously be true. For if individ uality is phenomenal, Maya, then death, the withdrawal, a. it were, from the phenomenal world, means the extinctior of consciousness. There remains perhaps the possibility o absorption in the one Will. But Schopenhauer seems to im ply, though he does not express himself clearly, that for the man who has denied the Will death means total extinction In life he has reduced existence to a tenuous thread, and a death it is finally destroyed. The man has reached the fina goal of the denial of the Will to live.

Schopenhauer does indeed speak of another possibility.[1] As we have already seen, he admits that the thing-in-itself the ultimate reality, may possibly possess attributes which we do not and cannot know. If so, these may remain wher Will has denied itself as Will. Hence there is presumably the possibility of a state being achieved through self-renunciatior which does not amount to nothingness. It could hardly be a state of knowledge, for the subject-object relationship is phe nomenal. But it might resemble the incommunicable experi ence to which mystics refer in obscure terms.

But though it is open to anyone to press this admission i he wishes, I should not myself care to do so. Partly, I suppose Schopenhauer feels bound to make the admission in view o his own statement that we know the ultimate reality in it self-manifestation as Will and not in itself, apart from phe nomena. Partly he may feel that the possibility cannot be excluded that the experiences of the mystics are not ade quately explicable in terms of his philosophy of the Will. Bu it would be going too far, were one to represent Schopen hauer as suggesting that either theism or pantheism may be true. Theism he stigmatizes as childish and unable to satisfy the mature mind. Pantheism he judges to be even more ab surd and, in addition, to be incompatible with any mora convictions. To identify a world filled with suffering and evi and cruelty with the Godhead or to interpret it as a theoph any in a literal sense is utter nonsense, worthy only of a Hegel. Moreover, it leads to a justification of all that happens, a justification which is incompatible with the demands of morality.

In any case, even if the ultimate reality possesses attributes other than those which justify its description as a blind Will, philosophy can know nothing about them. As far as philosophy is concerned, the thing-in-itself is Will. And the denial of the Will thus means for the philosopher the denial of reality, of all that there is, at least of all that he can know that there is. Hence philosophy at any rate must be content with the conclusion: 'no Will; no idea, no world'.[16] If the Will turns on itself and 'abolishes' itself, nothing is left.

4. The reader may perhaps be surprised that the philosophy of Schopenhauer has been considered under the general heading of the reaction to metaphysical idealism. And there is, of course, ground for such surprise. For in spite of Schopenhauer's constant abuse of Fichte, Schelling and Hegel his system undoubtedly belongs in some important respects to the movement of German speculative idealism. Will is indeed substituted for Fichte's Ego and Hegel's *Logos* or Idea, but the distinction between phenomenon and noumenon and the theory of the subjective and phenomenal character of space, time and causality are based on Kant. And it is not unreasonable to describe Schopenhauer's system as transcendental voluntaristic idealism. It is idealism in the sense that the world is said to be our idea or presentation. It is voluntaristic in the sense that the concept of Will rather than that of Reason or Thought is made the key to reality. And it is transcendental in the sense that the one individual Will is an absolute Will which manifests itself in the multiple phenomena of experience.

But though Schopenhauer's philosophy, when regarded from this point of view, appears as a member of the class of post-Kantian speculative systems which include those of Fichte, Schelling and Hegel, there are also considerable differences between it and the other three philosophies. For example, in the system of Hegel the ultimate reality is Reason, the self-thinking thought which actualizes itself as concrete spirit. The real is the rational and the rational the real. With Schopenhauer, however, reality is not so much rational as irrational: the world is the manifestation of a blind impulse or energy. There are, of course, certain similarities between the cosmic Reason of Hegel and the Schopenhauerian Will. For instance, for Hegel Reason has itself as an end, in the sense that it is thought which comes to think itself, and Schopenhauer's Will also has itself as an end, in the sense that it wills for the sake of willing. But there is a great difference between the idea of the universe as the life of self-unfolding Reason and the idea of the universe as the expression of a blind irrational impulse to existence or life. There are indeed elements of 'irrationalism' in German idealism itself. Schelling's theory of an irrational will in the Deity is a case in point. But with Schopenhauer the irrational character of existence becomes something to be emphasized; it is the cardinal truth rather than a partial truth, to be overcome in a higher synthesis.

This metaphysical irrationalism in Schopenhauer's philosophy may be obscured by his theory of art which sets before us the possibility of transmuting the horrors of existence in the serene world of aesthetic contemplation. But it has important consequences. For one thing there is the substitution of a metaphysically-grounded pessimism for the metaphysically-grounded optimism of absolute idealism. For another thing the deductive character of metaphysical idealism, which is natural enough if reality is regarded as the self-unfolding of Thought or Reason, gives way to a much more empirical approach. To be sure, the comprehensive and metaphysical character of Schopenhauer's philosophy, together with its strongly-marked romantic elements, gives it a family-likeness to the other great post-Kantian systems. At the same time it lends itself very easily to interpretation as a very wide hypothesis based on generalization from empirical data. And though we naturally and rightly regard it as part of the general movement of post-Kantian speculative metaphysics, it also looks forward to the inductive metaphysics which followed the collapse of absolute idealism.

Further, when we look back on Schopenhauer's system from a much later point in history, we can see in it a transition-stage between the idealist movement and the later philosophies of Life. Obviously, from one point of view the system is simply itself and not a 'transition-stage'. But this does not exclude the point of view which relates the system to the general movement of thought and sees it as a bridge between rationalist idealism and the philosophy of Life in Germany and France. It may be objected, of course, that Schopenhauer emphasizes a no-saying attitude to life. Life is something to be denied rather than affirmed. But Schopenhauer's theory of renunciation and denial is reached only by means of a philosophy which first emphasizes the idea of the Will to live and interprets the world in the light of this idea. Both instinct and reason are described by Schopenhauer as biological instruments or tools, even if he subsequently goes on to speak of the detachment of the human intellect from this practical orientation. Hence he provides the material, as it were, for the substitution of the idea of Life as the central idea in philosophy for that of Thought. Schopenhauer's pessimism no longer appears in the later philosophies of Life; but this does not alter the fact that he brings the idea of Life into the centre of the picture. True, the idea of Life is present in, for example, the philosophies of Fichte and Hegel. But with Schopenhauer the term 'Life' receives a primarily biological significance, and reason (which is also, of course, a form of life) is interpreted as an instrument of Life in a biological sense.

5. After the death of Hegel and after the failure of the revolution of 1848 the climate of opinion was more prepared for a favourable reconsideration of Schopenhauer's anti-rationalist and pessimistic system, and it became more widely known and won some adherents. Among these was Julius Frauenstädt (1813–79) who was converted from Hegelianism to the philosophy of Schopenhauer in the course of protracted conversations with the philosopher at Frankfurt. He modified somewhat the position of his master, maintaining that space, time and causality are not mere subjective forms and that individuality and multiplicity are not mere appearance. But he defended the theory that the ultimate reality is Will and published an edition of Schopenhauer's writings.

Schopenhauer's writings helped to stimulate in Germany an interest in oriental thought and religion. Among the

philosophers who were influenced by him in this direction
we can mention Paul Deussen (1845–1919), founder of the
Schopenhauer-Gesellschaft (Schopenhauer Society) and a
friend of Nietzsche. Deussen occupied a chair in the university of Kiel. In addition to a general history of philosophy he published several works on Indian thought and
contributed to bringing about the recognition of oriental philosophy as an integral part of the history of philosophy in
general.

Outside philosophical circles Schopenhauer's influence
was considerable. And special mention can be made of his
influence on Richard Wagner. The theory that music is the
highest of the arts was naturally congenial to Wagner, and he
thought of himself as the living embodiment of the Schopenhauerian concept of genius.[17] One cannot, of course, reduce
Wagner's outlook on life to Schopenhauer's philosophy. Many
of the composer's ideas were formed before he made the
acquaintance of this philosophy, and in the course of time
he modified and changed his ideas. But when he had been
introduced to Schopenhauer's writings in 1854, he sent the
philosopher an appreciative letter. And it is said that *Tristan
und Isolde* in particular reflects Schopenhauer's influence.
One can also mention the writer Thomas Mann as one who
owed a debt to Schopenhauer.

Within philosophical circles Schopenhauer's influence was
felt more in the form of a stimulus in this or that direction
than in the creation of anything which could be called a
school. In Germany his writings exercised a powerful influence on Nietzsche in his youth, though he afterwards repudiated Schopenhauer's no-saying attitude to Life. One
can also mention the names of Wilhelm Wundt and Hans
Vaihinger as philosophers who derived some stimulus from
Schopenhauer, though neither man was a disciple of the
great pessimist. As for France, it has been already remarked
that we must avoid the not uncommon mistake of assuming
that similarity of ideas necessarily reveals derivation or bor-
rowing. The development of the philosophy of Life in France
explains itself, without the need of involving the name of
Schopenhauer. But this does not, of course, exclude a stimu-

lative influence, direct or indirect, by the German philosopher on certain French thinkers.

6. There is at any rate one philosopher of some note whose most obvious affinity is with Schopenhauer and who derived a great deal from him, namely Eduard von Hartmann (1842–1906), a retired artillery officer who gave himself to study and writing. Von Hartmann, who also acknowledged debts to Leibniz and Schelling, endeavoured to develop the philosophy of Schopenhauer in such a way as to lessen the gulf between it and Hegelianism. And he claimed to have worked out his own system on an empirical and scientific basis. His best known work is *The Philosophy of the Unconscious* (*Die Philosophie des Unbewussten*, 1869).

The ultimate reality, according to von Hartmann, is indeed unconscious, but it cannot be, as Schopenhauer thought, simply a blind Will. For the matter of that, even Schopenhauer could not avoid speaking as though the Will had an end in view. Hence we must recognize that the one unconscious principle has two correlative and irreducible attributes, Will and Idea. Or we can express the matter by saying that the one unconscious principle has two co-ordinate functions. As Will it is responsible for the *that*, the existence, of the world: as Idea it is responsible for the *what*, the nature, of the world.

In this way von Hartmann claims to effect a synthesis between Schopenhauer and Hegel. The former's Will could never produce a teleological world-process, and the latter's Idea could never objectify itself in an existent world. The ultimate reality must thus be Will and Idea in one. But it does not follow that the ultimate reality must be conscious. On the contrary, we must turn to Schelling and import the notion of an unconscious Idea behind Nature. The world has more than one aspect. Will manifests itself, as Schopenhauer taught, in pain, suffering and evil. But the unconscious Idea, as Schelling maintained in his philosophy of Nature, manifests itself in finality, teleology, intelligible development and an advance towards consciousness.

Not content with reconciling Schopenhauer, Hegel and Schelling, von Hartmann is also concerned with synthesizing Schopenhauerian pessimism and Leibnizian optimism. The manifestation of the unconscious Absolute as Will gives grounds for pessimism, while its manifestation as Idea gives grounds for optimism. But the unconscious Absolute is one. Hence pessimism and optimism must be reconciled. And this demands a modification of Schopenhauer's analysis of pleasure and enjoyment as 'negative'. The pleasures, for example, of aesthetic contemplation and of intellectual activity are certainly positive.

Now, inasmuch as von Hartmann maintains that the end or *telos* of the cosmic process is the liberation of the Idea from the servitude of the Will through the development of consciousness, we might expect that optimism would have the last word. But though von Hartmann does indeed emphasize the way in which the development of intellect renders possible the higher pleasures, in particular those of aesthetic contemplation, he at the same time insists that the capacity for suffering grows in proportion to intellectual development. For this reason primitive peoples and the uneducated classes are happier than civilized peoples and the more cultured classes.

To think, therefore, that progress in civilization and in intellectual development brings with it an increase in happiness is an illusion. The pagans thought that happiness was attainable in this world. And this was an illusion. The Christians recognized it as such and looked for happiness in heaven. But this too was an illusion. Yet those who recognize it as such tend to fall into a third illusion, namely that of thinking that a terrestrial Paradise can be attained through unending progress. They fail to see two truths. First, increasing refinement and mental development increase the capacity for suffering. Secondly, progress in material civilization and well-being is accompanied by a forgetfulness of spiritual values and by the decadence of genius.

These illusions are ultimately the work of the unconscious principle which shows its cunning by inducing the human race in this way to perpetuate itself. But von Hartmann looks forward to a time when the human race in general will have so developed its consciousness of the real state of affairs that a cosmic suicide will take place. Schopenhauer was wrong in suggesting that an individual can attain annihilation by self-denial and asceticism. What is needed is the greatest possible development of consciousness, so that in the end humanity may understand the folly of volition, commit suicide and, with its own destruction, bring the world-process to an end. For by that time the volition of the unconscious Absolute, which is responsible for the existence of the world, will, von Hartmann hopes, have passed into or been objectified in humanity. Hence suicide on humanity's part will bring the world to an end.

Most people would describe this astonishing theory as pessimism. Not so von Hartmann. The cosmic suicide requires as its condition the greatest possible evolution of consciousness and the triumph of intellect over volition. But this is precisely the end aimed at by the Absolute as Idea, as unconscious Spirit. One can say, therefore, that the world will be redeemed by the cosmic suicide and its own disappearance. And a world which achieves redemption is the best possible world.

There are only two comments which I wish to make on von Hartmann's philosophy. First, if a man writes as much as von Hartmann did, he can hardly avoid making some true and apposite statements, be their setting what it may. Secondly, if the human race destroys itself, which is now a physical possibility, it is much more likely to be due to its folly than to its wisdom or, in von Hartmann's language, to the triumph of Will rather than to that of Idea.

Chapter Fifteen

THE TRANSFORMATION OF
IDEALISM (1)

Introductory remarks – Feuerbach and the transformation of theology into anthropology – Ruge's criticism of the Hegelian attitude to history – Stirner's philosophy of the ego.

1. When considering the influence of Hegel we noted that after the philosopher's death there emerged a right and a left wing. And something was said about the differences between them in regard to the interpretation of the idea of God in the philosophy of Hegel and about the system's relation to Christianity. We can now turn to consider some of the more radical representatives of the left wing who were concerned not so much with interpreting Hegel as with using some of his ideas to transform metaphysical idealism into something quite different.

These thinkers are commonly known as the Young Hegelians. This term ought indeed to signify the younger generation of those who stood under the influence of Hegel, whether they belonged to the right or to the left wing or to the centre. But it has come to be reserved in practice for the radical members of the left wing, such as Feuerbach. From one point of view they might well be called anti-Hegelians. For they represent a line of thought which culminated in dialectical materialism, whereas a cardinal tenet of Hegel is that the Absolute must be defined as Spirit. From another point of view, however, the name 'anti-Hegelian' would be a misnomer. For they were concerned to set Hegel on his feet, and even if they transformed his philosophy, they made use, as already mentioned, of some of his own ideas. In other words, they represent a left-wing development of Hegelianism, a development which was also a transformation. We find both continuity and discontinuity.

2. Ludwig Feuerbach (1804–72) studied Protestant theol-

ogy at Heidelberg and then went to Berlin where he attended
Hegel's lectures and gave himself to the study of philosophy. In 1828 he became an unsalaried lecturer (*Privatdozent*)
at the university of Erlangen. But finding no prospect of ad-
vancement in the academic career he retired into a life of
private study and writing. At the time of his death he was
living near Nuremberg.

If one were to look only at the titles of Feuerbach's writings, one would naturally conclude that he was first and foremost a theologian, or at any rate that he had strong theological interests. True, his earlier works are obviously concerned
with philosophy. For example, in 1833 he published a history of modern philosophy from Francis Bacon to Spinoza;
in 1837 an exposition and criticism of Leibniz's system; in
1838 a work on Bayle; and in 1839 an essay devoted to criticism of Hegel's philosophy. But then come his important
works, such as *The Essence of Christianity* (*Das Wesen des
Christentums*, 1841), *The Essence of Religion* (*Das Wesen
der Religion*, 1845) and *Lectures on the Essence of Religion*
(*Vorlesungen über das Wesen der Religion*, 1851). And
these titles, together with such others as *On Philosophy and
Christianity* (*Ueber Philosophie und Christentum*, 1839)
and *The Essence of Faith in Luther's sense* (*Das Wesen des
Glaubens im Sinne Luthers*, 1844), clearly suggest that the
author's mind is preoccupied with theological problems.

In a certain sense this impression is quite correct. Feuerbach himself asserted that the main theme of his writings
was religion and theology. But he did not mean by this statement that he believed in the objective existence of a God
outside human thought. He meant that he was principally
concerned with clarifying the real significance and function of
religion in the light of human life and thought as a whole.
Religion was not for him an unimportant phenomenon, an
unfortunate piece of superstition of which we can say that it
would have been better if it had never existed and that its
effect has been simply that of retarding man's development.
On the contrary, the religious consciousness was for Feuerbach an integral stage in the development of human consciousness in general. At the same time he regarded the idea
of God as a projection of man's ideal for himself and religion

as a temporal, even if essential, stage in the development of human consciousness. He can be said, therefore, to have substituted anthropology for theology.

Feuerbach reaches this position, the substitution of anthropology for theology, through a radical criticism of the Hegelian system. But the criticism is in a sense internal. For it is presupposed that Hegelianism is the highest expression of philosophy up to date. Hegel was 'Fichte mediated through Schelling',[1] and 'the Hegelian philosophy is the culminating point of speculative systematic philosophy'.[2] But though in the system of Hegel idealism, and indeed metaphysics in general, has attained its most complete expression, the system is not tenable. What is required is to set Hegel on his feet. In particular we have to find our way back from the conceptual abstractions of absolute idealism to concrete reality. Speculative philosophy has tried to make a transition 'from the abstract to the concrete, from the ideal to the real'.[3] But this was a mistake. The passage or transition from the ideal to the real has a part to play only in practical or moral philosophy, where it is a question of realizing ideals through action. When it is a matter of theoretical knowledge, we must start with the real, with Being.

Hegel, of course, starts with Being. But the point is that for Feuerbach Being in this context is Nature, not Idea or Thought.[4] 'Being is subject and thought is predicate.'[5] The fundamental reality is spatio-temporal Nature; consciousness and thought are secondary, derived. True, the existence of Nature can be known only by a conscious subject. But the being which distinguishes itself from Nature knows that it is not the ground of Nature. On the contrary, man knows Nature by distinguishing himself from his ground, sensible reality. 'Nature is thus the ground of man.'[6]

We can say indeed with Schleiermacher that the feeling of dependence is the ground of religion. But 'that on which man depends and feels himself to be dependent is originally nothing else but Nature'.[7] Thus the primary object of religion, if we view religion historically and not simply in the form of Christian theism, is Nature. Natural religion ranges from the deification of objects such as trees and fountains up to the idea of the Deity conceived as the physical cause of natural things. But the foundation of natural religion in all its phases is man's feeling of dependence on external sensible reality. 'The divine essence which manifests itself in Nature is nothing else but Nature which reveals and manifests itself to man and imposes itself on him as a divine being.'[8]

Man can objectify Nature only by distinguishing himself from it. And he can return upon himself and contemplate his own essence. What is this essence? 'Reason, will, heart. To a perfect man there belong the power of thought, the power of willing, the power of the heart.'[9] Reason, will and love in unity constitute the essence of man. Further, if we think any of these three perfections in itself, we think of it as unlimited. We do not conceive, for example, the power of thought as being in itself limited to this or that object. And if we think the three perfections as infinite, we have the idea of God as infinite knowledge, infinite will and infinite love. Monotheism, at least when God is endowed with moral attributes, is thus the result of man's projection of his own essence raised to infinity. 'The divine essence is nothing else but the essence of man; or, better, it is the essence of man when freed from the limitations of the individual, that is to say, actual corporeal man, objectified and venerated as an independent Being distinct from man himself.'[10]

In *The Essence of Christianity* Feuerbach concentrates on the idea of God as a projection of human self-consciousness, whereas in *The Essence of Religion*, in which religion is considered historically, he lays emphasis on the feeling of dependence on Nature as the ground of religion. But he also brings the two points of view together. Man, conscious of his dependence on external reality, begins by venerating the forces of Nature and particular natural phenomena. But he does not rise to the concept of personal gods or of God without self-projection. In polytheism the qualities which differentiate man from man are deified in the form of a multiplicity of anthropomorphic deities, each with his or her peculiar characteristics. In monotheism it is that which unifies men, namely the essence of man as such, which is projected into a transcendent sphere and deified. And a powerful factor in making the transition to some form of monotheism is the consciousness that Nature not only serves man's physical needs but can also be made to serve the purpose which man freely sets before himself. For in this way he comes to think of Nature as existing for him, and so as a unity which embodies a purpose and is the product of an intelligent Creator. But in thinking the Creator man projects his own essence. And if we strip from the idea of God all that is due to this projection, we are left simply with Nature. Hence, though religion is ultimately grounded on man's feeling of dependence on Nature, the most important factor in the formation of the concept of an infinite personal Deity is man's projection of his own essence.

Now, this self-projection expresses man's alienation from himself. 'Religion is the separation of man from himself: he sets God over against himself as an opposed being. God is not what man is, and man is not what God is. God is the infinite Being, man the finite; God is perfect, man is imperfect; God is eternal, man is temporal; God is almighty, man is powerless; God is holy, man is sinful. God and man are extremes: God is the absolutely positive, the essence of all realities, while man is the negative, the essence of all nothingness.'[11] Thus by projecting his essence into a transcendent sphere and objectifying it as God man reduces himself to a pitiful, miserable sinful creature.

In this case, of course, religion is something to be overcome. But it does not follow that religion has not played an essential role in human life. On the contrary, man's objectification of his own essence in the idea of God forms an integral stage in the explicit development of his self-awareness. For he has first to objectify his essence before he can become aware of it as *his* essence. And in the highest or most perfect form of religion, namely Christianity, this objectification reaches the point at which it calls for its own overcoming. Man is a social being, and the power of love belongs to his essence. He is an 'I' in relation to a 'Thou'. And in the Christian religion awareness of this fact finds a projected expression in the doctrine of the Trinity. Further, in the doctrine of the Incarnation, 'the Christian religion has united the word *Man* with the word *God* in the one name *God-Man*, thus making humanity an attribute of the supreme Being'.[12] What remains is to reverse this relation by making Deity an attribute of man. 'The new philosophy has, in accordance with the truth, made this attribute (humanity) the substance; it has made the predicate the subject. The new philosophy is . . . the *truth* of Christianity.'[13]

This last statement recalls to mind Hegel's view of the relation between the absolute religion and the absolute philosophy. But it is certainly not Feuerbach's intention to suggest that 'the new philosophy' can coexist with Christianity in the same mind. On the contrary, the new philosophy abandons the name of Christianity precisely because it gives the rational truth-value of the Christian religion and, in so doing, transforms it from theology into anthropology. Philosophy's elucidation of Christianity is no longer Christianity. Once a man understands that 'God' is a name for his own idealized essence projected into a transcendent sphere, he overcomes the self-alienation involved in religion. And the way then lies open to the objectification of this essence in man's own activity and social life. Man recovers faith in himself and in his own powers and future.

The abandonment of theology involves the abandonment of historic Hegelianism. For 'the Hegelian philosophy is the last place of refuge, the last rational prop of theology'.[14] And 'he who does not give up the Hegelian philosophy does not give up theology. For the Hegelian doctrine that Nature, reality, is posited by the Idea is simply the *rational* expression of the theological doctrine that Nature has been created by God. . . .'[15] Yet for the overcoming of theology we have to make use of the Hegelian concept of self-alienation. Hegel spoke of the return of absolute Spirit to itself from its self-alienation in Nature. For this concept we must substitute that of man's return to himself. And this means 'the transformation of theology into anthropology, and its dissolution therein'.[16] Yet philosophical anthropology is itself religion. For it gives the truth of religion in the highest form that religion has attained. 'What yesterday was still religion is not religion today, and what is accounted atheism today is accounted religion tomorrow.'[17]

With the substitution of anthropology for theology man becomes his own highest object, an end to himself. But this does not mean egoism. For man is by essence a social being:

he is not simply *Mensch* but *Mit-Mensch*. And the supreme principle of philosophy is 'the unity between man and man',[18] a unity which should find expression in love. 'Love is the universal law of intelligence and nature—it is nothing else but the realization of the unity of the species on the plane of feeling.'[19]

Feuerbach is obviously alive to the fact that Hegel emphasized man's social nature. But he insists that Hegel had an erroneous idea of the ground of unity in the species. In absolute idealism men are thought to be united in proportion as they become one with the life of universal spirit, interpreted as self-thinking Thought. It is thus on the level of pure thought that human unity is primarily achieved. But here again Hegel needs to be set squarely on his feet. The special nature of man is grounded on the biological level, 'on the *reality* of the *difference* between I and Thou',[20] that is, on sexual differentiation. The relation between man and woman manifests unity-in-difference and difference-in-unity. This distinction between male and female is not indeed simply a biological distinction. For it determines distinct ways of feeling and thinking and thus affects the whole personality. Nor is it, of course, the only way in which man's social nature is manifested. But Feuerbach wishes to emphasize the fact that man's nature as *Mit-Mensch* is grounded on the fundamental reality, which is sensible reality, not pure thought. In other words, sexual differentiation shows that the individual human being is incomplete. The fact that the 'I' calls for the 'Thou' as its complement is shown in its primary and basic form in the fact that the male needs the female and the female the male.

One might expect that with this insistence on man's special nature, on the unity of the species and on love, Feuerbach would go on to develop the theme of a supranational society or to propose some form of international federation. But in point of fact he is sufficiently Hegelian to represent the State as the living unity of men and the objective expression of the consciousness of this unity. 'In the State the powers of man divide and develop only to constitute an infinite being through this division and through their reunion; many human beings, many powers are one power. The

State is the essence of all realities, the State is the providence of man. . . . The true State is the unlimited, infinite, true, complete, divine Man . . . the absolute Man.'[21]

From this it follows that 'politics must become our religion',[22] though, paradoxically, atheism is a condition of this religion. Religion in the traditional sense, says Feuerbach, tends to dissolve rather than to unite the State. And the State can be for us an Absolute only if we substitute man for God, anthropology for theology. 'Man is the fundamental essence of the State. And the State is the actualized, developed and explicit totality of human nature.'[23] Justice cannot be done to this truth if we continue to project human nature into a transcendent sphere in the form of the concept of God.

The State which Feuerbach has in mind is the democratic republic. Protestantism, he remarks, put the monarch in the place of the Pope. 'The Reformation destroyed *religious* Catholicism, but in its place the modern era set *political* Catholicism'.[24] The so-called modern era has been up to now a Protestant Middle Ages. And it is only through the dissolution of the Protestant religion that we can develop the true democratic republic as the living unity of men and the concrete expression of man's essence.

If regarded from a purely theoretical standpoint, Feuerbach's philosophy is certainly not outstanding. For example, his attempt to dispose of theism by an account of the genesis of the idea of God is superficial. But from the historical point of view his philosophy possesses real significance. In general, it forms part of a movement away from a theological interpretation of the world to an interpretation in which man himself, considered as a social being, occupies the centre of the stage. Feuerbach's substitution of anthropology for theology is an explicit acknowledgement of this. And to a certain extent he is justified in regarding Hegelianism as a half-way house in the process of this transformation. In particular, the philosophy of Feuerbach is a stage in the movement which culminated in the dialectical materialism and the economic theory of history of Marx and Engels. True, Feuerbach's thought moves within the framework of the idea of the State as the supreme expression of social unity and of the concept of political rather than of economic man. But his transformation of idealism into materialism and his insistence on overcoming man's self-alienation as manifested in religion prepared the ground for the thought of Marx and Engels. Marx may have criticized Feuerbach severely, but he certainly owed him a debt.

3. In view of Feuerbach's preoccupation with the subject of religion the shift of emphasis in the Hegelian left wing from logical, metaphysical and religious problems to problems of a social and political nature is perhaps better illustrated by Arnold Ruge (1802–80). Ruge's first two works, written when he was more or less an orthodox Hegelian, were on aesthetics. But his interest came to centre on political and historical problems. In 1838 he founded the *Hallische Jahrbücher für deutsche Wissenschaft und Kunst*, having among his collaborators David Strauss, Feuerbach and Bruno Bauer (1809–82). In 1841 the review was renamed *Deutsche Jahrbücher für Wissenschaft und Kunst*, and at this time Marx began to collaborate with it. Early in 1843, however, the periodical, which had become more and more radical in tone and had aroused the hostile attention of the Prussian government, was suppressed; and Ruge moved to Paris where he founded the *Deutsch-französische Jahrbücher*. But a break between Ruge and Marx and the dispersal of other contributors brought the life of the new review to a speedy close. Ruge went to Zürich. In 1847 he returned to Germany, but after the failure of the revolution of 1848 he crossed over into England. In his last years he became a supporter of the new German empire. He died at Brighton.

Ruge shared Hegel's belief that history is a progressive advance towards the realization of freedom, and that freedom is attained in the State, the creation of the rational General Will. He was thus prepared to give full marks to Hegel for having utilized Rousseau's concept of the *volonté generale* and for having grounded the State on the universal will which realizes itself in and through the wills of individuals. At the same time he criticized Hegel for having given an interpretation of history which was closed to the future, in the sense that it left no room for novelty. In the Hegelian system, according to Ruge, historical events and institutions were portrayed as examples or illustrations of a dialectical scheme which worked itself out with logical necessity. Hegel failed to understand the uniqueness and non-repeatable character of historical events, institutions and epochs. And his deduction of the Prussian monarchical constitution was a sign of the closed character of his thought, that is, of its lack of openness to the future, to progress, to novelty.

The basic trouble with Hegel, in Ruge's view, was that he derived the scheme of history from the system. We ought not to presuppose a rational scheme and then derive the pattern of history from it. If we do this, we inevitably end by justifying the actual state of affairs. Our task is rather that of *making* history rational, of bringing, for example, new institutions into being which will be more rational than those already in existence. In other words, in place of Hegel's predominantly speculative and theoretical attitude to history and to social and political life we need to substitute a practical and revolutionary attitude.

This does not mean that we have to abandon the idea of a teleological movement in history. But it does mean that the philosopher should endeavour to discern the movement and demands of the spirit of the time (*der Zeitgeist*) and that he should criticize existing institutions in the light of these demands. Hegel's career fell in the period after the French revolution, but he had little understanding of the real movement of the *Zeitgeist*. He did not see, for instance, that the realization of freedom of which he talked so much could not be achieved without radical changes in the institutions which he canonized.

We can see in Ruge's attitude an attempt to combine belief in a teleological movement in history with a practical and revolutionary attitude. And his criticism of Hegel was congenial to Marx. The great idealist was primarily concerned with understanding history, with seeing the rational in the real. Ruge and Marx were concerned with making history, with understanding the world in order to change it. But Ruge refused to follow Marx in the path of communism. In his opinion Marx's idea of man was very one-sided, and he opposed to it what he called an integral humanism. It is not only man's material and economic needs which require to be satisfied but also his spiritual needs. However, the break between the two men was by no means due simply to ideological differences.

4. A counterblast to the general movement of thought in left-wing Hegelianism came from the somewhat eccentric philosopher Max Stirner (1806–56) whose real name was Johann Kaspar Schmidt. After attending the lectures of Schleiermacher and Hegel at Berlin Stirner taught in a school for a few years and then gave himself to private study. His best known work is *The Individual and His Property* (*Der Einzige und sein Eigentum*, 1845).

At the beginning of this work Stirner quotes Feuerbach's statement that man is man's supreme being and Bruno Bauer's assertion that man has just been discovered. And he invites his readers to take a more careful look at this supreme being and new discovery. What do they find? What he himself finds is the ego, not the absolute ego of Fichte's philosophy but the concrete individual self, the man of flesh and blood. And the individual ego is a unique reality which seeks from the start to preserve itself and so to assert itself. For it has to preserve itself in the face of other beings which threaten, actually or potentially, its existence as an ego. In other words, the ego's concern is with itself.

It is precisely this unique individual ego which most philosophers pass over and forget. In Hegelianism the individual self was belittled in favour of absolute Thought or Spirit. Paradoxically, man was supposed to realize his true self or essence in proportion as he became a moment in the life of the universal Spirit. An abstraction was substituted for concrete reality. And Feuerbach's philosophy is tarred with the same brush. To be sure, Feuerbach is right in claiming that man should overcome the self-alienation involved in the religious attitude and rediscover himself. For in Judaism and Christianity freedom, the very essence of man, was projected outside the human being in the concept of God, and man was enslaved. He was told to deny himself and obey. But though Feuerbach is justified in his polemics against religious self-alienation and against the abstractions of Hegelianism, he fails to understand the significance of the unique individual and offers us instead the abstraction of Humanity or of absolute Man and the fulfilment of selfhood in and through the State. Similarly, even if in humanistic socialism Humanity is substituted for the Christian God and the Hegelian Absolute, the individual is still sacrificed on the altar of an abstraction. In fine, the left-wing Hegelians can be subjected to the same sort of criticism which they level against Hegel himself.

In place of such abstractions as Absolute Spirit, Humanity and the universal essence of man Stirner enthrones the unique and free individual. In his view freedom is realized through owning. And, as this unique individual, I own all that I can appropriate. This does not mean, of course, that I have in fact to make everything my property. But there is no reason why I should not do so, other than my inability to do it or my own free decision not to do it. I proceed out of and return into the 'creative nothing', and while I exist my concern is with myself alone. My endeavour should be that of expressing my unique individuality without allowing myself to be enslaved or hampered by any alleged higher power such as God or the State or by any abstraction such as Humanity or the universal Moral Law. Subservience to such fictitious entities weakens my sense of my own uniqueness.

Stirner's philosophy of egoism possesses a certain interest and significance in so far as it represents the protest of the concrete human person against the worship of the collectivity or of an abstraction. Moreover some may wish to see in it some spiritual affinity with existentialism. And there is at least some ground for this. It can hardly be said that emphasis on the theme of property is a characteristic of existentialism, but the theme of the unique free individual certainly is.[25] Stirner's philosophy has been mentioned here, however, not for any anticipation of later thought but rather as a phase in the movement of revolt against metaphysical idealism. One can say perhaps that it represents an expression of the nominalistic reaction which over-emphasis on the universal always tends to evoke. It is, of course, an exaggeration. A healthy insistence on the uniqueness of the individual self is coupled with a fantastic philosophy of egoism.

But the protest against an exaggeration very often takes the form of an exaggeration in the opposite direction.

Apart, however, from the fact that Stirner was far from being a great philosopher, his thought was out of harmony with the *Zeitgeist*, and it is not surprising if Marx saw in it the expression of the alienated isolated individual in a doomed bourgeois society. Marx and Engels may have incorporated in their philosophy the very features which Stirner so disliked, substituting the economic class for Hegel's national State, the class war for the dialectic of States, and Humanity for absolute Spirit. But the fact remains that their philosophy was, for good or ill, to possess a great historical importance, whereas Max Stirner is remembered only as an eccentric thinker whose philosophy has little significance except when it is seen as a moment in the perennially recurrent protest of the free individual against the voraciously devouring universal.

Chapter Sixteen

THE TRANSFORMATION OF
IDEALISM (2)

Introductory remarks – The lives and writings of Marx and Engels and the development of their thought – Materialism – Dialectical materialism – The materialist conception of history – Comments on the thought of Marx and Engels.

1. Confronted with the thought of Marx and Engels the historian of philosophy finds himself in a rather difficult situation. On the one hand the contemporary influence and importance of their philosophy is so obvious that the not uncommon practice of according it little more than a passing mention in connection with the development of left-wing Hegelianism scarcely seems to be justified. Indeed, it might seem more appropriate to treat it as one of the great modern visions of human life and history. On the other hand it would be a mistake to allow oneself to be so hypnotized by the indubitable importance of Communism in the modern world as to tear its basic ideology from its historical setting in nineteenth-century thought. Marxism is indeed a living philosophy in the sense that it inspired and gave impetus and coherence to a force which, for good or ill, exercises a vast influence in the modern world. It is accepted, doubtless with varying degrees of conviction, by a great many people today. At the same time it is arguable that its continued life as a more or less unified system is primarily due to its association with an extra-philosophical factor, a powerful social-political movement, the contemporary importance of which nobody would deny. It is true, of course, that the connection is not accidental. That is to say, Communism did not adopt a system of ideas which lay outside the process of its own birth and development. But the point is that it is the Communist Party which has saved Marxism from undergoing the fate of other nineteenth-century philosophies by turning it into a

faith. And the historian of nineteenth-century philosophy is justified in dwelling primarily on the thought of Marx and Engels in its historical setting and in prescinding from its contemporary importance as the basic creed of a Party, however powerful this Party may be.

The present writer has therefore decided to confine his attention to some aspects of the thought of Marx and Engels themselves and to neglect, except for some brief references, the subsequent development of their philosophy as well as its impact on the modern world through the medium of the Communist Party. When it is a question of an inevitably somewhat overcrowded account of philosophy in Germany during the nineteenth century, this restriction does not really stand in need of any defence. But as the importance of Communism in our day may lead the reader to think that a more extended treatment would have been desirable and even that this volume should have culminated in the philosophy of Marx, it may be as well to point out that to depict Marxism as the apex and point of confluence of nineteenth-century German philosophical thought would be to give a false historical picture under the determining influence of the political situation in the world today.

2. Karl Marx (1818–83) was of Jewish descent. His father, a liberal Jew, became a Protestant in 1816, and Marx himself was baptized in 1824. But his father's religious convictions were by no means profound, and he was brought up in the traditions of Kantian rationalism and political liberalism. After his school education at Trier he studied at the universities of Bonn and Berlin. At Berlin he associated with the Young Hegelians, the members of the so-called *Doktorklub*, especially with Bruno Bauer. But he soon became dissatisfied with the purely theoretical attitude of left-wing Hegelianism, and this dissatisfaction was intensified when in 1842 he began to collaborate in editing at Cologne the newly-founded *Rheinische Zeitung*, of which he soon became the chief editor. For his work brought him into closer contact with concrete political, social and economic problems, and he became convinced that theory must issue in practical activity, in action, if it is to be effective. This may indeed seem to be obvious, even a tautology. But the point is that Marx was al-

ready turning away from the Hegelian notion that it is the philosopher's business simply to understand the world and that we can trust, as it were, to the working out of the Idea or of Reason. Criticism of traditional ideas and existing institutions is not sufficient to change them unless it issues in political and social action. In fact, if religion signifies man's alienation from himself, so also in its own way does German philosophy. For it divorces man from reality, making him a mere spectator of the process in which he is involved.

At the same time reflection on the actual situation led Marx to adopt a critical attitude towards the Hegelian theory of the State. And it was apparently in this period, between 1841 and 1843, that he wrote a criticism of Hegel's concept of the State under the title *Kritik des Hegelschen Staatsrechts*. According to Hegel objective spirit reaches its highest expression in the State, the family and civil society being moments or phases in the dialectical development of the idea of the State. The State, as the full expression of the Idea in the form of objective Spirit, is for Hegel the 'subject', while the family and civil society are 'predicates'. But this is to put things the wrong way round. The family and civil society, not the State, are the 'subject': they form the basic realities in human society. Hegel's State is an abstract universal, a governmental and bureaucratic institution which stands apart from and over against the life of the people. In fact there is a contradiction between public and private concerns. Transposing on to the political plane Feuerbach's idea of religion as an expression of man's self-alienation, Marx argues that in the State as conceived by Hegel man alienates his true nature. For man's true life is conceived as existing in the State whereas in point of fact the State stands over against individual human beings and their interests. And this contradiction or gulf between public and private concerns will last until man becomes socialized man and the political State, exalted by Hegel, gives way to a true democracy in which the social organism is no longer something external to man and his real interests.

Marx also attacks Hegel's idea of insistence on private property as the basis of civil society. But he has not yet arrived at an explicit communistic theory. He appeals rather for the abolition of the monarchy and the development of social democracy. The idea, however, of a classless economic society is implicit in his criticism of Hegel's political State and in his notion of true democracy. Further, his concern with man as such and his internationalism are also implicit in his criticism of Hegel.

Early in 1843 the life of the *Rheinische Zeitung* was brought to a close by the political authorities, and Marx went to Paris where he collaborated with Ruge in editing the *Deutsch-französische Jahrbücher*. In the first and only number which appeared he published two articles, one a criticism of Hegel's *Philosophy of Right*, the other a review of essays by Bruno Bauer on Judaism. In the first of these articles Marx refers to Feuerbach's analysis of religion as a self-alienation on man's part and asks why it occurs. Why does man create the illusory world of the supernatural and project into it his own true self? The answer is that religion reflects or expresses the distortion in human society. Man's political, social and economic life is incapable of fulfilling his true self, and he creates the illusory world of religion and seeks his happiness therein, so that religion is man's self-administered opium. Inasmuch as religion prevents man from seeking his happiness where alone it can be found, it must indeed be attacked. But a criticism of religion is of little value if it is divorced from political and social criticism, for it attacks the effect while neglecting the cause. Further, criticism by itself is in any case inadequate. We cannot change society simply by philosophizing about it. Thought must issue in action, that is, in social revolution. For philosophical criticism raises problems which can be solved only in this way. In Marx's language philosophy must be overcome, this overcoming being also the realization (*Verwirklichung*) of philosophy. It must leave the plane of theory and penetrate to the masses. And when it does so, it is no longer philosophy but takes the form of a social revolution which must be the work of the most oppressed class, namely the proletariat. By abolishing private property consciously and explicitly the proletariat will emancipate itself and, together with itself, the whole of society. For egoism and social injustice are bound up with the institution of private property.

In certain obvious respects Marx's way of thinking is influenced by Hegel's. For example, the idea of alienation and its overcoming is of Hegelian origin. But it is equally obvious that he rejects the notion of history as the self-manifestation or self-expression of the Absolute defined as Spirit. His concept of theory as realizing itself through practice or action reminds us indeed of Hegel's concept of the concrete self-unfolding of the Idea. But the fundamental reality is for him, as for Feuerbach, Nature rather than the Idea or *Logos*. And in his political and economic manuscripts of 1844 Marx emphasizes the difference between his own position and that of Hegel.

True, Marx retains a profound admiration for Hegel. He praises him for having recognized the dialectical character of all process and for having seen that man develops or realizes himself through his own activity, through self-alienation and its overcoming. At the same time Marx sharply criticizes Hegel for his idealist concept of man as self-consciousness and for having conceived human activity as being primarily the spiritual activity of thought. Hegel did indeed look on man as expressing himself outwardly in the objective order and then returning to himself on a higher plane. But his idealism involved the tendency to do away with the objective order by interpreting it simply in relation to consciousness. Hence the process of self-alienation and its overcoming was for him a process in and for thought rather than in objective reality.

Whether Marx does justice to Hegel may be open to question. But in any case he opposes to the primacy of the Idea the primacy of sensible reality. And he maintains that the fundamental form of human work is not thought but manual labour in which man alienates himself in the objective product of his labour, a product which, in society as at present constituted, does not belong to the producer. This alienation cannot be overcome by a process of thought in which the idea of private property is regarded as a moment in the dialectical movement to a higher idea. It can be overcome only through a social revolution which abolishes private property and effects the transition to communism. The dialectical movement is not a movement of thought about reality: it is the movement of reality itself, the historical process. And

the negation of the negation (the abolition of private property) involves the positive occurrence of a new historical situation in which man's self-alienation is overcome in actual fact
and not simply for thought.

This insistence on the unity of thought and action and on
the overcoming of man's self-alienation through social revolution and the transition to communism, an insistence which
shows itself in the articles of 1843 and the manuscripts of
1844, can be regarded, in part at least, as the result of a marriage between left-wing Hegelianism and the socialist movement with which Marx came into contact at Paris. Dissatisfied
with the predominantly critical and theoretical attitude of
the Young Hegelians, Marx found at Paris a much more dynamic attitude. For besides studying the classical English
economists, such as Adam Smith and Ricardo, he made the
personal acquaintance of German socialists in exile and of
French socialists such as Proudhon and Louis Blanc, as well
as of revolutionaries such as the Russian Bakunin. And even
if he had already shown an inclination to emphasize the need
for action, this personal contact with the socialist movement
had a profound influence upon his mind. At the same time
he came to the conclusion that though the socialists were
more in touch with reality than were the German philosophers, they failed to make an adequate appraisal of the situation and its demands. They needed an intellectual instrument to give unity of vision, purpose and method. And
though Marx spoke of the overcoming of philosophy and did
not regard his own theory of history as a philosophical system, it is clear not only that this is in fact what it became
but also that it owed much to a transformation of Hegelianism.

The most important personal contact, however, which
Marx made at Paris was his meeting with Engels who arrived
in the city from England in 1844. The two men had indeed
met one another a couple of years before, but the period of
their friendship and collaboration dates from 1844.

Friedrich Engels (1820–95) was the son of a rich indus-
trialist, and he took up a position in his father's firm at an
early age. While doing his military service at Berlin in 1841
he associated with the circle of Bruno Bauer and adopted an

Hegelian position. The writings of Feuerbach, however, turned his mind away from idealism to materialism. In 1842 he went to Manchester to work for his father's firm and interested himself in the ideas of the early English socialists. It was at Manchester that he wrote his study of the working classes in England (*Die Lage der arbeitenden Klassen in England*) which was published in Germany in 1845. He also composed for the *Deutsch-französische Jahrbücher* his *Outlines of a Critique of National Economy* (*Umrisse einer Kritik der Nationalökonomie*).

An immediate result of the meeting between Marx and Engels in Paris was their collaboration in writing *The Holy Family* (*Die heilige Family*, 1845) directed against the idealism of Bruno Bauer and his associates who appeared to think that 'criticism' was a transcendent being which had found its embodiment in the 'Holy Family', namely the members of Bauer's circle. In opposition to the idealist emphasis on thought and consciousness Marx and Engels maintained that the forms of the State, law, religion and morality were determined by the stages of the class-war.

At the beginning of 1845 Marx was expelled from France and went to Brussels where he composed eleven theses against Feuerbach, ending with the famous statement that whereas philosophers have only tried to understand the world in different ways, the real need is to change it. When he had been joined by Engels the two men collaborated in writing *The German Ideology* (*Die deutsche Ideologie*) which remained unpublished until 1932. The work is a criticism of contemporary German philosophy as represented by Feuerbach, Bauer and Stirner and of the German socialists, and it is important for its outline of the materialist conception of history. The fundamental historical reality is social man in his activity in Nature. This material or sensible activity is man's basic life, and it is life which determines consciousness, not, as the idealists imagine, the other way round. In other words, the fundamental factor in history is the process of material or economic production. And the formation of social classes, the warfare between classes and, indirectly, the forms of political life, of law and of ethics are all determined by the varying successive modes of production. Further, the whole

historical process is moving dialectically towards the prole-
tarian revolution and the coming of communism, not the
self-knowledge of absolute Spirit or any such philosophical
illusion.

In 1847 Marx published in French his *Poverty of Philosophy* (*Misère de la philosophie*), a reply to Proudhon's *Philosophy of Poverty* (*Philosophie de la misère*). In it he
attacks the notion of fixed categories, eternal truths and natural laws which in his view is characteristic of bourgeois
economics. For example, after accepting the description of
property as theft Proudhon goes on to envisage a socialist
system which will strip property of this character. And this
shows that he regards the institution of private property as
an eternal or natural value and as a fixed economic category.
But there are no such values and categories. Nor is there any
philosophy which can be worked out *a priori* and then applied to the understanding of history and society. There can
be only a critical knowledge based on the analysis of concrete historical situations. In Marx's view the dialectic is not
a law of thought which is expressed in reality: it is immanent
in the actual process of reality and is reflected in thought
when the mind correctly analyses concrete situations.

Faithful, however, to his idea of the unity of thought and
action, Marx was by no means content to criticize the short-
comings of German ideologists such as Bauer and Feuerbach
and of socialists such as Proudhon. He joined the Communist
League and in 1847 was commissioned, together with Engels,
to draw up a summary statement of its principles and aims.
This was the famous *Communist Manifesto* or *Manifesto of
the Communist Party* which appeared in London early in
1848, shortly before the beginning of the series of revolutions
and insurrections which took place in Europe during that
year. When the active phase of the revolutionary movement
started in Germany, Marx and Engels returned to their na-
tive land. But after the failure of the revolution Marx, who
had been brought to trial and acquitted, retired to Paris, only
to be expelled from France for the second time in 1849. He
went to London where he remained for the rest of his life,
receiving financial aid from his friend Engels.

In 1859 Marx published at Berlin his *Contribution to a*

Critique of Political Economy (*Zur Kritik der politischen Oekonomie*) which is important, as is also the *Manifesto*, for its statement of the materialist conception of history. And, again uniting action with theory, he founded in 1864 the International Working Men's Association, commonly known as the First International. Its life, however, was beset with difficulties. For example, Marx and his friends considered that it was necessary for authority to be centralized in the hands of the committee if the proletariat was to be led successfully to victory, whereas others, such as Bakunin the anarchist, refused to accept a dictatorship of the central committee. Besides, Marx soon found himself at loggerheads with the French and German socialist groups. After the congress at The Hague in 1872 the central committee was transferred to New York at the instance of Marx. And the First International did not long survive.

The first volume of Marx's famous work *Capital* (*Das Kapital*) appeared at Hamburg in 1867. But the author did not continue the publication. He died in March 1883, and the second and third volumes were published posthumously by Engels in 1885 and 1894 respectively. Further manuscripts were published in several parts by K. Kautsky in 1905–10. In the work Marx maintains that the bourgeois or capitalist system necessarily involves a class antagonism. For the value of a community is crystallized labour, as it were. That is to say, its value represents the labour put into it. Yet the capitalist appropriates to himself part of this value, paying the worker a wage which is less than the value of the commodity produced. He thus defrauds or exploits the worker. And this exploitation cannot be overcome except by the abolition of capitalism. Marx refers, of course, to contemporary abuses in the economic system, such as the practice of keeping wages as low as possible. But exploitation should not be understood only in this sense. For if the so-called labour theory of value is once accepted, it necessarily follows that the capitalist system involves exploitation or defrauding of the worker. And the payment of high wages would not alter this fact.

In 1878 Engels published as a book, commonly known as *Anti-Dühring*, some articles which he had written against the then influential German socialist Eugen Dühring. One chapter was written by Marx. Engels also occupied himself with composing his *Dialectics of Nature (Dialektik der Natur)*. But he was too taken up with bringing out the second and third volumes of Marx's *Capital* and with efforts to resuscitate the International to be able to finish the work. And it was not published until 1925, when it appeared at Moscow. Engels lacked his friend's philosophical training, but he had wide interests, and it was he rather than Marx who applied dialectical materialism to the philosophy of Nature. The results were not perhaps such as to enhance Engels' reputation as a philosopher among those who do not accept his writings as part of a creed.

Of Engels' other publications mention should be made of his work on *The Origin of the Family, Private Property and the State (Der Ursprung der Familie, des Privateigentums und des Staats, 1884)* in which he tries to derive the origin of class divisions and of the State from the institution of private property. In 1888 a series of articles by Engels were published together as a book under the title *Ludwig Feuerbach and the End of the Classical German Philosophy (Ludwig Feuerbach und der Ausgang der klassischen deutschen Philosophie)*. Engels died of cancer in August 1895.

3. Whether or not Hegel meant that the Concept (*der Begriff*) or logical Idea is a subsistent reality which externalizes or alienates itself in Nature, is a disputable question. But both Marx and Engels understood him in this sense, namely as holding that the *Logos* is the primary reality which expresses itself in its opposite, namely unconscious Nature, and then returns to itself as Spirit, thus actualizing, as it were, its own essence or definition. Thus in his preface to the second German edition of *Capital* Marx states that 'for Hegel the thought-process, which he goes so far as to transform into an independent Subject under the name "Idea", is the demiurge of the real, the real being simply its external appearance'.[1] And in his book on Feuerbach Engels asserts that 'with Hegel the dialectic is the self-development of the Concept. The absolute Concept is not only present from eternity—who knows where?—but it is also the real living soul of the whole existent world. . . . It alienates itself in the sense that it transforms itself into Nature where, without

consciousness of itself and disguised as natural necessity, it goes through a new process of development and finally comes again to self-consciousness in man'.[2]

As against this metaphysical idealism Marx and Engels accepted Feuerbach's thesis that the primary reality is Nature. Thus Engels speaks of the liberating effect of Feuerbach's *Essence of Christianity*, which restored materialism to its throne. 'Nature exists independently of all philosophy; it is the basis on which we human beings, ourselves products of Nature, have grown. Apart from Nature and human beings nothing exists; and the higher beings which our religious fantasy created are only the fantastic reflection of our own essence . . . the enthusiasm was general; we were all for the moment followers of Feuerbach. One can see in the *Holy Family* how enthusiastically Marx welcomed the new conception, and how much he was influenced by it, in spite of all critical reservations'.[3]

In this passage Engels speaks of the re-enthronement of materialism. And both Marx and Engels were, of course, materialists. But this obviously does not mean that they denied the reality of mind or that they identified the processes of thought in a crude manner with material processes. What materialism meant for them was in the first place the denial that there is any Mind or Idea which is prior to Nature and expresses itself in Nature. It was certainly not equivalent to denying that human beings have minds. In his *Dialectics of Nature* Engels speaks of the law of the transformation of quantity into quality, and *vice versa*, as the law by which changes in Nature take place.[4] A transformation of this kind occurs when a series of quantitative changes is succeeded by an abrupt qualitative change. Thus when matter has reached a certain pattern of complicated organization mind emerges as a new qualitative factor.

To be sure, the question of the power of the mind is left somewhat obscure by Marx and Engels. In the preface to his *Critique of Political Economy* Marx makes the famous statement that 'it is not the consciousness of human beings which determines their being, but it is, on the contrary, their social being which determines their consciousness.'[5] And Engels remarks that 'we conceived the concepts in our heads once

more from a materialist point of view as copies of real thi
instead of conceiving real things as copies of this or that
of the absolute Concept'.[6] And such passages tend to su
that human thought is no more than a copy or reflecti
material economic conditions or of the processes of Nature.
In other words, they tend to suggest the passive character of
the human mind. But we have already seen that in his theses
against Feuerbach Marx asserts that whereas philosophers
have only tried to understand the world, it is man's business
to change it. Hence it is not really surprising if in the first
volume of *Capital* we find him comparing the human worker
with the spider and the bee and remarking that even the
worst builder can be distinguished from the best bee by the
fact that the former conceives the product of his work before
he constructs it whereas the latter does not. In the human
worker there is the will which has an end in view and which
externalizes itself.[7] Indeed, if Marx and Engels wish to maintain, as they do, the need for revolutionary activity, for correctly analysing the situation and acting accordingly, they obviously cannot maintain at the same time that the mind is
no more than a kind of pool on the surface of which natural
processes and economic conditions are passively mirrored.
When they are engaged in setting Hegel on his feet, that is,
in substituting materialism for idealism, they tend to stress
the copy-idea of human concepts and thought-processes. But
when they are speaking of the need for social revolution and
for its preparation, they clearly have to attribute to the human mind and will an active role. Their utterances may not
be always perfectly consistent, but their materialism is basically an assertion of the priority of matter, not a denial of
the reality of mind.

4. Although, however, Marx and Engels regarded their materialism as a counterblast to Hegel's idealism, they certainly
did not look on themselves as being simply opponents of
Hegel. For they recognized their indebtedness to him for the
idea of the dialectical process of reality, that is, a process by
way of negation followed by a negation of the negation, which
is also an affirmation of a higher stage. Another way of putting the same thing is to say that process or development
takes the form of the contradiction of an existing situation

or state of affairs, followed by the contradiction of the contradiction, this contradiction being an overcoming of the first. It is not so much a question of thesis, antithesis and synthesis, as of negation and its negation, though the second negation can be regarded as in some sense a 'synthesis', inasmuch as it is a transition to a higher stage in the dialectical process.

This idea of development as a dialectical process is essential to the thought of Marx and Engels. Obviously, a man can accept the thesis of the priority of matter to mind and some form of what is now called emergent evolution without thereby being a Marxist. The materialism of Marx and Engels is dialectical materialism, to use the descriptive term which is now in general use, even if Marx himself did not employ it.

Marx and Engels were indeed at pains to distinguish between their conception of the dialectic and that of Hegel. In their view Hegel, having seen that thought moves dialectically, hypostatized this process as the process of absolute Thought, the self-development of the Idea. Thus the movement of the dialectic in the world and in human history was regarded by Hegel as the reflection or phenomenal expression of the movement of Thought. For Marx and Engels, however, the dialectical movement is found first of all in reality, that is to say, in Nature and history. The dialectical movement of human thought is simply a reflection of the dialectical process of reality. And this reversal of the relation between thought and reality was for them an essential part of the business of setting Hegel on his feet. At the same time Marx and Engels made no secret of the fact that the idea of the dialectic was derived from Hegel. Hence they regarded their materialism as being essentially a post-Hegelian materialism, and not as a mere return to an earlier type of materialist theory.

Now, though Marx affirms with Feuerbach the priority of matter to mind, he is not really interested in Nature as such, considered apart from man. Sometimes indeed he seems to imply that Nature does not exist except for man. But this must not be taken as meaning that Nature possesses no ontological reality except as object of consciousness. It would be absurd to interpret Marx as an idealist. What he means is that Nature first exists for man when man differentiates himself from it, though at the same time he recognizes a relation between himself and Nature. An animal is a natural product, and we see it as related to Nature. But the animal is not conscious of these relations as such: they do not exist 'for it'. Hence Nature cannot be said to exist 'for the animal'. With the emergence of consciousness, however, and the subject-object relation Nature begins to exist for man. And this is essential for what we may call the becoming of man. To be man, man must objectify himself. And he cannot do so, except by distinguishing himself from Nature.

But man is orientated towards Nature in the sense that he has needs which can be satisfied only through objects other than himself. And Nature is orientated towards man in the sense that it is the means of satisfying these needs. Further, man's satisfaction of his needs involves activity or work on his part. And in a sense the spontaneous satisfaction of a basic physical need by appropriating a ready-made object, so to speak, is work. But it is not specifically human work or activity, not at least if it is considered simply as a physical act. A man may, for example, stoop down and drink from a stream to quench his thirst. But so do many animals. Work becomes specifically human when man consciously transforms a natural object to satisfy his needs, and when he employs means or instruments to do so. In other words, the fundamental form of human work and man's fundamental relation to Nature is his productive activity, his conscious production of the means of satisfying his needs. Man is basically economic man, though this is not to say that he cannot be anything but economic man.

Man cannot, however, objectify himself and become man unless he is also object for another. In other words, man is a social being: a relation to his fellows is essential to his being as man. And the basic form of society is the family. We can say, therefore, that the fundamental reality to which Marx directs his attention is productive man as standing in a twofold relation, to Nature and to other human beings. Or, inasmuch as the term 'productive man' already implies a relation to Nature, we can say that the fundamental reality considered by Marx is productive man in society.

For Marx, therefore, man is basically not a contemplative but an active being, this activity being primarily the material one of production. And the relations between man and Nature are not static but changing relations. He uses means of production to satisfy his needs, and therefore fresh needs present themselves, leading to a further development in the means of production. Further, corresponding to each stage in the development of means of production for the satisfaction of man's needs there are social relations between men. And the dynamic interaction between the means or forces of production and the social relations between men constitute the basis of history. Speaking of man's basic physical needs Marx asserts that 'the first historical fact is the production of the means which enable man to satisfy these needs'.[8] But, as we have seen, this leads to the appearance of fresh needs, to a development in the means of production and to new sets of social relations. Hence the so-called first historical fact contains in itself, as it were in germ, the whole history of man. And this history is for Marx the 'locus', so to speak, of the dialectic. But an account of the dialectic of history according to Marx is best reserved for the next section. It is sufficient to note here that his theory of history is materialist in the sense that the basic factor in history is for him man's economic activity, his activity of production to satisfy his physical needs.

Attention has already been drawn to the fact that Engels extended the dialectic to Nature itself, thus developing what may be called a philosophy of Nature. And there has been some dispute about whether this extension was compatible with the attitude of Marx. Of course, if one assumes that for Marx Nature exists for us only as the field for transformation by human work and that the dialectical movement is confined to history, which presupposes a dynamic relation between man and his natural environment, the extension of the dialectic to Nature in itself would constitute not only a novelty but also a change in the Marxist conception of the dialectic. There might perhaps be a dialectical movement in the development of man's scientific knowledge, but this movement could hardly be attributed to Nature in itself, considered apart from man. It would not be merely a case of Marx having concentrated on human history to the practical exclusion of a philosophy of Nature. It would be a case of an exclusion in principle. But it must be remembered that in Marxism the dialectical movement of history is not the expression of the interior movement of absolute Thought: it is the movement of reality itself. It can be reproduced in the human mind, but in the first instance it is the movement of objective reality. Unless, therefore, we choose to press certain of Marx's utterances to the extent of turning him into an idealist, it does not seem to me that his position excludes in principle the notion of a dialectic of Nature. Moreover, Marx was well aware that his friend was working at a dialectic of Nature, and he appears to have approved or at any rate not to have shown disapproval. So even if it is arguable that Engels was unfaithful to the thought of Marx and that he was laying the foundation of a mechanistic version of dialectical materialism, in which the movement of history would be regarded as simply a continuation of the necessary movement of autodynamic matter, I should not care to commit myself to the assertion that the extension of the dialectic to Nature in itself was excluded by Marx. Given some of his statements, it may be that he ought to have excluded it. But it does not appear that he did so in point of fact.

However this may be, in what he calls his 'recapitulation of mathematics and the natural sciences'[9] Engels was struck by the fact that in Nature nothing is fixed and static but that all is in movement, change, development. And, as he tells us himself, he was particularly impressed by three factors; first, the discovery of the cell, through the multiplication and differentiation of which plant and animal bodies have developed; secondly, the law of the transformation of energy; and, thirdly, Darwin's statement of the theory of evolution. Reflecting on Nature as revealed by contemporary science Engels came to the conclusion that 'in Nature the same dialectical laws of movement assert themselves in the confusion of innumerable changes which govern the apparent contingency of events in history'.[10]

In his *Dialectics of Nature*[11] Engels summarizes these laws as those of the transformation of quantity into quality, of the mutual penetration of opposites and of the negation of the negation. Some often-quoted examples of this last law, the negation of the negation, are to be found in *Anti-Dühring*. Engels speaks, for instance, of the barley-seed which is said to be negated when it sprouts and the plant begins to grow. The plant then produces a multiplicity of seeds and is itself negated. Thus as 'result of this negation of the negation we have again the original barley-seed, though not as such but tenfold, twentyfold or thirtyfold'.[12] Similarly, the larva or caterpillar negates the egg out of which it comes, is transformed in the course of time into a butterfly and is then itself negated in its death.

Whether logical terms such as 'negation' and 'contradiction' are appropriate in this context is, to put it mildly, disputable. But we need not labour this point. Instead we can note that Engels draws an important conclusion in regard to human thought and knowledge from the nature of the twofold field of application of the dialectic, namely Nature and human history.[13] In his view it was Hegel's great discovery that the world is a complex not of finished things but of processes. And it is true both of Nature and of human history that each is a process or complex of processes. From this it follows that human knowledge, as a mirror of this twofold reality, is itself a process which does not and cannot reach a fixed and absolute system of truth. Hegel saw that 'truth lay in the process of knowing itself, in the long historical development of science which rises from lower to ever higher levels of knowledge without ever arriving, through the discovery of a so-called absolute truth, to the point where it can proceed no further, where nothing remains but to lay one's hands on one's lap and wonder at the absolute truth which has been attained'.[14] There is not and cannot be an absolute system of philosophy which only needs to be learned and accepted. Indeed, inasmuch as absolute truth is precisely what philosophers have had in view, we can say that with Hegel philosophy comes to an end. Instead we have a dialectically-advancing progressive scientific knowledge of reality which is always open to further change and development.

Like Marx, therefore, Engels attacks the notion of 'eternal truths'. He finds himself compelled to admit that there are truths which nobody can doubt without being considered mad; for example, that 'two and two make four, that the three angles of a triangle are equal to two right angles, that Paris lies in France, that a man who eats nothing dies of hunger and so on'.[15] But such truths, says Engels, are trivialities or commonplaces. And nobody would dignify them with the solemn title of 'eternal truths' unless he wished to draw from their existence the conclusion that in the field of human history there is an eternal moral law, an eternal essence of justice, and so on. But it is precisely this sort of conclusion which is erroneous. Just as hypotheses in physics and biology are subject to revision and even to revolutionary change, so is morality.

Marx and Engels, therefore, did not present their interpretation of reality as being the absolute and final system of philosophy. True, they regarded it as science rather than as speculative philosophy. And this means, of course, that they regarded it as supplanting all previous interpretations, whether idealist or materialist. At the same time science was not for them something which could ever attain a fixed and final form. If reality is a dialectical process, so is human thought, in so far, that is to say, as it reflects reality and does not take refuge in an illusory world of eternal truths and fixed essences.

Taken by itself, this denial of eternal truths, stable positions and final solutions suggests that a detached attitude towards their philosophy would be the appropriate one for Marx and Engels to maintain. But they did not look on it as being simply a theoretical exercise in interpreting the world and history. And it was precisely the detached, theoretical attitude which they decried in Hegel. But the implications of their view of dialectical materialism as a practical instrument or weapon is a topic which must be left aside for the moment.

5. As we have seen, the Marxist theory of history is materialist in the sense that the fundamental situation is depicted as a relation between man, considered as a material being, and Nature: it is man producing by his physical activity the means of satisfying his basic needs. But we must add that historical materialism does not mean only this. It means in addition that man's productive activity determines, directly or indirectly, his political life, his law, his morality,

his religion, his art, his philosophy. In the present context materialism does not involve, as has been already remarked, denying the reality of mind or consciousness. Nor does it involve denying all value to the cultural activities which depend on mind. But it maintains that the cultural superstructure in general depends on and is in some sense determined by the economic substructure.

In the economic substructure Marx distinguishes two elements, the material forces of production and the productive relations, the second element depending upon the first. 'In the social production of their life human beings enter into determinate necessary relations which are independent of their will, productive relations (*Produktionsverhältnisse*) which correspond with a determinate stage in the development of their material forces of production (*Produktivkräfte*). The totality of these productive relations forms the economic structure of society'.[16] In this passage the economic structure of a society is indeed identified with the totality of its productive relations. But inasmuch as these relations are said to correspond with a certain level of development of the productive forces of the society in question, and inasmuch as the emergence of conflicts between the productive forces and the productive relations in a given society is an essential feature in Marx's picture of human history, it is obvious that we must distinguish two main elements in the economic structure of society, a structure which is also described by Marx as a mode of production (*Produktionsweise*).

The term 'material forces of production' (or 'material productive powers') obviously covers all the material things which are used by man as artificial instruments in his productive activity, that is, in the satisfaction of his physical needs, from primitive flint instruments up to the most complicated modern machinery. It also includes natural forces in so far as they are used by man in the process of production. And the term can apparently also cover all such objects as are required for productive activity, even if they do not enter into it directly.[17]

Now, if the term is applied exclusively to things distinct from man himself, man is obviously presupposed. Marx tends to speak of the forces of production as doing this or that, but he is not so stupid as to suppose that these forces develop themselves without any human agency. 'The first condition of all human history is naturally the existence of living human individuals.'[18] And in the *Communist Manifesto* he speaks of the bourgeoisie as revolutionizing the instruments of production and thereby the productive relations. However, in the *German Ideology* he remarks that the production of life, whether of one's own life by work or of that of another through procreation, always involves a social relation, in the sense of the collaboration of several individuals. And after observing that it follows from this that a given mode of production is always linked to a given mode of collaboration, he asserts that this mode of collaboration is itself a 'productive force'.[19] He means, of course, that the social relation between men in the process of production can itself react on men's needs and on the productive forces. But if the mode of collaboration in the labour-process can be reckoned as a productive force, there seems to be no reason why, for example, the proletariat should not be accounted a productive force, even if the term is generally used by Marx for instruments or means of production rather than for man himself.[20] In any case it is notoriously difficult to pin him down to a precise and universal use of such terms.

The term 'productive relations' means above all property-relations. Indeed, in the *Critique of Political Economy* we are told that 'property relations' (*Eigentumsverhältnisse*) is simply a juristic expression for 'productive relations'.[21] However, in general the term 'productive relations' refers to the social relations between men as involved in the labour-process. As we have seen, these relations are said to depend on the stage of development of the productive forces. And the two together constitute the economic substructure.

This economic substructure is said to condition the superstructure. 'The mode of production of material life conditions the social, political and mental (*geistigen*) life-process in general. It is not the consciousness of human beings which determines their being, but it is, on the contrary, their social being which determines their consciousness.'[22] Obviously, the statement that the economic substructure 'conditions' (*bedingt*) the superstructure is ambiguous. The statement is not at all startling if it is taken in a very weak sense. It becomes interesting only in proportion as the meaning of the term 'conditions' approaches 'determines'. And it has indeed frequently been taken in this strong sense. Thus it has been maintained, for example, that the celestial hierarchy (from God down to the choirs of angels and the company of the saints) of mediaeval theology was simply an ideological reflection of the mediaeval feudal structure which was itself determined by economic factors. Again, the rise of the bourgeoisie and the arrival of the capitalist mode of production were reflected in the transition from Catholicism to Protestantism. According to Engels the Calvinist doctrine of predestination reflected the supposed economic fact that in commercial competition success or failure does not depend on personal merits but on incomprehensible and uncontrollable economic powers. Yet it was also Engels who protested that the doctrine of Marx and himself had been misunderstood. They had never meant that man's ideas are simply a pale reflection of economic conditions in the sense that the relation of dependence is exclusively unilateral. Ideas (that is to say, men inspired by ideas) can react on the substructure which has conditioned them.

The fact of the matter is, I think, that in their reversal of the idealist conception of history Marx and Engels not unnaturally emphasized the determining influence of the economic substructure. But, having once stated their vision of the world in terms which suggested that for them the world of consciousness and ideas was simply determined by the mode of economic production, they found themselves compelled to qualify this simple outlook. Political and legal structures are more directly determined by the economic substructure than are ideological superstructures such as religion and philosophy. And human ideas, though conditioned by economic conditions, can react on these conditions. In fact they had to allow for such reaction if they wished to allow for revolutionary activity.

To turn now to a more dynamic aspect of history. According to Marx 'at a certain stage in their development a society's forces of production come into conflict [literally

'contradiction', *Widerspruch*] with the existing produ
relations'.[23] That is to say, when in a given social epoch t,
forces of production have developed to such a point that the
existing productive relations, especially property-relations,
have become a fetter on the further development of the forces
of production, there is a contradiction within the economic
structure of society, and a revolution takes place, a qualitative
change to a new economic structure, a new social epoch. And
this change in the substructure is accompanied by changes in
the superstructure. Man's political, juristic, religious, artistic
and philosophical consciousness undergoes a revolution which
depends on and is subsidiary to the revolution in the economic sphere.

A revolution of this kind, the change to a new social epoch,
does not take place, Marx insists, until the forces of production have developed to the fullest extent that is compatible
with the existing productive relations and the material conditions for the existence of the new form of society are already present within the old. For this is the state of affairs
which comprises a contradiction, namely that between the
forces of production and the existing social relations. The
qualitative change in the economic structure of society or
mode of production does not occur until a contradiction has
matured, as it were, within the old society through a series of
quantitative changes.

Now, if the theory is expressed simply in this way, it gives
the impression of being simply a technological and mechanical theory. That is to say, it seems as though social revolution, the transition from one social epoch to another, took
place inevitably and mechanically, and as though man's consciousness of the need for a change and his revolutionary activity constituted mere epiphenomena which exercised no real
influence on the cause of events. But though this interpretation would fit in with the general doctrine that it is the material conditions of life which determine consciousness and
not the other way round, it could scarcely fit in with Marx's
insistence on the unity of theory and practice and on the
need for the active preparation of the proletariat's revolutionary overthrow of the capitalist economy. Hence, although
Marx sometimes tends to speak as though the material forces

of production were the real revolutionary agent, we have to introduce the idea of the class war and of human agency.

Marx and Engels envisage at the dawn of history a state of primitive communism in which the land was possessed and tilled by the tribe in common and in which there was no class-division. Once, however, private property had been introduced, a division of society into economic classes soon followed. Marx is aware, of course, that social distinctions in civilized society form a more or less complicated pattern. But his general tendency is to simplify the situation by representing the fundamental distinction as being that between the oppressors and the oppressed, the exploiters and the exploited. In all forms of society, therefore, which presuppose the institution of private property, there is an antagonism between classes, an antagonism now latent, now open. And 'the history of all society hitherto is the history of class struggle'.[24] The State becomes the organ or instrument of the dominant class. So does the law. And the dominant class also tries to impose its own moral conceptions. In the Marxist dialectic of history, therefore, the concept of the class replaces Hegel's concept of the national State, and the class war replaces national wars.[25]

This class war or class struggle becomes particularly significant at the period when in a given social epoch the forces of production have developed to such a point that the existing social relations, especially property-relations, are turned into a drag and a fetter. For the hitherto dominant class (individual defections apart) endeavours to maintain the existing productive relations, while it is in the interest of a rising class to overthrow these relations. And when the contradiction between the forces of production and the productive relations has been perceived by the rising class whose interest it is to overthrow the existing and antiquated social order, revolution takes place. Then the new dominant class in its own turn uses the State and the law as its instruments. This process inevitably continues until private property has been abolished and, with it, the division of society into mutually antagonistic classes.

In the preface to his *Contribution to the Critique of Political Economy* Marx observes that we can distinguish in broad outline four progressive social epochs which together form the prehistory (*die Vorgeschichte*) of mankind. The first of these, the asiatic, called by Engels the *gens* organization, is that of primitive communism. As we have seen, this was marked by communal ownership of land, associated labour and absence of private property. But with the institution of private property, associated by Engels with the change from matriarchy to patriarchy and with improvements in methods of production, the accumulation of private wealth was rendered possible. It was possible, for example, for a man to produce more than he required for his own needs. Hence there arose a division between rich and poor, and a new form of economic organization was required. If we ask what was the new productive force which was responsible for the transition, special mention is made of iron, though the subject is not developed. In any case the growth of private property and wealth made it necessary for the prospective rich to have labour at their disposal. But as under primitive communism there was no free labour available, slaves had to be obtained through captives in war.

We thus pass to the antique or ancient period, characterized by slavery and by the class antagonism between freemen and slaves. On this economic structure, represented, for instance, by Greece and Rome, there arose corresponding legal and political institutions and the splendid ideological superstructure of the classical world.

Although Marx and Engels mention various historical factors which contributed to the transition from the antique to the feudal epoch, which reached its culminating phase in the Middle Ages, no convincing explanation is offered of the productive force or forces which were responsible for the transition. However, it took place, and the feudal economy was reflected in the political and legal institutions of the time, as well as, though more indirectly, in mediaeval religion and philosophy.

During the mediaeval period a middle class or bourgeoisie gradually developed. But its wealth-amassing propensities were hampered by factors such as feudal restrictions and guild regulations, as also by the lack of free labour for hire. With the discovery of America, however, and the opening-up of markets in different parts of the world, a powerful impetus was given to commerce, navigation and industry. New sources of wealth became available, and at the close of the Middle Ages land-enclosure by the nobility and other factors contributed to the formation of a class of dispossessed people ready to be hired and exploited. The time was ripe for a change, and the guild-system was overthrown by the new middle class in favour of the early phase of capitalist society. Finally, steam and machinery revolutionized industry; the world market was opened up; means of communication underwent a remarkable development; and the bourgeoisie pushed into the background the classes which had lingered from the Middle Ages.

In feudal society, as Marx is aware, the pattern of organization was too complicated to permit of its being reduced to one simple class antagonism, as between barons and serfs. But in capitalist society, to which he naturally devotes most of his attention, we can see, Marx argues, a growing simplification. For there has been a tendency for capital to become concentrated in ever fewer hands, in great combines of a more or less international or cosmopolitan character. At the same time many of the small capitalists have sunk into the ranks of the proletariat[26] which has also tended to take on an international character. Hence we are faced by two prominent classes, the exploiters and the exploited. The term 'exploitation' suggests, of course, the imposition of long hours of work for starvation wages. But though Marx does indeed inveigh against the abuses of the earlier phases of the industrial revolution, the primary meaning of the term is for him technical, not emotive. As we have seen, according to the doctrine expounded in *Capital* the whole value of a commodity is, as it were, crystallized labour; it is due to the labour expended in its production. Hence the wage-system is necessarily exploitation, irrespective of the amount of the wages paid. For in every case the capitalist filches from the worker. The fact that a given capitalist is a humane man who does his best to improve wages and conditions of work makes no difference to the basic situation which is a necessary antagonism between the two classes.

Now, the bourgeoisie has developed the forces of production to a hitherto unknown and undreamed-of extent. But at the same time it has developed them to the point at which they can no longer co-exist with the existing productive relations. According to Marx, this fact is shown, for example, by the periodic recurrence of economic crises. Hence the time is approaching for the overthrow of the capitalist system. And the task of revolutionary activity, particularly of the Communist Party, is to turn the proletariat from a class in itself, to use Hegelian language, into a class for itself, a class conscious of itself and of its mission. The proletariat will then be able to sweep away the capitalist system, seize the organ of the State and use it to establish the dictatorship of the proletariat which will prepare the way for communist society. In this society the political State will wither away. For the State is an instrument for the maintenance of its own position by a dominant class in face of another class or other classes. And under communism class divisions and the class war will disappear.

In view of the fact that the bourgeoisie itself develops the forces of production we may be inclined to ask, what is the new productive force which emerges and which is fettered by the capitalist mode of production? But Marx is ready with his answer. And in the *Poverty of Philosophy* he tells us that the greatest of all productive forces is 'the revolutionary class itself'.[27] This is the productive force which enters into conflict with the existing economic system and overthrows it by revolution.

Human history is thus a dialectical progress from primitive communism to developed communism. And from one point of view at least the intermediary stages are necessary. For it is through them that the forces of production have been developed and that productive relations have been correspondingly changed in such a manner that developed communism is rendered not only possible but also the inevitable result. But the Marxist theory of history is also an instrument or weapon, not merely a spectator's analysis of historical situations. It is the instrument by which the proletariat, through its vanguard the Communist Party, becomes conscious of itself and of the historical task which it has to perform.

The theory is also, however, a philosophy of man. Marx

assumes the Hegelian thesis that to realize himself man must objectify himself. And the primary form of self-objectification is in labour, production. The product is, as it were, man-in-his-otherness. But in all societies based on private property this self-objectification takes the form of self-alienation or self-estrangement. For the worker's product is treated as something alien to himself. In capitalist society it belongs to the capitalist, not to the worker. Further, this economic self-alienation is reflected in a social self-alienation. For membership of a class does not represent the whole man. Whichever class he belongs to, there is, so to speak, something of himself in the other class. Thus class antagonism expresses a profound division, a self-estrangement, in the nature of man. Religion also represents, as Feuerbach said, human self-alienation. But, as we have seen, self-alienation in the religious consciousness is for Marx a reflection of a profounder self-alienation in the social-economic sphere. And this cannot be overcome except through the abolition of private property and the establishment of communism. If self-alienation on the economic and social level is overcome, its religious expression will disappear. And at last the whole man, the non-divided man, will exist. Human ethics will take the place of class ethics, and a genuine humanism will reign.

It follows from this that the overthrow of the capitalist system by the proletariat is not merely a case of the replacement of one dominant class by another. It is indeed this, but it is also much more. The dictatorship of the proletariat is a temporary phase which prepares the way for the classless communist society from which self-alienation will be absent. In other words, by its revolutionary act the international proletariat saves not simply itself but all mankind. It has a messianic mission.

6. There is no great difficulty in giving a certain plausibility to the materialist theory of history. For example, if I wish to illustrate the conditioning by the economic structure of political and legal forms and of the ideological superstructure, there is a large variety of facts to which I can appeal. I can point to the connection between the then existing economic and class structure and the ferocious penalties which were once inflicted in England for theft, or to the connection

between the economic interests of plantation-owners in the southern States of America and the absence of strong moral feeling against slavery. I can draw attention to the connections between the economic life of a hunting tribe and its ideas of life after death or between class divisions and the lines of the hymn 'The rich man in his castle, the poor man at his gate, God made them high and lowly and ordered their estate'. I can refer to the evident influence of Greek political structures on Plato's picture of the ideal State or, for the matter of that, to the influence of existing conditions in the world of industry on the thought of Marx and Engels.

But though the Marxist theory of the relation between the economic substructure and the superstructure can be rendered plausible, this plausibility depends in large part on one's selecting certain data, slurring over others and circumventing awkward questions. For example, to maintain the theory I have to slur over the fact that Christianity became the dominant religion in the late Roman empire and was then accepted by the peoples who built up the feudal society of the Middle Ages. And I have to avoid awkward questions about the relation between the development of the forces of production and the origins of Islam. If such questions are pressed, I refer to factors which lie outside my original explanation of the ideological superstructure, while at the same time I continue to assert the truth of this explanation. And I blithely admit that the superstructure can itself exercise an influence on the substructure and that changes can take place in the former independently of changes in the latter, while at the same time I refuse to admit that these concessions are inconsistent with my original position. Why, indeed, should I admit this? For I have spoken of the relation between the substructure and the superstructure as a 'conditioning' of the latter by the former. And I can understand this term in a weak or in a strong sense according to the demands of the particular situation which I am considering.

We have seen that for Marx and Engels the dialectic is not something imposed on the world from without, the expression of absolute Thought or Reason. The dialectic as thought is the reflection of the inner movement of reality, of its immanent laws of development. And in this case the movement is presumably necessary and inevitable. This does not mean, of course, that human thought has no part to play. For there is continuity between Nature, human society and the world of ideas. We have already quoted Engels' statement that 'dialectic is nothing else but the science of the general laws of movement and development in Nature, human society and thought'.[28] But the total process would then be the necessary working-out of immanent laws. And in this case there does not seem to be much room for revolutionary activity. Or, rather, revolutionary activity would be a phase of an inevitable process.

From one point of view this mechanical view of the dialectic seems to be required by the conviction of Marx and Engels that the coming of communism is inevitable. But if the dialectic as operating in human history is, as Engels at any rate suggests, continuous with the dialectic as operating in Nature, that is, if it is ultimately a question of the self-development of auto-dynamic matter, it is difficult to see why the process should ever stop or reach a stage where contradictions and antagonisms disappear. Indeed, there is a passage in the *Dialectics of Nature* where Engels remarks that matter goes through an eternal cycle and that with an 'iron necessity' it will exterminate its highest product, namely the thinking mind, and produce it again somewhere else at another time.[29]

But this idea hardly fits in with the apocalyptic aspect of Marxism, which requires the vision of history as moving towards a goal, a terrestrial Paradise. The two ways of looking at the matter are perhaps compatible up to a point. That is to say, it is possible to look on each cycle as leading up to a peak point, as it were. But the more one emphasizes the teleological aspect of history, its movement from primitive communism, the age of innocence, through the Fall, as represented by the introduction of private property and the consequent emergence of selfishness, exploitation and class antagonism, up to the recovery of communism at a higher level and the overcoming of man's self-alienation, so much the more does one tend to reintroduce surreptitiously the notion of the working out of a plan, the realization of an Idea.

In other words, there is a fundamental ambiguity in Marxism. If some aspects are stressed, we have a mechanistic interpretation of the historical process. If other aspects are stressed, the system seems to demand the reintroduction of what Marx and Engels called idealism. Nor is this surprising. For in part Marxism is a transformation of idealism, and elements of this particular source linger on. The alliance between dialectic and materialism is not altogether an easy one. For, as Marx and Engels were well aware, dialectics originally referred to a movement of thought. And though they located the movement of the dialectic primarily in the object of thought and only secondarily and by way of reflection in human thinking, this transposition inevitably tends to suggest that the historical process is the self-development of an Idea. The alternative is to interpret the process as a purely mechanical one.[30]

This is a matter of some importance. Left to itself, so to speak, Marxism tends to divide into divergent lines of thought. It is possible to emphasize the ideas of necessity, inevitability, determinism, and it is possible to emphasize the ideas of deliberate revolutionary activity and of free action. It is possible to emphasize the materialist element, and it is possible to emphasize the dialectical element. It is also possible, of course, to attempt to hold together all these different aspects, in spite of the ambiguities to which this attempt gives rise. But it is significant that even in the Soviet Union different lines of interpretation and development have manifested themselves. If the emergence of these different lines of thought has been held in check, this has been due to the constraining force of the Party Line, to an extra-philosophical factor and not to any intrinsic consistency and lack of ambiguity in the thought of Marx and Engels themselves.

From one point of view criticism of the type suggested in the foregoing paragraphs[31] is beside the point. That is to say, if we choose to regard Marxism as an interesting 'vision' of the world, detailed criticism necessarily seems pedantic and tiresome. Philosophers who provide striking visions of the world are inclined to take one aspect of reality and to use it as a key to unlock all doors. And detailed criticism, it may be said, is out of place. For it is the very exaggeration involved in the vision which enables us to see the world in a new light.

When we have done so, we can forget about the exaggeration: the vision has accomplished its purpose. Thus the philosophy of Marx and Engels enables us to see the importance and far-reaching influence of man's economic life, of the so-called substructure. And it is largely because of the exaggerations involved that it can have this effect, breaking the rigidity of other pictures or interpretations of the world. Once we have seen what Marx and Engels are drawing attention to, we can forget Marxism as expounded in their writings: the essence of their vision passes into the common outlook. It is pedantic to worry about such detailed questions as the precise relation between freedom and necessity, the precise meaning of 'condition', the exact extent to which morality and values are thought to be relative, and so on.

This attitude is indeed understandable. But the Marxist theory of history is not simply a striking nineteenth-century vision of the world which has made its contribution to human thought and then relapsed into the historical background. It is a living and influential system which professes to be a scientific analysis of historical development, an analysis which permits prediction, and it is at the same time the creed or faith of groups whose importance in the modern world nobody would deny. It is therefore appropriate to point out that the transformation of this philosophy into the dogmatic creed of a powerful Party has arrested the natural development of the different lines of thought to which its diverse aspects might otherwise be expected to have given rise.

The Communist theoretician would perhaps reply that it is not a question of the philosophy of Marx and Engels having been adopted by a Party and transformed into a weapon or instrument. For it was this from the beginning. And it is precisely this fact which distinguishes it from all previous philosophies. Marx always thought of his philosophy as a means of transforming the world and not simply as an interpretation of it. But though this is doubtless true, the question then arises whether Marxism falls under its own concept of ideologies as relative to a passing economic structure or whether it transcends this status and represents absolute truth. If Marxism is relative to the situation in which the proletariat is opposed to the bourgeoisie, it should pass away when this antagonism has been overcome. If, however, it represents absolute truth, how is this claim to be reconciled with what Marx and Engels have to say about eternal truths, natural laws and so on?

And yet all criticism based on the internal ambiguities of the philosophy of Marx and Engels seems in a certain sense to be futile. It may have an effect on those, if any, who are attracted to Marxism simply because they think that it is 'scientific'. But it is not likely to have much effect on those who are primarily attracted by the ideal of human society which Marxism represents. What is needed is the delineation of another ideal, based on a more adequate view of man and his vocation and on a more adequate view of the nature of reality.

The philosophy of Marx and Engels has, of course, undergone some development. Attention has been paid, for example, to the theory of knowledge. And certain modern Thomists seem to think that among contemporary philosophical traditions Marxism, as represented by the philosophers of the Soviet Union, offers them a common basis of discussion because of its insistence on realism in epistemology and ontology. This is a theme which goes beyond the scope of this book. But one may remark that even if realism in the sense intended is common to Thomism and to Marxism, Thomism is for the Marxist an 'idealist' system. For it maintains the priority of Mind or Spirit to matter. And it was precisely this doctrine which Marx and Engels were concerned to deny when they affirmed the truth of materialism.

Chapter Seventeen

KIERKEGAARD

Introductory remarks – Life and writings – The individual and the crowd – The dialectic of the stages and truth as subjectivity – The idea of existence – The concept of dread – The influence of Kierkegaard.

1. In the chapters on the development of Schelling's thought mention was made of the distinction which he came to draw between negative and positive philosophy. The former moves in the realm of ideas: it is a deduction of concepts or essences. The latter is concerned with the *that* of things, with existence. Positive philosophy cannot simply dispense with negative philosophy. At the same time negative philosophy by itself by-passes actual existence. And its chief modern representative is Hegel.

Among Schelling's hearers at Berlin, when he expounded this distinction, was the Dane, Søren Kierkegaard. For the way in which the German thinker developed his own idea of positive philosophy Kierkegaard had little sympathy. But he was in full agreement with Schelling's attack on Hegel. Not that Kierkegaard was lacking in admiration for Hegel or in appreciation of the magnitude of his achievement. On the contrary, he regarded Hegel as the greatest of all speculative philosophers and as a thinker who had achieved a stupendous intellectual *tour de force*. But this, in Kierkegaard's opinion, was precisely the trouble with Hegelianism, namely that it was a gigantic *tour de force* and nothing more. Hegel sought to capture all reality in the conceptual net of his dialectic, while existence slipped through the meshes.

Existence, as will be explained presently, was for Kierkegaard a category relating to the free individual. In his use of the term, to exist means realizing oneself through free choice between alternatives, through self-commitment. To exist, therefore, means becoming more and more an individual and less and less a mere member of a group. It means, one can say, transcending universality in favour of individuality Hence Kierkegaard has scant sympathy with what he took to be Hegel's view, that a man realizes his true self or essence in proportion as he transcends his particularity and becomes a spectator of all time and existence as a moment in the life of universal thought. Hegelianism, in Kierkegaard's opinion, had no place for the existing individual: it could only universalize him in a fantastic manner. And what could not be universalized it dismissed as unimportant, whereas in point of fact it is that which is most important and significant. To merge or sink oneself in the universal, whether this is conceived as the State or as universal Thought, is to reject personal responsibility and authentic existence.

Kierkegaard's emphasis on self-commitment through free choice, a self-commitment whereby the individual resolutely chooses one alternative and rejects another, is an aspect of his general tendency to underline antitheses and distinctions rather than to gloss them over. For example, God is not man, and man is not God. And the gulf between them cannot be bridged by dialectical thinking. It can be bridged only by the leap of faith, by a voluntary act by which man relates himself to God and freely appropriates, as it were, his relation as creature to the Creator, as a finite individual to the transcendent Absolute. Hegel, however, confounds what ought to be distinguished. And his dialectical mediation between the infinite and the finite, between God and man, leaves us in the end with neither God nor man but only with the pale ghost of hypostatized thought, dignified by the name of absolute Spirit.

With this emphasis on the individual, on choice, on self-commitment, Kierkegaard's philosophical thought tends to become a clarification of issues and an appeal to choose, an attempt to get men to see their existential situation and the great alternatives with which they are faced. It is certainly not an attempt to master all reality by thought and to exhibit it as a necessary system of concepts. This idea was quite foreign and repugnant to his mind. In his view speculative systematic philosophy, the greatest example of which was for him absolute idealism, radically misrepresented human exist-

ence. The really important problems, that is, the problems
which are of real importance for man as the existing individual, are not solved by thought, by adopting the absolute
standpoint of the speculative philosopher, but by the act of
choice, on the level of existence rather than on that of detached, objective reflection.

As one might expect, Kierkegaard's philosophy is intensely
personal. In one sense, of course, every philosopher worthy
of the name is a personal thinker. For it is he who does the
thinking. But with Kierkegaard there is a closer connection
between his life and his philosophy than in the case of many
other philosophers. He does not simply take over traditional
problems or the problems most discussed in contemporary
philosophical circles and then attempt to solve them in a
purely objective and disinterested spirit. His problems arise
out of his own life, in the sense that in the first instance they
arise for him in the form of alternatives presented for his
own personal choice, a choice involving a radical self-commitment. His philosophy is, as it were, a lived philosophy. And
one of his objections to Hegelianism is that one cannot live
by it. Obviously, Kierkegaard has to universalize. Without
universalization there would be only autobiography. At the
same time it is abundantly clear that it is the actor who
speaks rather than the spectator.

From one point of view this feature of his philosophy constitutes its weakness. That is to say, his thought may appear
too subjective, too hostile to objectivity. In fact, some would
refuse it the name of philosophy at all. But from another
point of view the intensely personal character of Kierkegaard's
thought constitutes its strength. For it gives to his writing a
degree of seriousness and depth which sets it entirely outside
the concept of philosophy as a game or as an academic pastime for those who have the requisite aptitude and inclination.

In view of the fact that Kierkegaard's thought is developed
in conscious opposition to Hegelianism or, if preferred, to
speculative philosophy as represented by absolute idealism,
as well as for chronological reasons, I have included the
chapter on his philosophy in this part of the present volume.
But if one were to neglect chronology and take effective in-

fluence as a standard, one would have to postpone consideration of his thought to a later stage. For though he was one of the most passionate thinkers of his period, he excited very little real interest at the time. A Dane, he was first discovered, so to speak, by the Germans in the first decades of the present century, and he has exercised a profound influence on some phases of the existentialist movement and on modern Protestant theology of the type represented by Karl Barth. Kierkegaard's preoccupation with Hegelianism as the dominant philosophy of his time and cultural milieu constitutes the dating element in his thought. But the ideas which he opposed to Hegelianism have a quite independent significance, and they have exercised a widespread influence in another and later cultural context.

2. Søren Aabye Kierkegaard was born at Copenhagen on May 15th, 1813. He was given an extremely religious upbringing by his father, a man who suffered from melancholia and imagined that the curse of God hung over him and his family.[1] And Kierkegaard was himself affected to some degree by this melancholy, concealed beneath a display of sarcastic wit.

In 1830 Kierkegaard matriculated in the university of Copenhagen and chose the faculty of theology, doubtless in accordance with his father's wishes. But he paid little attention to theological studies and devoted himself instead to philosophy, literature and history. It was at this time that he gained his knowledge of Hegelianism. During this period Kierkegaard was very much the observer of life, cynical and disillusioned, yet devoted to the social life of the university. Estranged from his father and his father's religion, he spoke of the 'stuffy atmosphere' of Christianity and maintained that philosophy and Christianity were incompatible. Religious disbelief was accompanied by laxity in moral standards. And Kierkegaard's general attitude at this time fell under the heading of what he later called the aesthetic stage on life's way.

In the spring of 1836 Kierkegaard appears to have had a temptation to commit suicide, having been overcome by a vision of his inner cynicism. But in June of that year he underwent a kind of moral conversion, in the sense that he adopted moral standards and made an attempt, even if not always successful, to live up to them.[2] This period corresponds to the ethical stage in his later dialectic.

On May 19th, 1838, the year in which his father died, Kierkegaard experienced a religious conversion, accompanied by an 'indescribable joy'. He resumed the practice of his religion and in 1840 he passed his examinations in theology. He became engaged to Regina Olsen, but a year later he broke off the engagement. He evidently thought that he was unsuited for married life, a correct idea one would imagine. But he had also become convinced that he was a man with a mission, and that marriage would interfere with it.

In 1843 Kierkegaard published *Either-Or*, a title which well expresses his attitude to life and his abhorrence of what he took to be Hegel's 'Both-And', *Fear and Trembling* and *Repetition*. These works were followed in 1844 by *The Concept of Dread* and *Philosophical Fragments*, in 1845 by *Stages on Life's Way* and in 1846 by the *Concluding Unscientific Postscript* which, though its name may not suggest it, is a large and weighty tome. He also published some 'edifying discourses' in these years. The works of this period appeared under various pseudonyms, though the identity of the author was well enough known at Copenhagen. As far as the Christian faith was concerned, it was presented from the point of view of an observer, by indirect communication as Kierkegaard put it, rather than from the point of view of an apostle intent on direct communication of the truth.

In the spring of 1848 Kierkegaard enjoyed a religious experience which, as he wrote in his *Journal*, changed his nature and impelled him to direct communication. He did not at once abandon the use of pseudonyms, but with *Anti-Climacus* the change to a direct and positive presentation of the standpoint of Christian faith becomes apparent. The year 1848 saw the publication of *Christian Discourses*, and *The Point of View* was also composed at this time, though it was published only after Kierkegaard's death. *The Sickness unto Death* appeared in 1849.

Kierkegaard was meditating a frontal attack on the Danish State Church which, in his opinion, scarcely deserved any more the name of Christian. For as far as its official representatives at least were concerned, it appeared to him to have watered down Christianity to a polite moral humanism with a modicum of religious beliefs calculated not to offend the susceptibilities of the educated. However, to avoid wounding Bishop Mynster, who had been a friend of his father, Kierkegaard did not open fire until 1854, after the prelate's death. A vigorous controversy ensued in the course of which Kierkegaard maintained that what he represented was simply ordinary honesty. The emasculated Christianity of the established Church should recognize and admit that it was not Christianity.

Kierkegaard died on November 4th, 1855. At his funeral there was an unfortunate scene when his nephew interrupted the Dean to protest against the appropriation by the Danish Church of a man who had so vigorously condemned it.

3. There is an obvious sense in which every human being is and remains an individual, distinct from other persons and things. In this sense of individuality even the members of an enraged mob are individuals. At the same time there is a sense in which the individuality of the members of such a mob is sunk in a common consciousness. The mob is possessed, as it were, by a common emotion, and it is a notorious fact that a mob is capable of performing actions which its members would not perform precisely as individuals.

This is indeed an extreme example. But I mention it to show in a simple way that we can quite easily give a cash value to the idea of man's being more or less of an individual. One might, of course, take less dramatic examples. Suppose that my opinions are dictated predominantly by what 'one thinks', my emotive reactions by what 'one feels', and my actions by the social conventions of my environment. To the extent that this is the case I can be said to think, feel and act as a member of 'the One', as a member of an impersonal collectivity, rather than as this individual. If, however, I become aware of my anonymous status, so to speak, and begin to form my own principles of conduct and to act resolutely in accordance with them, even if this means acting in a way quite opposed to the customary ways of acting of my social environment, there is a sense in which I can be said to have become more of an individual, in spite of the fact that in another sense I am no more and no less an individual than I was before.

If space permitted, these concepts would obviously require careful analysis. But even in this unanalysed state they may serve to facilitate understanding of the following quotation from Kierkegaard. 'A crowd—not this crowd or that, the crowd now living or the crowd long deceased, a crowd of humble people or of superior people, of rich or of poor, etc. —a crowd in its very concept is the untruth, by reason of the fact that it renders the individual completely impenitent and irresponsible, or at least weakens his sense of responsibility by reducing it to a fraction.'[3] Kierkegaard is not, of course, concerned simply with the dangers of allowing oneself to become a member of a crowd in the sense of a mob. His point is that philosophy, with its emphasis on the universal rather than on the particular, has tried to show that man realizes his true essence in proportion as he rises above what is contemptuously regarded as his mere particularity and becomes a moment in the life of the universal. This theory, Kierkegaard argues, is false, whether the universal is considered as the State or as the economic or social class or as Humanity or as absolute Thought. 'I have endeavoured to express the thought that to employ the category "race" to indicate what it is to be a man, and especially as an indication of the highest attainment, is a misunderstanding and mere paganism, because the race, mankind, differs from an animal race not merely by its general superiority as a race, but by the *human* characteristic that every single individual within the race (not merely distinguished individuals but every individual) is more than the race. For to relate oneself to God is a far higher thing than to be related to the race and through the race to God.'[4]

The last sentence of this quotation indicates the general direction of Kierkegaard's thought. The highest self-actualization of the individual is the relating of oneself to God, not as the universal, absolute Thought, but as the absolute Thou. But further explanation of what Kierkegaard means by becoming the individual is best reserved for the context of his theory of the three stages. For the moment it is sufficient to notice that it means the opposite of self-dispersal in 'the One' or self-submerging in the universal, however this may be conceived. The exaltation of the universal, the collectivity, the totality, is for Kierkegaard 'mere paganism'. But he also insists that historic paganism was orientated towards Christianity, whereas the new paganism is a falling away or an apostasy from Christianity.[5]

4. In *The Phenomenology of Spirit* Hegel expounded his masterly dialectic of the stages by which the mind awakens to self-consciousness, to universal consciousness and to the standpoint of absolute Thought. Kierkegaard also expounds a dialectic. But it is radically different from that of Hegel. In the first place it is the process by which spirit is actualized in the form of individuality, the individual existent, not in the form of the all-comprehensive universal. In the second place the transition from one stage to the next is accomplished not by thinking but by choice, by an act of the will, and in this sense by a leap. There is no question of overcoming antitheses by a process of conceptual synthesis: there is a choice between alternatives, and the choice of the higher alternative, the transition to a higher stage of the dialectic, is a willed self-commitment of the whole man.

The first stage or sphere is described as the aesthetic.[6] And it is characterized by self-dispersal on the level of sense. The aesthetic man is governed by sense, impulse and emotion. But we must not conceive him as being simply and solely the grossly sensual man. The aesthetic stage can also be exemplified, for instance, in the poet who transmutes the world into an imaginative realm and in the romantic. The essential features of the aesthetic consciousness are the absence of fixed universal moral standards and of determinate religious faith and the presence of a desire to enjoy the whole range of emotive and sense experience. True, there can be discrimination. But the principle of discrimination is aesthetic rather than obedience to a universal moral law considered as the dictate of impersonal reason. The aesthetic man strives after infinity, but in the sense of a bad infinity which is nothing else but the absence of all limitations other than those imposed by his own tastes. Open to all emotional and sense experience, sampling the nectar from every flower, he hates all that would limit his field of choice and he never gives definite form to his life. Or, rather, the form of his life is its very formlessness, self-dispersal on the level of sense.

To the aesthetic man his existence seems to be the expression of freedom. Yet he is more than a psycho-physical organism, endowed with emotive and imaginative power and the capacity for sense enjoyment. 'The soulish-bodily synthesis in every man is planned with a view to being spirit, such is the building; but the man prefers to dwell in the cellar, that is, in the determinants of sensuousness.'[7] And the aesthetic consciousness or attitude to life may be accompanied by a vague awareness of this fact, by a vague dissatisfaction with the dispersal of the self in the pursuit of pleasure and sense enjoyment. Further, the more aware a man becomes that he is living in what Kierkegaard calls the cellar of the building, the more subject he becomes to 'despair'. For he finds that there is no remedy, no salvation, at the level on which he stands. He is faced, therefore, with two alternatives. Either he must remain in despair on the aesthetic level or he must make the transition to the next level by an act of choice, by self-commitment. Mere thinking will not do the trick for him. It is a question of choice; either-or.

The second stage is the ethical. A man accepts determinate moral standards and obligations, the voice of universal reason, and thus gives form and consistency to his life. If the aesthetic stage is typified by Don Juan, the ethical stage is typified by Socrates. And a simple example of the transition from the aesthetic to the moral consciousness is for Kierkegaard that of the man who renounces the satisfaction of his sexual impulse according to passing attraction and enters into the state of marriage, accepting all its obligations. For marriage is an ethical institution, an expression of the universal law of reason.

Now, the ethical stage has its own heroism. It can produce what Kierkegaard calls the tragic hero. 'The tragic hero renounces himself in order to express the universal.'[8] This is what Socrates did, and Antigone was prepared to give her life in defence of the unwritten natural law. At the same time the ethical consciousness as such does not understand sin. The ethical man may take account of human weakness, of course; but he thinks that it can be overcome by strength of will, enlightened by clear ideas. In so far as he exemplifies the attitude characteristic of the ethical consciousness as such he believes in man's moral self-sufficiency. Yet in point of fact a man can come to realize his own inability to fulfil the moral law as it should be fulfilled and to acquire perfect virtue. He can come to an awareness of his lack of self-sufficiency and of his sin and guilt. He has then arrived at the point at which he is faced with the choice or rejection of the standpoint of faith. Just as 'despair' forms, as it were, the antithesis to the aesthetic consciousness, an antithesis which is overcome or resolved by ethical self-commitment, so consciousness of sin forms the antithesis to the ethical stage, and this antithesis is overcome only by the act of faith, by relating oneself to God.

To affirm one's relationship to God, the personal and transcendent Absolute, is to affirm oneself as spirit. 'By relating itself to its own self and by willing to be itself, the self is grounded transparently in the Power which constituted it. And this formula . . . is the definition of faith.'[9] Every man is, as it were, a mixture of the finite and the infinite. Considered precisely as finite, he is separated from God, alienated from him. Considered as infinite, man is not indeed God, but he is a movement towards God, the movement of the spirit. And the man who appropriates and affirms his relationship to God in faith becomes what he really is, the individual before God.

To emphasize the difference between the second and third stages Kierkegaard uses as a symbol Abraham's willingness to sacrifice his son Isaac at God's command. The tragic hero, such as Socrates, sacrifices himself for the universal moral law; but Abraham, as Kierkegaard puts it, does nothing for the universal. 'So we stand in the presence of the paradox. Either the Individual as the Individual can stand in an absolute relation to the Absolute, and then ethics is not supreme, or Abraham is lost: he is neither a tragic hero nor an aesthetic hero.'[10] Needless to say, Kierkegaard does not intend to enunciate the general proposition that religion involves the negation of morality. What he means is that the man of faith is directly related to a personal God whose demands are absolute and cannot be measured simply by the standards of the human reason. At the back of Kierkegaard's mind there is doubtless the memory of his behaviour towards Regina Olsen. Marriage is an ethical institution, the expression of the universal. And if ethics, the universal, is supreme, Kierkegaard's conduct was inexcusable. He was justified only if he had a personal mission from God whose absolute demands are addressed to the individual. Obviously, I do not intend to suggest that Kierkegaard is universalizing his own experience in the sense of assuming that everyone has the same specific experience. He universalizes it in the sense that he reflects on its general significance.

As Kierkegaard's dialectic is one of discontinuity, in the sense that the transition from one stage to another is made by choice, by self-commitment, and not through a continuous process of conceptual mediation, he not unnaturally plays down the role of reason and emphasizes that of will when he is treating of religious faith. In his view faith is a leap. That is to say, it is an adventure, a risk, a self-commitment to an objective uncertainty. God is the transcendent Absolute, the absolute Thou; he is not an object the existence of which can be proved. True, God reveals himself to the human conscience in the sense that man can become aware of his sin and alienation and his need of God. But man's response is a venture, an act of faith in a Being who lies beyond the reach of speculative philosophy. And this act of faith is not something which can be performed once and for all. It has to be constantly repeated. It is true that God has revealed himself in Christ, the God-Man. But Christ is the Paradox, to the Jews a stumbling-block and to the Greeks foolishness. Faith is always a venture, a leap.

Looked at from one point of view Kierkegaard's account of the standpoint of faith is a vigorous protest against the way in which speculative philosophy, represented principally by Hegelianism, blurs the distinction between God and man and rationalizes the Christian dogmas, turning them into philosophically-demonstrated conclusions. In the Hegelian system 'the qualitative distinction between God and man is pantheistically abolished'.[11] The system does indeed hold out the attractive prospect of 'an illusory land, which to a mortal eye might appear to yield a certainty higher than that of faith'.[12] But the mirage is destructive of faith, and its claim to represent Christianity is bogus. 'The entirely unsocratic tract of modern philosophy is that it wants to make itself and us believe that it is Christianity.'[13] In other words, Kierkegaard refuses to admit that in this life there can be a higher standpoint than that of faith. The vaunted transformation of faith into speculative knowledge is an illusion.

But though in such passages it is Hegelianism which Kierkegaard has principally in mind, there is no adequate ground for saying that he would have had much sympathy with the idea of proving God's existence by metaphysical argument provided that an unequivocally theistic idea of God were maintained. In his view the fact that man is held eternally accountable for belief or disbelief shows that belief is not a matter of accepting the conclusion of a demonstrative argument but rather a matter of will. Catholic theologians would obviously wish to make some distinctions here. But Kierkegaard was not a Catholic theologian. And the point is that he deliberately emphasized the nature of faith as a leap. It was not simply a case of opposition to Hegelian rationalism.

This comes out clearly in his famous interpretation of truth as subjectivity. '*An objective uncertainty held fast in an appropriation-process of the most passionate inwardness is the truth*, the highest truth attainable for an *existing* individual.'[14] Kierkegaard is not denying that there is any such thing as objective, impersonal truth. But mathematical truths, for example, do not concern the 'existing individual' as such. That is to say, they are irrelevant to a man's life of total self-commitment. He accepts them. He cannot do otherwise. But he does not stake his whole being on them. That on which I stake my whole being is not something which I cannot deny without logical contradiction or something which is so obviously true that I cannot deny it without palpable absurdity. It is something which I can doubt but which is so important to me that if I accept it, I do so with a passionate self-commitment. It is in a sense *my* truth. 'The truth is precisely the venture which chooses an objective uncertainty with the passion of the infinite. I contemplate the order of nature in the hope of finding God, and I see omnipotence and wisdom; but I also see much else that disturbs my mind and excites anxiety. The sum of all this is an objective uncertainty. But it is for this very reason that the inwardness becomes as intense as it is, for it embraces this objective uncertainty with the entire passion of the infinite.'[15]

Obviously, truth as so described is precisely what Kierkegaard means by faith. The definition of truth as subjectivity and the definition of faith are the same. 'Without risk there is no faith. Faith is precisely the contradiction between the infinite passion of the individual's inwardness and the objective uncertainty.'[16] Kierkegaard does indeed assert more than once that the eternal truth is not in itself a paradox. But it becomes paradoxical in relation to us. One can indeed see some evidence in Nature of God's work, but at the same time one can see much which points in the opposite direction. There is, and remains, 'objective uncertainty', whether we look at Nature or at the Gospels. For the idea of the God-Man is itself paradoxical for the finite reason. Faith grasps the objectively uncertain and affirms it; but it has to maintain itself, as it were, over a fathomless sea. Religious truth exists only in the 'passionate' appropriation of the objectively uncertain.[17]

In point of fact Kierkegaard does not say that there are no rational motives at all for making the act of faith and that it is a purely arbitrary act of capricious choice. But he certainly takes delight in minimizing the rational motives for religious belief and in emphasizing the subjectivity of truth and the nature of faith as a leap. Hence he inevitably gives the impression that faith is for him an arbitrary act of the will. And Catholic theologians at least criticize him on this score. But if we prescind from the theological analysis of faith and concentrate on the psychological aspect of the matter, there is no difficulty in recognizing, whether one is Catholic or Protestant, that there are certainly some who understand very well from their own experience what Kierkegaard is driving at when he describes faith as a venture or risk. And, in general, Kierkegaard's phenomenological analysis of the three distinct attitudes or levels of consciousness which he describes possess a value and a stimulative power which is not destroyed by his characteristic exaggerations.

5. In the passage quoted above which gives Kierkegaard's unconventional definition of truth mention is made of the '*existing* individual'. It has already been explained that the term 'existence', as used by Kierkegaard, is a specifically human category which cannot be applied, for example, to a stone. But something more must be said about it here.

To illustrate his use of the concept of existence Kierkegaard employs the following analogy. A man sits in a cart and holds the reins, but the horse goes along its accustomed path without any active control by the driver, who may be asleep. Another man actively guides and directs his horse. In one sense both men can be said to be drivers. But in another sense it is only the second man who can be said to be driving. In an analogous manner the man who drifts with the crowd, who merges himself in the anonymous 'One', can be said to exist in one sense of the term, though in another sense he cannot be said to exist. For he is not the 'existing individual' who strives resolutely towards an end which cannot be realized once and for all at a given moment and is thus in a constant state of becoming, making himself, as it were, by his repeated acts of choice. Again, the man who contents himself with the role of spectator of the world and of life and transmutes everything into a dialectic of abstract concepts exists indeed in one sense but not in another. For he wishes to understand everything and commits himself to nothing. The 'existing individual', however, is the actor rather than the spectator. He commits himself and so gives form and direction to his life. He ex-ists towards an end for which he actively strives by choosing this and rejecting that. In other words, the term 'existence' has with Kierkegaard more or less the same sense as the term 'authentic existence' as used by some modern existentialist philosophers.

If understood simply in this way, the term 'existence' is neutral, in the sense that it can be applied within any of the three stages of the dialectic. Indeed, Kierkegaard says explicitly that 'there are three spheres of existence: the aesthetic, the ethical, the religious'.[18] A man can 'exist' within the aesthetic sphere if he deliberately, resolutely and consistently acts as the aesthetic man, excluding alternatives. In this sense Don Juan typifies the existing individual within the aesthetic sphere. Similarly, the man who sacrifices his own inclinations to the universal moral law and constantly strives after the fulfilment of a moral ideal which beckons him ever forward is an existing individual within the ethical sphere. 'An existing individual is himself in process of becoming. . . . In existence the watchword is always *forward*.'[19]

But though the term 'existence' has indeed this wide field of application, it tends to take on a specifically religious connotation. Nor is this in any way surprising. For man's highest form of self-realization as spirit is for Kierkegaard his self-relating to the personal Absolute. 'Existence is a synthesis of the infinite and the finite, and the existing individual is both infinite and finite.'[20] But to say that the existing individual is infinite is not to identify him with God. It is to say that his becoming is a constant striving towards God. 'Existence itself, the act of existing, is a striving . . . (and) the striving is infinite.'[21] 'Existence is the child that is born of the infinite and the finite, the eternal and the temporal, and is therefore a constant striving.'[22] One can say, therefore, that existence comprises two moments: separation or finiteness and a constant striving, in this context towards God. The striving must be constant, a constant becoming, because the self-relating to God in faith cannot be accomplished once and for all: it has to take the form of a constantly repeated self-commitment.

It can hardly be claimed that Kierkegaard's definition or descriptions of existence are always crystal clear. At the same time the general notion is intelligible enough. And it is clear that for him the existing individual *par excellence* is the individual before God, the man who sustains the standpoint of faith.

6. In the writings of the existentialists the concept of dread[23] is conspicuous. But the term is used by different writers in different ways. With Kierkegaard it has a religious setting. And in *The Concept of Dread* it has a close association with the idea of sin. However, one can, I think, broaden the range of application and say that dread is a state which

precedes a qualitative leap from one stage in life's way to another.

Dread is defined by Kierkegaard as a 'sympathetic antipathy and an antipathetic sympathy'.[24] Take the case of the small boy who feels an attraction for adventure, 'a thirst for the prodigious, the mysterious'.[25] The child is attracted by the unknown, yet at the same time is repelled by it, as a menace to his security. Attraction and repulsion, sympathy and antipathy, are interwoven. The child is in a state of dread, but not of fear. For fear is concerned with something quite definite, real or imagined, a snake under the bed, a wasp threatening to sting, whereas dread is concerned with the as yet unknown and indefinite. And it is precisely the unknown, the mysterious, which both attracts and repels the child.

Kierkegaard applies this idea to sin. In the state of innocence, he says, spirit is in a dreaming state, in a state of immediacy. It does not yet know sin. Yet it can have a vague attraction, not for sin as something definite, but for the use of freedom and so for the possibility of sin. 'Dread is the possibility of freedom.'[26] Kierkegaard uses Adam as an illustration. When Adam, in the state of innocence, was told not to eat the fruit of the tree of the knowledge of good and evil under pain of death, he could not know what was meant either by evil or by death. For the knowledge could be obtained only by disobeying the prohibition. But the prohibition awoke in Adam 'the possibility of freedom . . . the alarming possibility of being able'.[27] And he was attracted and repelled by it at the same time.

But there is also, Kierkegaard says, a dread in relation to the good. Let us suppose, for example, a man sunk in sin. He may be aware of the possibility of emerging from this state and he may be attracted by it. But at the same time he may be repelled by the prospect, inasmuch as he loves his state of sin. He is then possessed by dread of the good. And this is really a dread of freedom, if, that is to say, we suppose that the man is in the enslaving grip of sin. Freedom is for him the object of a sympathetic antipathy and an antipathetic sympathy. And this dread is itself the possibility of freedom.

The notion of dread may perhaps become clearer if we can apply it in this way. A man, let us suppose, has become conscious of sin and of his utter lack of self-sufficiency. And he is faced with the possibility of the leap of faith,[28] which, as we have seen, means self-commitment to an objective uncertainty, a leap into the unknown. He is rather like the man on the edge of the precipice who is aware of the possibility of throwing himself over and who feels attraction and repulsion at the same time. True, the leap of faith means salvation, not destruction. 'The dread of possibility holds him as its prey, until it can deliver him saved into the hands of faith. In no other place does he find repose. . . .'[29] This seems to imply that dread is overcome by the leap. But in so far at least as the maintenance of the standpoint of faith involves a repeated self-commitment to an objective uncertainty, it would appear that dread recurs as the emotive tonality of the repeated leap.

7. Kierkegaard was first and foremost a religious thinker. And though for his actual contemporaries he was pretty well a voice crying in the wilderness, his idea of the Christian religion has exercised a powerful influence on important currents of modern Protestant theology. Mention has already been made of the name of Karl Barth, whose hostility to 'natural theology' is very much in tune with Kierkegaard's attitude towards any invasion by metaphysics into the sphere of faith. It may be said, of course, and with justice, that in the type of theology represented by Karl Barth it is a case not so much of following Kierkegaard as of making a renewed contact with the original well-spring of Protestant thought and spirituality. But inasmuch as some of Kierkegaard's ideas were distinctively Lutheran, this was just one of the effects which his writings could and did exercise.

At the same time his writings are obviously capable of exercising an influence in other directions. On the one hand he had some very hard things to say about Protestantism, and we can discern a movement in his thought not only away from emasculated Protestantism but also from Protestantism as such. It is not my purpose to argue that if he had lived longer, he would have become a Catholic. Whether he would or not is a question which we cannot possibly answer. Hence it is unprofitable to discuss it. But in point of fact his writings have had the effect of turning some people's minds towards Catholicism which, as he remarked, has always maintained the ideal at any rate of what he called No. 1 Christianity. On the other hand one can envisage the possibility of his writings contributing to turn people away from Christianity altogether. One can imagine a man saying, 'Yes, I see the point. Kierkegaard is quite right. I am not really a Christian. And, what is more, I do not wish to be. No leaps for me, no passionate embracing of objective uncertainties.'

It is not so surprising, therefore, if in the development of the modern existentialist movement we find certain Kierke-gaardian themes divorced from their original religious setting and employed in an atheistic system. This is notably the case in the philosophy of M. Sartre. With Karl Jaspers indeed, who of all the philosophers commonly classified as existen-tialists[30] stands nearest to Kierkegaard, the religious setting of the concept of existence is to a large extent retained.[31] But the philosophy of M. Sartre reminds us that the concepts of authentic existence, of free self-commitment and of dread are capable of displacement from this setting.

These remarks are certainly not meant to imply that the origins of modern existentialism can be attributed simply to the posthumous influence of Kierkegaard. This would be a gross misstatement. But Kierkegaardian themes recur in ex-istentialism, though the historical context has changed. And writers on the existentialist movement are perfectly justified in seeing in the Danish thinker its spiritual ancestor, though not, of course, its sufficient cause. At the same time Kierke-gaard has exercised a stimulative influence on many people who would not call themselves existentialists or, for the mat-ter of that, professional philosophers or theologians of any kind. As was remarked in the first section of this chapter, his philosophical thought tends to become both an attempt to get men to see their existential situation and the alternatives with which they are faced and an appeal to choose, to com-mit themselves, to become 'existing individuals'. It is also, of course, a protest in the name of the free individual or person against submergence in the collectivity. Kierkegaard indeed exaggerates. And the exaggeration becomes more evi-dent when the concept of existence is deprived of the reli-gious significance which he gave it. But exaggeration so often serves to draw attention to what is after all worth saying.

PART III

LATER CURRENTS OF THOUGHT

Chapter Eighteen

NON-DIALECTICAL MATERIALISM

Introductory remarks – The first phase of the materialist movement – Lange's criticism of materialism – Haeckel's monism – Ostwald's energeticism – Empirio-criticism considered as an attempt to overcome the opposition between materialism and idealism.

1. The collapse of absolute idealism was soon followed by the rise of a materialistic philosophy which did not stem, as did dialectical materialism, from left-wing Hegelianism but professed to be based on and to follow from serious reflection on the empirical sciences. Science has, of course, no intrinsic connection with philosophical materialism, even if the philosophies of Nature expounded by Schelling and Hegel did little to foster the conviction that the natural complement of science is metaphysical idealism. Further, the leading German philosophers, apart from Marx, have certainly not been materialists. Hence I do not propose to devote much space to the nineteenth-century materialist movement in Germany. But it is as well to understand that there was such a movement. And though it did not represent any profound philosophical thought, it was none the less influential. Indeed, it was precisely because of its lack of profundity and its appeal to the prestige of science that a book such as Büchner's *Force and Matter* enjoyed a wide vogue and passed through a great number of editions.

2. Among the German materialists prominent in the middle of the nineteenth century were Karl Vogt (1817–95), Heinrich Czolbe (1819–73), Jakob Moleschott (1822–93) and Ludwig Büchner (1824–99). Vogt, a zoologist and professor at Giessen for a time, is memorable for his statement that the brain secretes thought as the liver secretes bile. His general outlook is indicated by the title of his polemical work against the physiologist Rudolf Wagner, *Blind Faith and Sci-*

ence (*Kohlerglaube und Wissenschaft*, 1854, literally *Faith of a Charcoal-burner and Science*). Rudolf Wagner had openly professed belief in divine creation, and Vogt attacked him in the name of science. Czolbe, author of a *New Exposition of Sensualism* (*Neue Darstellung des Sensualismus*, 1855) and of attacks on Kant, Hegel and Lotze, derived consciousness from sensation, which he interpreted in a manner reminiscent of Democritus. At the same time he admitted the presence in Nature of organic forms which are not susceptible of a purely mechanistic explanation.

Moleschott was a physiologist and doctor who had to abandon his chair at Utrecht in consequence of the opposition aroused by his materialistic theories. Subsequently he became a professor in Italy where he exercised a considerable influence on minds inclined to positivism and materialism. In particular he influenced Cesare Lombroso (1836–1909), the famous professor of criminal anthropology at Turin, who translated into Italian Moleschott's *The Cycle of Life* (*Der Kreislauf des Lebens*, 1852). In Moleschott's view the whole history of the universe can be explained in terms of an original matter, of which force or energy is an intrinsic and essential attribute. There is no matter without force, and no force without matter. Life is simply a state of matter itself. Feuerbach prepared the way for the destruction of all anthropomorphic, teleological interpretations of the world, and it is the task of modern science to continue and complete this work. There is no good reason for making a dichotomy between the natural sciences on the one hand and the study of man and his history on the other. Science can use the same principles of explanation in both cases.

The best known product of the earlier phase of German materialism is probably Büchner's *Force and Matter* (*Kraft und Stoff*, 1855), which became a kind of popular textbook of materialism and was translated into a number of foreign languages. The author condemned out of hand all philosophy which could not be understood by the ordinary educated reader. And for this very reason the book enjoyed considerable popularity. As its title indicates, force and matter are taken as sufficient principles of explanation. The spiritual soul, for example, is thrown overboard.

3. In 1866 Friedrich Albert Lange (1828–75) published his famous *History of Materialism* (*Geschichte des Materialismus*) in which he subjected the materialist philosophy to well-founded criticism from the point of view of a Neo-Kantian. If it is considered simply as a methodological principle in natural science, materialism is to be affirmed. That is to say, the physicist, for example, should proceed as though there were only material things. Kant himself was of this opinion. The natural scientist is not concerned with spiritual reality. But though materialism is acceptable as a methodological principle in the field of natural science, it is no longer acceptable when it has been transformed into a metaphysics or general philosophy. In this form it becomes uncritical and naïve. For example, in empirical psychology it is quite right and proper to carry as far as possible the physiological explanation of psychical processes. But it is a sure sign of an uncritical and naïve outlook if it is supposed that consciousness itself is susceptible of a purely materialist interpretation. For it is only through consciousness that we know anything at all about bodies, nerves and so on. And the very attempt to develop a materialist reduction of consciousness reveals its irreducible character.

Further, the materialists betray their uncritical mentality when they treat matter, force, atoms and so forth as though they were things-in-themselves. In point of fact they are concepts formed by the mind or spirit in its effort to understand the world. We have indeed to make use of such concepts, but it is naïve to assume that their utility shows that they can properly be made the basis for a dogmatist materialist metaphysics. And this is what philosophical materialism really is.

4. Lange's criticism dealt a telling blow at materialism, all the more so because he did not confine himself to polemics but was at pains to show what was, in his opinion, the valid element in the materialist attitude. But, as one might expect, his criticism did not prevent a recrudescence of materialism, a second wave which appealed for support to the Darwinian theory of evolution as a proved factor which showed that the origin and development of man was simply a phase of cosmic evolution in general, that man's higher activities could be

adequately explained in terms of this evolution, and that at no point was it necessary to introduce the notion of creative activity by a supramundane Being. The fact that there is no necessary connection between the scientific hypothesis of biological evolution and philosophical materialism was indeed clear to some minds at the time. But there were many people who either welcomed or attacked the hypothesis, as the case might be, because they thought that materialism was the natural conclusion to draw from it.

The characteristic popular expression of this second phase of the materialist movement in Germany was Haeckel's *The Riddle of the Universe* (*Die Welträtsel*, 1899). Ernst Haeckel (1834–1919) was for many years professor of zoology at Jena, and a number of his works treated simply of the results of his scientific research. Others, however, were devoted to expounding a monistic philosophy based on the hypothesis of evolution. Between 1859, the year which saw the publication of Darwin's *The Origin of Species by Means of Natural Selection*, and 1871, when Darwin's *The Descent of Man* appeared, Haeckel published several works on topics connected with evolution and made it clear that in his opinion Darwin had at last set the evolutionary hypothesis on a really scientific basis. On this basis Haeckel proceeded to develop a general monism and to offer it as a valid substitute for religion in the traditional sense. Thus in 1892 he published a lecture, with additional notes, bearing the title *Monism as Link between Religion and Science* (*Der Monismus als Band zwischen Religion und Wissenschaft*). And similar attempts to find in his monism a fulfilment of man's need for religion can be seen in *The Riddle of the Universe* and in *God-Nature, Studies in Monistic Religion* (*Gott-Natur, Studien über monistische Religion*, 1914).

Reflection on the world has given rise, Haeckel asserts, to a number of riddles or problems. Some of these have been solved, while others are insoluble and are no real problems at all. 'The monistic philosophy is ultimately prepared to recognize only one comprehensive riddle of the universe, the problem of substance.'[1] If this is understood to mean the problem of the nature of some mysterious thing-in-itself behind phenomena, Haeckel is prepared to grant that we are perhaps as unable to solve it as were 'Anaximander and Empedocles 2400 years ago'.[2] But inasmuch as we do not even know that there is such a thing-in-itself, discussion of its nature is fruitless. What has been made clear is 'the comprehensive law of substance',[3] the law of the conservation of force and matter. Matter and force or energy are the two attributes of substance, and the law of their conservation, when interpreted as the universal law of evolution, justifies us in conceiving the universe as a unity in which natural laws are eternally and universally valid. We thus arrive at a monistic interpretation of the universe which is based on the proofs of its unity and of the causal relation between all phenomena. Further, this monism destroys the three principal dogmas of dualistic metaphysics, namely 'God, freedom and immortality'.[4]

Kant's theory of two worlds, the physical, material world and the moral, immaterial world, is thus excluded by the monistic philosophy. But it does not follow that there is no place in monism for an ethics, provided that it is grounded on the social instincts of man and not on some imagined categorical imperative. Monism acknowledges as its highest moral ideal the achievement of a harmony between egoism and altruism, self-love and love of the neighbour. 'Before all others it is the great English philosopher Herbert Spencer whom we have to thank for finding in the theory of evolution a basis for this monistic ethics.'[5]

Haeckel protests that materialism is an entirely inappropriate epithet to apply to his monistic philosophy. For while it does indeed reject the idea of immaterial spirit, it equally rejects the idea of a dead, spiritless matter. 'In every atom both are inseparably combined.'[6] But to say that in every atom spirit and matter (*Geist und Materie*) are combined is really to say that in every atom force and 'stuff' (*Kraft und Stoff*) are combined. And though Haeckel asserts that his philosophy might just as well be labelled spiritualism as materialism, it is evidently what most people would describe as materialism, an evolutionary version of it, it is true, but none the less materialism. His account of the nature of consciousness and reason makes this quite clear, whatever he may say to the contrary.

If the term 'materialism' is objectionable to Haeckel, so also is the term 'atheism'. The monistic philosophy is pantheistic, not atheistic: God is completely immanent and one with the universe. 'Whether we describe this impersonal "Almighty" as "God-Nature" (*Theophysis*) or as "All-God" (*Pantheos*) is ultimately a matter of indifference.'[7] It does not seem to have occurred to Haeckel that if pantheism consists in calling the universe 'God' and if religion consists in cultivating science, ethics and aesthetics as directed respectively towards the ideals of truth, goodness and beauty, pantheism is distinguishable from atheism only by the possible presence of a certain emotive attitude towards the universe in those who call themselves pantheists which is not present in those who call themselves atheists. Haeckel does indeed make the suggestion that 'as the ultimate cause of all things "God" is the hypothetical "original ground of substance"'.[8] But this concept is presumably the same as that of the ghostly impersonal thing-in-itself which, as we have seen, Haeckel elsewhere dismisses from consideration. Hence his pantheism cannot amount to much more than calling the universe 'God' and entertaining a certain emotive attitude towards it.

5. In 1906 a German Monist Society (Monistenbund) was founded at Munich under the patronage of Haeckel,[9] and in 1912 *The Monist Century* (*Das monistische Jahrhundert*) was published by Ostwald, the then president of the Monist Society.

Wilhelm Ostwald (1853–1932) was a famous chemist, professor of chemistry first at Riga and afterwards at Leipzig, a recipient of the Nobel Prize (1909) and founder of the *Annalen der Naturphilosophie* (1901–21), in the last issue of which there appeared the German text of Ludwig Wittgenstein's *Tractatus logico-philosophicus*. In 1906 he resigned from his chair at Leipzig, and in subsequent years he published a considerable number of writings on philosophical topics.

In 1895 Ostwald published a book on *The Overcoming of Scientific Materialism* (*Die Ueberwindung des wissenschaftlichen Materialismus*). But the so-called overcoming of materialism meant for him the substitution of the concept of energy for that of matter. The fundamental element of reality is energy which in a process of transformations takes a variety of distinct forms. The different properties of matter are different forms of energy; and psychic energy, which can be either unconscious or conscious, constitutes another distinct level or form. The different forms or levels are irreducible, in the sense that one distinct form cannot be identified with another. At the same time they arise through transformation of the one ultimate reality, namely energy. Hence 'energeticism' is a monistic theory. It hardly fits in perhaps with Ostwald's own canons of scientific method, which exclude anything approaching metaphysical hypotheses. But when he turned to the philosophy of Nature he was in any case going beyond the limits of empirical science.

6. It is only in its crudest form that materialism involves the assertion that all processes are material. But a philosophy could not be classified as materialist unless it at any rate maintained the priority of matter and that processes which cannot be properly described as material are emergents from matter or epiphenomenal to material processes. Similarly, though idealism does not involve the assertion that all things are ideas in any ordinary sense, a philosophy could not be properly described as a system of metaphysical idealism unless it at any rate held that Thought or Reason or Spirit is prior and that the material world is its expression or externalization. In any case the dispute between materialism and idealism presupposes a *prima facie* distinction between matter and spirit or thought. An attempt is then made to overcome the opposition by subordinating one term of the distinction to the other. One way, therefore, of excluding the dispute between materialism and idealism is to reduce reality to phenomena which cannot properly be described either as material or as spiritual.

We find such an attempt in the phenomenalism of Mach and Avenarius, which is commonly known as empirio-criticism. This is not to say that the two philosophers in question were simply concerned with overcoming the opposition between materialism and idealism. Mach, for instance, was largely concerned with the nature of physical science. At the same time they regarded their phenomenalism as eliminating the dualisms which give rise to metaphysical essays in unification. And it is from this point of view that their theory is considered here.

Richard Avenarius (1843–96), professor of physics at Zürich and author of a *Critique of Pure Experience* (*Kritik der reinen Erfahrung*, 1888–90) and *The Human Concept of the World* (*Der menschliche Weltbegriff*, 1891), sought to reveal the essential nature of pure experience, that is, of experience stripped of all added interpretation. And he found the immediate data or elements of experience in sensations. These depend on changes in the central nervous system which are conditioned by the environment acting either as an external stimulus or by way of the process of nutrition. Further, the more the brain develops, the more is it excited by constant elements in the environment. Thus the impression of a familiar world is produced, a world in which one can feel secure. And increase in these feelings of familiarity and security is accompanied by a decrease in the impression of the world as enigmatic, problematic and mysterious. In fine, the unanswerable problems of metaphysics tend to be eliminated. And the theory of pure experience, with its reduction of both the outer and the inner worlds to sensations, excludes those dichotomies between the physical and the psychical, thing and thought, object and subject, which have formed the basis for such rival metaphysical theories as materialism and idealism.

A similar theory was produced, though by way of a rather different approach, by Ernst Mach (1838–1916) who was for many years a professor in the university of Vienna and published, in addition to works concerned with physical science, *Contributions to the Analysis of Sensations* (*Beiträge zur Analyse der Empfindungen*, 1886), and *Knowledge and Error* (*Erkenntnis und Irrtum*, 1905). Experience is reducible to sensations which are neither purely physical nor purely psychical but rather neutral. Mach thus tries to get behind the distinctions which philosophers have used as a basis for the construction of metaphysical theories. But he is more concerned with purifying physical science from metaphysical elements than with developing a general philosophy.[10] Arising out of our biological needs, science aims at control of Nature by enabling us to predict. For this purpose we have to practise an economy of thought, uniting phenomena by means of the fewest and simplest concepts possible. But though these concepts are indispensable instruments for rendering scientific prediction possible, they do not give us insight into causes or essences or substances in a metaphysical sense.

In *Materialism and Empirio-Criticism* (1909) Lenin maintained that the phenomenalism of Mach and Avenarius leads inevitably to idealism and thence to religious belief. For if things are reduced to sensations or sense-data, they must be mind-dependent. And as they can hardly be dependent simply on the individual human mind, they must be referred to a divine mind.

Historically, the phenomenalism of Mach and Avenarius formed part of the line of thought which issued in the neopositivism of the Vienna Circle in the twenties of the present century. It can hardly be said to have led to a revival of idealism, and much less of theism. It does not follow, however, that Lenin's point of view has nothing to be said for it. For example, as Avenarius had no intention of denying that there were things in some sense before there were human beings, he maintained that sensations could exist before minds, as possible sensations. But unless the reduction of things to sensations is interpreted as equivalent to the statement, with which not even the most resolute realist would quarrel, that physical objects are in principle capable of being sensed if there is any sentient subject at hand, it becomes difficult to avoid some such conclusion as that drawn by Lenin. One can, of course, try to do so by speaking of *sensibilia* rather than of sensations. But in this case one either reinstates physical objects over against the mind or becomes involved in the same difficulty as before. Besides, it is absurd, in the opinion of the present writer, to reduce the self to a complex or succession of *sensibilia*. For the presence of the self as irreducible to *sensibilia* is a condition of the possibility of attempting such a reduction. Hence one would be left with the self on the one hand and *sensibilia* on the other, in other words with a dualism of the very type which empirio-criticism was concerned to overcome.[11] Mach's attempt to purify physical science from metaphysics is one thing: phenomenalism as a philosophical theory is quite another.

Chapter Nineteen

THE NEO-KANTIAN MOVEMENT

Introductory remarks – The Marburg School – The School of Baden – The pragmatist tendency – E. Cassirer; concluding observations – Some notes on Dilthey.

1. In 1865 Otto Liebmann (1840–1912), in his *Kant und die Epigonen*, raised the cry of 'Back to Kant!' This demand for a return to Kant was indeed perfectly understandable in the circumstances. On the one hand idealist metaphysics had produced a crop of systems which, when the first flush of enthusiasm had passed away, seemed to many to be incapable of providing anything which could properly be called knowledge and thus to justify Kant's attitude towards metaphysics. On the other hand materialism, while speaking in the name of science, proceeded to serve up its own highly questionable form of metaphysics and was blind to the limitations placed by Kant to the use which could legitimately be made of scientific concepts. In other words, both the idealists and the materialists justified by their fruits the limitations which Kant had set to man's theoretical knowledge. Was it not desirable, therefore, to turn back to the great thinker of modern times who by a careful critique of human knowledge had succeeded in avoiding the extravagances of metaphysics without falling into the dogmatism of the materialists? It was not a question of following Kant slavishly, but rather of accepting his general position or attitude and working on the lines which he had followed.

The Neo-Kantian movement became a powerful force in German philosophy. It became in fact the academic philosophy or 'School Philosophy' (*Schulphilosophie*), as the Germans say, and by the turn of the century most of the university chairs of philosophy were occupied by people who were in some degree at least representatives of the movement. But Neo-Kantianism assumed pretty well as many shapes as it had representatives. And we cannot possibly mention them all here. Some general indications of the principal lines of thought will have to suffice.

2. A distinction is drawn within the Neo-Kantian movement between the Schools of Marburg and Baden. The Marburg School can be said to have concentrated principally on logical, epistemological and methodological themes. And it is associated above all with the names of Hermann Cohen (1842–1918) and Paul Natorp (1854–1924).

Cohen, who was nominated professor of philosophy in the university of Marburg in 1876, concerned himself with both the exegesis and the development of Kant's thought. In a wide sense his principal theme is the unity of the cultural consciousness and its evolution, and whether he is writing on logic, ethics, aesthetics or religion[1] it is noticeable that he is constantly referring to the historical development of the ideas which he is treating and to their cultural significance at different stages of their development. This aspect of his thought makes it less formalistic and abstract than Kant's, though the wealth of historical reflections does not facilitate an immediate grasp of Cohen's personal point of view.

In the first volume of his *System of Philosophy* (*System der Philosophie*, 1902–12) Cohen abandons Kant's doctrine of sensibility, the transcendental aesthetic, and devotes himself entirely to the logic of pure thought or pure knowledge (*die reine Erkenntnis*), especially of the pure or *a priori* knowledge which lies at the basis of mathematical physics. True, logic possesses a wider field of application. But 'the fact that logic must have a relation which extends beyond the field of mathematical natural science to the field of the mental sciences (*Geisteswissenschaften*) in no way affects the fundamental relation of logic to knowledge in mathematical natural science'.[2] Indeed, 'the establishment of the relation between metaphysics and mathematical natural science is Kant's decisive act'.[3]

In the second volume, devoted to the ethics of the pure will (*Ethik des reinen Willens*), Cohen remarks that 'ethics, as the doctrine of man, becomes the centre of philosophy'.[4] But the concept of man is complex and comprises the two principal aspects of man, namely as an individual and as a member of society. Thus the deduction of the adequate concept of man moves through several phases or moments until the two aspects are seen as interpenetrating one another. In his discussion of this matter Cohen observes that philosophy has come to look on the State as the embodiment of man's ethical consciousness. But the empirical or actual State is only too evidently the State 'of the ruling classes'.[5] And the power-State (*der Machtstaat*) can become the State which embodies the principles of right and justice (*der Rechtsstaat*) only when it ceases to serve particular class-interests. In other words, Cohen looks forward to a democratic socialist society which will be the true expression of the ethical will of man considered both as a free individual person and as essentially orientated towards social life and the attainment of a common ideal end.

As the whole system of philosophy is conceived 'from the point of view of the unity of the cultural consciousness'[6] and as this consciousness is certainly not completely characterized by science and morals, Cohen devotes the third volume to aesthetics. As Kant saw, a treatment of aesthetics forms an intrinsic part of systematic philosophy.

Natorp, who also occupied a chair at Marburg, was strongly influenced by Cohen. In his *Philosophical Foundations of the Exact Sciences* (*Die philosophischen Grundlagen der exakten Wissenschaften*, 1910) he tries to show that the logical development of mathematics does not require any recourse to intuitions of space and time. His philosophy of mathematics is thus considerably more 'modern' than Kant's. As for ethics, Natorp shared Cohen's general outlook, and on the basis of the idea that the moral law demands of the individual that he should subordinate his activity to the elevation of humanity he developed a theory of social pedagogy. It can also be mentioned that in a well-known work, *Plato's Theory of Ideas* (*Platons Ideenlehre*, 1903), Natorp attempted to establish an affinity between Plato and Kant.

Both Cohen and Natorp endeavoured to overcome the dichotomy between thought and being which seemed to be implied by the Kantian theory of the thing-in-itself. Thus according to Natorp 'both, namely thought and being, exist and have meaning only in their constant mutual relations to one another'.[7] Being is not something static, set over against the activity of thought; it exists only in a process of becoming which is intrinsically related to this activity. And thought is a process which progressively determines its object, being. But though Cohen and Natorp sought to unite thought and being as related poles of one process, it would not have been possible for them to eliminate effectively the thing-in-itself without deserting the Kantian standpoint and making the transition to metaphysical idealism.

3. While the Marburg School emphasized inquiry into the logical foundations of the natural sciences, the School of Baden emphasized the philosophy of values and reflection on the cultural sciences. Thus for Wilhelm Windelband[8] (1848–1915) the philosopher is concerned with inquiry into the principles and presuppositions of value-judgments and with the relation between the judging subject or consciousness and the value or norm or ideal in the light of which the judgment is made.

Given this account of philosophy, it is obvious that ethical and aesthetic judgments provide material for philosophical reflection. The moral judgment, for example, is clearly axiological in character rather than descriptive. It expresses what ought to be rather than what is the case in the world. But Windelband includes also logical judgments. For just as ethics is concerned with moral values, so is logic concerned with a value, namely truth. It is not everything which is thought that is true. The true is that which ought to be thought. Thus all logical thought is guided by a value, a norm. The ultimate axioms of logic cannot be proved; but we must accept them if we value truth. And we must accept truth as an objective norm or value unless we are prepared to reject all logical thinking.

Logic, ethics and aesthetics, therefore, presuppose the values of truth, goodness and beauty. And this fact compels us to postulate a transcendental norm-setting or value-positing consciousness which lies, as it were, behind empirical consciousness. Further, inasmuch as in their logical, ethical and aesthetic judgments all individuals appeal implicitly to universal absolute values, this transcendental consciousness forms the living bond between individuals.

Absolute values, however, require a metaphysical anchoring (*eine metaphysische Veränkerung*). That is to say, recognition and affirmation of objective values leads us to postulate a metaphysical foundation in a supersensible reality which we call God. And there thus arises the values of the holy. 'We do not understand by the holy a particular class of universally valid values, such as the classes constituted by the true, the good and the beautiful, but rather all these values themselves in so far as they stand in relation to a supersensible reality.'[9]

Windelband's philosophy of values was developed by Heinrich Rickert (1863–1936), his successor in the chair of philosophy at Heidelberg. Rickert insists that there is a realm of values which possess reality but cannot properly be said to exist.[10] They possess reality in the sense that the subject recognizes and does not create them. But they are not existing things among other existing things. In value-judgments, however, the subject brings together the realm of values and the sensible world, giving valuational significance to things and events. And though values themselves cannot be properly said to exist, we are not entitled to deny the possibility of their being grounded in an eternal divine reality which transcends our theoretical knowledge.

In accordance with his general outlook Rickert emphasizes the place of the idea of value in history. Windelband had maintained[11] that natural science is concerned with things in their universal aspects, as exemplifying types, and with events as repeatable, that is, as exemplifying universal laws, whereas history is concerned with the singular, the unique. The natural sciences are 'nomothetic' or law-positing, whereas history (that is, the science of history) is 'idiographic'.[12] Rickert agrees that the historian is concerned with the singular and unique, but insists that he is interested in persons and events only with reference to values. In other words, the ideal of historiography is a science of culture which depicts historical development in the light of the values recognized by different societies and cultures.

As far as one particular aspect of his thought is concerned, Hugo Münsterberg (1863–1916), who was a friend of Rickert, can be associated with the Baden School of Neo-

Kantianism. In his *Philosophy of Values* (*Philosophie der Werte*, 1908), he expounded the idea of giving meaning to the world in terms of a system of values. But as professor of experimental psychology at Harvard he gave his attention mainly to the field of psychology, where he had been strongly influenced by Wundt.

4. We have seen that Windelband regarded the existence of a supersensible divine reality as a postulate of the recognition of absolute values. At the same time he was concerned to argue that the term 'postulate', as used in this context, means much more than 'useful fiction'. There were, however, some Neo-Kantians who interpreted Kant's postulate-theory in a definitely pragmatist sense.

Thus Friedrich Albert Lange (1828–75), who has already been mentioned as a critic of materialism, interpreted metaphysical theories and religious doctrines as belonging to a sphere between knowledge and poetry. If such theories and doctrines are presented as expressing knowledge of reality, they are open to all the objections raised by Kant and other critics. For we cannot have theoretical knowledge of metaphenomenal reality. But if they are interpreted as symbols of a reality which transcends knowledge and if at the same time their value for life is emphasized, they become immune from objections which have point only if cognitive value is claimed for metaphysics and theology.

The useful-fiction version of the theory of postulates was developed in a more systematic way by Hans Vaihinger (1852–1933), author of the celebrated work *The Philosophy of As-If* (*Die Philosophie des Als-Ob*, 1911). With him metaphysical theories and religious doctrines become only particular instances of the application of a general pragmatist view of truth. Only sensations and feelings are real: otherwise the whole of human knowledge consists of 'fictions'. The principles of logic, for example, are fictions which have proved their real utility in experience. And to say that they are undeniably true is to say that they have been found indispensably useful. Hence the question to ask in regard, say, to a religious doctrine is whether it is useful or valuable to act as though it were true rather than whether it is true. Indeed, the question whether the doctrine is 'really' true or not

hardly arises, not simply because we have no means of knowing whether it is true or not but rather because the concept
of truth is given a pragmatist interpretation.[13]

This pragmatist fictionalism evidently goes a long way beyond the position of Kant. Indeed, it really deprives the Kantian theory of postulates of its significance, inasmuch as it
does away with the sharp contrast established by Kant between theoretical knowledge on the one hand and the postulates of the moral law on the other. But though I have included Vaihinger among the Neo-Kantians, he was strongly
influenced by the vitalism and fiction-theory of Nietzsche on
whom he published a well-known work, *Nietzsche as Philosopher* (*Nietzsche als Philosoph*, 1902).

5. As we have seen, Neo-Kantianism was by no means
a homogeneous system of thought. On the one hand we have
a philosopher such as Alois Riehl (1844–1924), professor
at Berlin, who not only rejected decisively all metaphysics
but also maintained that value-theory must be excluded
from philosophy in the proper sense.[14] On the other hand
we have a philosopher such as Windelband who developed
the theory of absolute values in such a way as practically to
reintroduce metaphysics, even if he still spoke about 'postulates'.

Such differences naturally become all the more marked in
proportion as the field of application of the term 'Neo-Kantian' is extended. For instance, the term has sometimes been
applied to Johannes Volkelt (1848–1930), professor of philosophy at Leipzig. But as Volkelt maintained that the human spirit can enjoy an intuitive certitude of its unity with
the Absolute, that the Absolute is infinite spirit, and that
creation can be conceived as analogous to aesthetic production, the propriety of calling him a Neo-Kantian is obviously
questionable. And in point of fact Volkelt was strongly
influenced by other German philosophers besides Kant.

It will have been noticed that most of the philosophers
mentioned lived into the twentieth century. And the Neo-
Kantian movement has indeed had one or two eminent representatives in comparatively recent times. Notable among
these is Ernst Cassirer (1874–1945) who occupied chairs successively at Berlin, Hamburg, Göteborg and Yale in the

United States. The influence of the Marburg School contributed to directing his attention to problems of knowledge. And the fruit of his studies was his three-volume work on *The Problem of Knowledge in the Philosophy and Science of the Modern Era* (*Das Erkenntnisproblem in der Philosophie und Wissenschaft der neueren Zeit*, 1906–20). This was followed in 1910 by a work on the concepts of substance and function (*Substanzbegriff und Funktionsbegriff*). Cassirer was struck by the progressive mathematization of physics, and he concluded that in modern physics sensible reality is transformed into and reconstructed as a world of symbols. Further reflection on the function of symbolism led him to develop a large-scale *Philosophy of Symbolic Forms* (*Philosophie der symbolischen Formen*, 1923–9) in which he maintained that it is the use of symbols which distinguishes man from the animals. It is by means of language that man creates a new world, the world of culture. And Cassirer used the idea of symbolism to unlock many doors. For example, he tried to explain the unity of the human person as a functional unity which unites man's different symbolic activities. He devoted special attention to the function of symbolism in the form of myth, and he studied such activities as art and historiography in the light of the idea of symbolic transformation.

But though Neo-Kantianism lasted on into the present century, it can scarcely be called a twentieth-century philosophy. The emergence of new movements and lines of thought has pushed it into the background. It is not so much that the subjects with which it dealt are dead. It is rather that they are treated in different settings or frameworks of thought. Inquiry into the logic of the sciences and the philosophy of values are cases in point. Further, epistemology or theory of knowledge no longer enjoys the central position which Kant and his disciples attributed to it.

This is not to say, of course, that the influence of Kant is exhausted. Far from it. But it is not felt, at any rate on a significant scale, in the continuance of any movement which could appropriately be called Neo-Kantian. Further, Kant's influence is sometimes exercised in a direction which is thoroughly un-Kantian. For example, while positivists believe that Kant was substantially right in excluding metaphysics from the field of knowledge, there is a current of thought in modern Thomism which has interpreted and developed Kant's transcendental method for the very un-Kantian purpose of establishing a systematic metaphysics.

6. This is a convenient place at which to make a few remarks about Wilhelm Dilthey (1833–1911), who occupied chairs successively at Basel, Kiel, Breslau and finally Berlin, where he succeeded Lotze as professor of philosophy. True, though Dilthey entertained a profound admiration for Kant he cannot properly be described as a Neo-Kantian. He did indeed endeavour to develop a critique of historical reason (*Kritik der historischen Vernunft*) and a corresponding theory of categories. And this activity can be regarded from one point of view as an extension of Kant's critical work to what the Germans call the *Geisteswissenschaften*. At the same time he insisted that the categories of the historical reason, that is, of reason engaged in understanding and interpreting history, are not *a priori* categories which are then applied to some raw materials to constitute history. They arise out of the living penetration by the human spirit of its own objective manifestation in history. And in general, especially from 1883 onwards, Dilthey drew a sharp distinction between the abstractness of Kant's thought and his own concrete approach. However, the fact that we have already had occasion in this chapter to refer to the distinction between the natural sciences and the *Geisteswissenschaften* provides, I think, sufficient reason for mentioning Dilthey here.

The fact that the term 'mental sciences' is a misleading translation of *Geisteswissenschaften* can easily be seen by considering the examples given by Dilthey. Alongside the natural sciences, he says, there has grown up a group of other sciences which together can be called the *Geisteswissenschaften* or *Kulturwissenschaften*. Such are 'history, national economy, the sciences of law and of the State, the science of religion, the study of literature and poetry, of art and music, of philosophical world-views, and systems, finally psychology'.[15] The term 'mental sciences' tends to suggest only psychology. But in a similar list of examples Dilthey does not even mention psychology.[16] The French are accustomed to speak of 'the moral sciences'. But in English this term suggests primarily ethics. Hence I propose to speak of 'the cultural sciences'. It is true that this term would not normally suggest national economy. But it is sufficient to say that the term is being used to cover what Dilthey calls *Kulturwissenschaften* or *Geisteswissenschaften*.

It is clear that we cannot distinguish between the cultural sciences on the one hand and the natural sciences on the other by the simple expedient of saying that the former are concerned with man whereas the latter are not. For physiology is a natural science; yet it treats of man. And the same can be said of experimental psychology. Nor can we say simply that the natural sciences are concerned with the physical and sensible, including the physical aspects of man, whereas the cultural sciences are concerned with the psychical, the interior, with that which does not enter into the sensible world. For it is evident that in the study of art, for instance, we are concerned with sensible objects such as pictures rather than with the psychical states of the artists. True, works of art are studied as objectifications of the human spirit. But they are none the less sensible objectifications. Hence we must find some other way of distinguishing between the two groups of sciences.

Man stands in a living felt unity with Nature, and his primary experience of his physical milieu are personal lived experiences (*Erlebnisse*), not objects of reflection from which man detaches himself. To construct the world of natural science, however, man has to prescind from the aspect of his impressions of his physical milieu under which they are his personal lived experiences; he has to put himself out of the picture as far as he can[17] and develop an abstract conception of Nature in terms of relations of space, time, mass and motion. Nature has to become for him the central reality, a law-ordered physical system, which is considered, as it were, from without.

When, however, we turn to the world of history and culture, the objectifications of the human spirit, the situation is different. It is a question of penetration from within. And the individual's personal lived relations with his own social milieu become of fundamental importance. For example, I cannot understand the social and political life of ancient Greece as an objectification of the human spirit if I exclude my own lived experiences of social relations. For these form the basis of my understanding of the social life of any other epoch. True, a certain unity in the historical and social life of humanity is a necessary condition of the possibility of my own *Erlebnisse* providing a key to the understanding of history. But the 'original cell of the historical world,'[18] as Dilthey calls it, is precisely the individual's *Erlebnis*, his lived experience of interaction with his own social milieu.

But though what Dilthey calls *Erlebnisse* are a necessary condition for the development of the cultural sciences, they do not by themselves constitute a science of any kind. Understanding (*Verstehen*) is also necessary. And what we have to understand in history and the other cultural sciences is not the human spirit in its interiority, so to speak, but the external objectification of this spirit, its objective expression, as in art, law, the State and so on. We are concerned in other words with the understanding of objective spirit.[19] And to understand a phase of objective spirit means relating its phenomena to an inner structure which finds expression in these phenomena. For example, the understanding of Roman law involves penetrating beneath the external apparatus, so to speak, to the spiritual structure which finds expression in the laws. It means penetrating what can be called the spirit of Roman law, just as understanding Baroque architecture would involve penetrating the spirit, the structure of purposes and ideals, which found expression in this style. We can say, therefore, that 'the cultural sciences rest on the relation of lived experience, expression and understanding'.[20] Expression is required because the underlying spiritual structure is grasped only in and through its external expression. Understanding is a movement from the outside to the inside. And in the process of understanding a spiritual object rises before our vision, whereas in the natural sciences a physical object is constructed (though not in the Kantian sense) in the process of scientific knowledge.

We have seen that a man's personal experience of his own social milieu is a necessary condition of his being able to live over again the experience of men in the past. *Erleben* is a condition of the possibility of *Nacherleben*. And the former renders the latter possible because of the continuity and fundamental unity of the developing historical-cultural reality which Dilthey describes as Life (*Leben*). Cultures are, of course, spatially and temporally distinct. But if we conceive the reciprocal relations between persons, under the conditions set by the external world, as a structural and developing unity which persists throughout spatial and temporal differentiations, we have the concept of Life. And in studying this Life the historical reason employs certain categories. As has already been remarked, these categories are not *a priori* forms or concepts applied to some raw material: 'they lie in the nature of Life itself'[21] and are conceptualized abstractly in the process of understanding. We cannot determine the exact number of such categories or turn them into a tidy abstract logical scheme for mechanical application. But among them we can name 'meaning, value, purpose, development, ideal'.[22]

These categories should not be understood in a metaphysical sense. It is not a question, for example, of defining the end or meaning of history in the sense of an end which the process of historical development is predestined to attain. It is a question rather of understanding the meaning which Life has for a particular society and the operative ideals which find expression in that society's political and legal institutions, in its art, religion and so on. 'The category of meaning signifies the relations of parts of Life to the whole.'[23] But 'our conception of the meaning of Life is always changing. Each life-plan expresses an idea of the meaning of Life. And the purpose which we set for the future conditions our account of the meaning of the past.'[24] If we say that the task for the future is to achieve this or that, our judgment conditions our understanding of the meaning of the past. And, of course, the other way round as well.

It can hardly be denied that Dilthey's thought contains a prominent element of historical relativism. For example, all world-views or *Weltanschauungen* are partial views of the world, relative to distinct cultural phases. And a study of such world-views or metaphysical systems would exhibit their relativity. At the same time Dilthey does not maintain that there is no universally valid truth at all. And he regards the study of Life, of history as a whole, as a constant approximation to an objective and complete self-knowledge by man.

Man is fundamentally an historical being, and he comes to know himself in history. This self-knowledge is never actually complete, but the knowledge which man attains through a study of history is no more purely subjective than is the knowledge attained through the natural sciences. How far Dilthey actually succeeds in overcoming pure historicism is doubtless open to discussion. But he certainly does not intend to assert an extreme relativism which would necessarily invalidate his conception of world-history.

At a time when the natural sciences appear to be threatening to engulf the whole field of knowledge, the question whether and how one could distinguish between the natural and the cultural sciences naturally becomes an issue of importance. And Dilthey's account of the matter was one of the most signal contributions to the discussion. What one thinks of its value seems to depend very largely on one's view of the historian's function. If, for example, one thinks that Dilthey's idea of getting behind the external expression to an inward spiritual structure (the 'spirit' of Roman law, of Baroque art and architecture, and so on) smacks of the transcendental metaphysics which Dilthey himself professed to reject, and if at the same time one disapproves of such transcendental metaphysics, one will hardly be disposed to accept Dilthey's account of the differences between the two groups of sciences. If, however, one thinks that an understanding of man's cultural life does in fact demand this passage from the external phenomena to the operative ideals, purposes and values which are expressed in them, one can hardly deny the relevance of the concepts of *Erleben* and *Nacherleben*. For historical understanding would then necessarily involve a penetration of the past from within, a reliving, so far as this is possible, of past experience, of past attitudes, valuations and ideals. And this would be at any rate one distinguishing characteristic of the historical and cultural sciences. For the physicist can scarcely be said to attempt to relive the experience of an atom or to penetrate behind the relations of infra-atomic particles to a spiritual structure expressed in them. To introduce such notions into mathematical physics would mean its ruin. Conversely, to fail to introduce them into the theory of the cultural sciences is to forget that 'he who explores history is the same who makes history'.[25]

Chapter Twenty

THE REVIVAL OF METAPHYSICS

Remarks on inductive metaphysics – Fechner's inductive metaphysics – The teleological idealism of Lotze – Wundt and the relation between science and philosophy – The vitalism of Driesch – Eucken's activism – Appropriation of the past: Trendelenburg and Greek thought; the revival of Thomism.

1. In spite of their own excursions into metaphysics both the materialists and the Neo-Kantians were opposed to the idea of metaphysics as a source of positive knowledge about reality, the former appealing to scientific thinking in justification of their attitude, the latter to Kant's theory of the limitations of man's theoretical knowledge. But there was also a group of philosophers who came to philosophy from some branch or other of empirical science and who were convinced that the scientific view of the world demands completion through metaphysical reflection. They did not believe that a valid system of metaphysics could be worked out *a priori* or without regard to our scientific knowledge. And they tended to look on metaphysical theories as hypothetical and as enjoying a higher or lower degree of probability. Hence in their case we can speak of inductive metaphysics.

Inductive metaphysics has, of course, had its notable representatives, above all perhaps Henri Bergson. But there are probably few people who would be prepared to claim that the German inductive metaphysicians of the second half of the nineteenth century were of the same stature as the great idealists. And one of the weak points of inductive metaphysics in general is that it tends to leave unexamined and unestablished the basic principles on which it rests. However, it is as well to realize that we cannot simply divide the German philosophers into two classes, those who constructed metaphysics in an *a priori* manner and those who rejected metaphysics in the name of science or in that of the limitations of the human mind. For there were also those who attempted to achieve a synthesis between science and metaphysics, not by trying to harmonize science with an already-made philosophical system but rather by trying to show that reflection on the world as known through the particular sciences reasonably leads to metaphysical theories.

2. Among the representatives of inductive metaphysics, we can mention Gustav Theodor Fechner (1801–87), for many years professor of physics at Leipzig and celebrated as one of the founders of experimental psychology. Continuing the studies of E. H. Weber (1795–1878) on the relation between sensation and stimulus, Fechner gave expression in his *Elements of Psychophysics* (*Elemente des Psychophysik*, 1860) to the 'law' which states that the intensity of the sensation varies in proportion to the logarithm of the intensity of the stimulus. Fechner also devoted himself to the psychological study of aesthetics, publishing his *Propaedeutics to Aesthetics* (*Vorschule der Aesthetik*) in 1876.

These studies in exact science did not, however, lead Fechner to materialist conclusions.[1] In psychology he was a parallelist. That is to say, he thought that psychical and physical phenomena correspond in a manner analogous to the relation between a text and its translation or between two translations of a text, as he explained in his *Zend-Avesta* (1851) and in his *Elements of Psychophysics*. In fact, the psychical and the physical were for him two aspects of one reality. And in accordance with this view he postulated the presence of a psychical life even in plants, though of a lower type than in animals.[2] Moreover, he extended this parallelism to the planets and stars and indeed to all material things, justifying this panpsychism by a principle of analogy which states that when objects agree in possessing certain qualities or traits, one is entitled to assume hypothetically that they agree also in other qualities, provided that one's hypotheses do not contradict established scientific facts.

This is hardly a very safe rule of procedure, but, to do Fechner justice, it should be added that he demanded some positive ground for metaphysical theories, as distinct from a mere absence of contradiction of scientific facts. At the same

time he also made use of a principle which is not calculated
to commend his metaphysics in the eyes of anti-metaphysi-
cians or, for the matter of that, of many metaphysicians themselves. I refer to the principle which states that an hypothesis
which has some positive ground and does not contradict any
established fact is to be the more readily embraced the more
it renders man happy.[3]

In the spirit of this principle Fechner contrasted what he
called the day-view with the night-view, to the detriment of
the latter.[4] The night-view, attributed not only to the materialists but also to the Kantians, is the view of Nature as
dumb and dead and as affording no real clue to its teleological
significance. The day-view is the vision of Nature as a living
harmonious unity, animated by a soul. The soul of the universe is God, and the universe considered as a physical system
is the divine externality. Fechner thus uses his principle of
analogy to extend psychophysical parallelism not only from
human beings to other classes of particular things but also
from all particular things to the universe as a whole. He employs it also as a basis for belief in personal immortality.
Our perceptions persist in memory and enter once again into
consciousness. So, we may suppose, our souls persist in the
divine memory but without simple absorption in the Deity.

Panpsychism is indeed a very ancient theory, and it is one
which tends to recur. It is far from being Fechner's private
invention. However, it is difficult to avoid the impression
that when Fechner leaves the purely scientific sphere and em-
barks on philosophy he becomes a kind of poet of the universe. But it is interesting to observe the pragmatist element
in his thought. We have seen that in his view, other things
being equal, the theory which makes for happiness is to be
preferred to the theory which does not. But Fechner does
not make it a matter simply of individual preference. Another of his principles states that the probability of a belief
increases in proportion to the length of its survival, especially
if acceptance of it increases together with the development
of human culture. And it is not surprising that William
James derived inspiration from Fechner.

3. A much more impressive figure as a philosopher is Rudolf Hermann Lotze (1817–81) who studied medicine and

philosophy at Leipzig, where he also listened to Fechner's lectures on physics. In 1844 he was nominated professor of philosophy at Göttingen and in 1881, shortly before his death, he accepted a chair of philosophy at Berlin. Besides works on physiology, medicine and psychology he published a considerable number of philosophical writings.[5] In 1841 there appeared a *Metaphysics*, in 1843 a *Logic*, in 1856–64 a large three-volume work entitled *Microcosm* (*Mikrokosmus*) on philosophical anthropology, in 1868 a history of aesthetics in Germany and in 1874–9 a *System of Philosophy* (*System der Philosophie*). After Lotze's death a series of volumes were published which were based on lecture-notes taken by his students. These covered in outline the fields of psychology, ethics, philosophy of religion, philosophy of Nature, logic, metaphysics, aesthetics and the history of post-Kantian philosophy in Germany. A three-volume collection of his minor writings (*Kleine Schriften*) appeared in 1885–91.

According to Lotze himself it was his inclination to poetry and art which originally turned his mind to philosophy. Hence it can be somewhat misleading to say that he came to philosophy from science. At the same time he had a scientific training at the university of Leipzig, where he enrolled in the faculty of medicine, and it is characteristic of his systematic philosophical thinking that he presupposed and took seriously what he called the mechanical interpretation of Nature.

For example, while recognizing, of course, the evident fact that there are differences in behaviour between living and non-living things, Lotze refused to allow that the biologist must postulate some special vital principle which is responsible for the maintenance and operation of the organism. For science, which seeks everywhere to discover connections which can be formulated in terms of general laws, 'the realm of life is not divided from that of inorganic Nature by a higher force peculiar to itself, setting itself up as something alien above other modes of action . . . but simply by the peculiar kind of connection into which its manifold constituents are woven. . . .'[6] That is to say, the characteristic behaviour of the organism can be explained in terms of the combination of material elements in certain ways. And it is the biologist's business to push this type of explanation as far as he can and not to have recourse to the expedient of invoking special vital principles. 'The connection of vital phenomena demands throughout a mechanical treatment which explains life not by a peculiar principle of operation but by a characteristic application of the general principles of physical process.'[7]

This mechanical interpretation of Nature, which is necessary for the development of science, should be extended as far as possible. And this is as true of psychology as of biology. At the same time we are certainly not entitled to rule out a priori the possibility of finding facts of experience which limit the applicability of the mechanical view. And we do find such facts. For example, the unity of consciousness, which manifests itself in the simple act of comparing two presentations and judging them to be like or unlike, at once sets a limit to the possibility of describing man's psychical life in terms of causal relations between distinct psychical events. It is not a question of inferring the existence of a soul as a kind of unalterable psychical atom. It is 'the fact of the unity of consciousness which is eo ipso at the same time the fact of the existence of a substance',[8] namely the soul. In other words, to affirm the existence of the soul is neither to postulate a logical condition of the unity of consciousness nor to infer from this unity an occult entity. For recognition of the unity of consciousness is at the same time recognition of the existence of the soul, though the proper way of describing the soul is obviously a matter for further reflection.

Thus there are certain empirical facts which set a limit to the field of application of the mechanical interpretation of Nature. And it is no good suggesting that further scientific advance can abolish these facts or show that they are not facts. This is quite evident in the case of the unity of consciousness. For any further scientific advances in empirical and physiological psychology depend on and presuppose the unity of consciousness. And as for Lotze reflection on the unity of consciousness shows that psychical states must be referred to an immaterial reality as their subject, the point at which the limitation of the mechanical interpretation of man's psychical life becomes decisively evident is also the point at which the need for a metaphysical psychology becomes clear.

It is not, however, Lotze's intention to construct a two-storey system, as it were, in which the mechanical interpretation of material Nature would form the lower storey and a superimposed metaphysics of spiritual reality the higher. For he argues that even as regards Nature itself the mechanical interpretation gives but a one-sided picture, valid indeed for scientific purposes but inadequate from a metaphysical point of view.

The mechanical interpretation of Nature presupposes the existence of distinct things which are in causal relations of interaction and each of which is relatively permanent, that is, in relation to its own changing states. But interaction between A and B is possible, according to Lotze, only if they are members of an organic unity. And permanence in relation to changing states can best be interpreted on an analogy with the permanent subject of change which is best known to us, namely the human soul as revealed in the unity of consciousness. We are thus led not only to the concept of Nature as an organic unity but also to the idea of things as in some sense psychical or spiritual entities. Further, the ground of this unity must be conceived on an analogy with the highest thing known to us, namely the human spirit. Hence the world of finite spirits is to be conceived as the self-expression of infinite Spirit or God. All things are immanent in God, and what the scientist sees as mechanical causality is simply the expression of the divine activity. God does not create a world and then sit back, as it were, while the world obeys the laws he has given it. The so-called laws are the divine action itself, the mode of God's operation.

From a rather hard-headed starting-point in the mechanical conception of Nature Lotze thus goes on to expound a metaphysical theory which recalls the monadology of Leibniz and which entails the conclusion that space is phenomenal. But though Lotze did indeed derive stimulus from Leibniz and Herbart, he also drew inspiration, as he himself says, from the ethical idealism of Fichte. He was not a disciple of Fichte, and he disapproved of the *a priori* method of the post-Kantian idealists, especially of Hegel. At the same time

Fichte's conception of the ultimate principle expressing itself in finite subjects with a view to a moral end exercised a powerful attraction on Lotze's mind. And it is to the philosophy of values that he turns for the key to the meaning of creation. Sense experience tells us nothing about the final cause of the world. But that the world cannot be without end or purpose is a moral conviction. And we must conceive God as expressing himself in the world for the realization of value, of a moral ideal which is being constantly fulfilled in and through the divine activity. As for our knowledge of what this end or aim is, we can come to some knowledge of it only by an analysis of the notion of the Good, of the highest value. A phenomenological analysis of values is thus an integral part of philosophy. Indeed, our belief in God's existence ultimately rests on our moral experience and appreciation of value.[9]

God is for Lotze a personal Being. The notion of impersonal spirit he dismisses as contrary to reason. As for the view of Fichte and other philosophers that personality is necessarily finite and limited and so cannot be predicated of the infinite, Lotze replies that it is only infinite spirit which can be personal in the fullest sense of the word: finitude involves a limitation of personality. At the same time all things are immanent in God, and, as we have seen, mechanical causality is simply the divine action. In this sense God is the Absolute. But he is not the Absolute in the sense that finite spirits can be considered modifications of the divine substance. For each exists 'for itself' and is a centre of activity. From a metaphysical point of view, says Lotze, pantheism could be accepted as a possible view of the world only if it renounced all inclination to conceive the infinite as anything else but Spirit. For the spatial world is phenomenal and cannot be identified with God under the name of Substance. From a religious point of view 'we do not share the inclination which commonly governs the pantheistic imagination to suppress all that is finite in favour of the infinite. . . .'[10]

Lotze's teleological idealism has obvious affinities with the post-Kantian idealist movement. And his vision of the world as an organic unity which is the expression of infinite Spirit's realization of ideal value may be said to have given fresh life to idealist thought. But he did not believe that we can deduce a metaphysical system, descriptive of existent reality, from ultimate principles of thought or self-evident truths. For the so-called eternal truths of logic are hypothetical in character, in the sense that they state conditions of possibility. Hence they cannot be used as premisses for an *a priori* deduction of existent reality. Nor can human beings achieve an absolute point of view and describe the whole process of reality in the light of a final end which they already know. Man's metaphysical interpretation of the universe must be based on experience. And, as we have seen, Lotze attributes a profound significance to the experience of value. For it is this experience which lies at the root of the conviction that the world cannot be simply a mechanical system without purpose or ethical value but must be conceived as progressively realizing a spiritual end. This is not to say that the metaphysician, once armed with this conviction, is entitled to indulge in flights of the imagination uncontrolled by logical thinking about the nature of reality. But in the philosopher's systematic interpretation of the universe there will inevitably be much that is hypothetical.

The influence of Lotze was considerable. For instance, in the field of psychology it was felt by Carl Stumpf (1848–1936) and Franz Brentano, of whom something will be said in the last chapter. But it was perhaps in the field of the philosophy of values that his influence was most felt. Among a number of English thinkers who derived stimulus from Lotze we may mention in particular James Ward (1843–1925). In America the idealist Josiah Royce (1855–1916) was influenced by Lotze's personalistic idealism.

4. Among the German philosophers of the second half of the nineteenth century who came from science to philosophy mention must be made of Wilhelm Wundt (1832–1920). After studying medicine Wundt gave himself to physiological and psychological research, and in 1863–4 he published a series of *Lectures on the Human and Animal Soul* (*Vorlesungen über die Menschen- und Tierseele*). After nine years as an 'extraordinary' professor of physiology at Heidelberg he was nominated to the chair of inductive philosophy at Zürich in 1874. In the following year he moved to Leipzig where he

occupied the chair of philosophy until 1918. And it was at Leipzig that he founded the first laboratory of experimental psychology. The first edition of his *Outlines of Physiological Psychology* (*Grundzüge der physiologischen Psychologie*) was published in 1874. In the philosophical field he published a two-volume *Logic* in 1880–3,[11] an *Ethics* in 1886, a *System of Philosophy* in 1889,[12] and a *Metaphysics* in 1907. But he did not abandon his psychological studies, and in 1904 he published a two-volume *Psychology of Peoples* (*Völkerpsychologie*) of which a new and greatly enlarged edition appeared in 1911–20.

When Wundt speaks about experimental psychology and the experimental method he is generally referring to introspective psychology and the introspective method. Or, more accurately, he regards introspection as the appropriate method of investigation for individual, as distinct from social, psychology. Introspection reveals, as its immediate data, a connection of psychical events or processes, not a substantial soul, nor a set of relatively permanent objects. For no one of the events revealed by introspection remains precisely the same from one moment to another. At the same time there is a unity of connection. And just as the natural scientist tries to establish the causal laws which operate in the physical sphere, so should the introspective psychologist endeavour to ascertain the fundamental laws of relation and development which give content to the idea of psychical causality. In interpreting man's psychical life Wundt lays emphasis on volitional rather than on cognitive elements. The latter are not denied, of course, but the volitional element is taken as fundamental and as providing the key for the interpretation of man's psychical life as a whole.

When we turn from the psychical life as manifested in introspection to human societies, we find common and relatively permanent products such as language, myth and custom. And the social psychologist is called on to investigate the psychical energies which are responsible for these common products and which together form the spirit or soul of a people. This spirit exists only in and through individuals, but it is not reducible to them when taken separately. In other words, through the relations of individuals in a society there arises a reality, the spirit of a people, which expresses itself in common spiritual products. And social psychology studies the development of these realities. It also studies the evolution of the concept of humanity and of the general spirit of man which manifests itself, for example, in the rise of universal instead of purely national religions, in the development of science, in the growth of the idea of common human rights, and so on. Wundt thus allots to social psychology a far-reaching programme. For its task is to study from a psychological point of view the development of human society and culture in all its principal manifestations.

Philosophy, according to Wundt, presupposes natural science and psychology. It builds upon them and incorporates them into a synthesis. At the same time philosophy goes beyond the sciences. Yet there can be no reasonable objection to this procedure on the ground that it is contrary to the scientific spirit. For in the particular sciences themselves explanatory hypotheses are constructed which go beyond the empirical data. At the level of knowledge of the understanding (*Verstandeserkenntnis*), the level at which sciences such as physics and psychology arise, presentations are synthesized with the aid of logical method and techniques. At the level of rational knowledge (*Vernunfterkenntnis*) philosophy, especially metaphysics, tries to construct a systematic synthesis of the results of the previous level. At all levels of cognition the mind aims at absence of contradiction in a progressive synthesis of presentations, which form the fundamental point of departure for human knowledge.

In his general metaphysical picture of reality Wundt conceives the world as the totality of individual agents or active centres which are to be regarded as volitional unities of different grades. These volitional unities form a developing series which tends towards the emergence of a total spirit (*Gesamtgeist*). In more concrete terms, there is a movement towards the complete spiritual unification of man or humanity, and individual human beings are called on to act in accordance with the values which contribute to this end. Metaphysics and ethics are thus closely connected, and both receive a natural completion in religious idealism. For the concept of a cosmic process directed towards an ideal leads to a religious view of the world.

5. We have seen that though Lotze went on to develop a metaphysical theory about the spiritual nature of reality, he would not allow that the biologist has any warrant for setting aside the mechanical interpretation of Nature which is proper to the empirical sciences and postulating a special vital principle to explain the behaviour of the organism. When, however, we turn to Hans Driesch (1867–1941) we find this onetime pupil of Haeckel being led by his biological and zoological researches to a theory of dynamic vitalism and to the conviction that finality is an essential category in biology. He became convinced that in the organic body there is an autonomous active principle which directs the vital processes and which cannot be accounted for by a purely mechanistic theory of life.

To this principle Driesch gave the name of *entelechy*, making use of an Aristotelian term. But he was careful to refrain from describing the entelechy or vital principle as psychical. For this term, he considered, is inappropriate in view both of its human associations and of its ambiguity.

Having formed the concept of entelechies Driesch proceeded to blossom out as a philosopher. In 1907–8 he gave the Gifford Lectures at Aberdeen, and in 1909 he published his two-volume *Philosophy of the Organic* (*Philosophie des Organischen*). In 1911 he obtained a chair of philosophy at Heidelberg, and subsequently he was professor first at Cologne and later at Leipzig. In his general philosophy[13] the concept of the organism was extrapolated to apply to the world as a whole, and his metaphysics culminated in the idea of a supreme entelechy, God. The picture was that of a cosmic entelechy, the teleological activity of which is directed towards the realization of the highest possible level of knowledge. But the question of theism or pantheism was left in suspense.

Through his attack on mechanistic biology Driesch exercised a considerable influence. But of those who agreed with him that a mechanistic interpretation was inadequate and that the organism manifests finality by no means all were prepared to accept the theory of entelechies. To mention two Englishmen who, like Driesch, came to philosophy from science and in due course delivered series of Gifford Lectures, Lloyd Morgan (1852–1936) rejected Driesch's neo-vitalism, while J. A. Thomson (1861–1933) tried to steer a middle path between what he regarded as the metaphysical Scylla of the entelechy theory and the Charybdis of mechanistic materialism.

6. The philosophers whom we have been considering in this chapter had a scientific training and either turned from the study of some particular science or sciences to philosophical speculation or combined the two activities. We can now consider briefly a thinker, Rudolf Eucken (1846–1926), who certainly did not come to philosophy from science but who was already interested as a schoolboy[14] in philosophical and religious problems and who devoted himself to the study of philosophy at the universities of Göttingen and Berlin. In 1871 he was appointed professor of philosophy at Basel, and in 1874 he accepted the chair of philosophy at Jena.

Eucken had little sympathy with the view of philosophy as a purely theoretical interpretation of the world. Philosophy was for him, as for the Stoics, a wisdom for life. Further, it was for him an expression of life. In his opinion the interpretation of philosophical systems as so many life-views (*Lebensanschauungen*) contained a profound truth, namely that philosophy is rooted in life and continuous with it. At the same time he wished to overcome the fragmentation of philosophy, its falling apart into purely personal reactions to life and ideals for life. And he concluded that if philosophy, as the expression of life, is to possess a more than subjective and purely personal significance, it must be the expression of a universal life which rescues man from his mere particularity.

This universal life is identified by Eucken with what he calls Spiritual Life (*das Geistesleben*). From the purely naturalistic point of view psychical life 'forms a mere means and instrument for the preservation of beings in the hard fight for existence'.[15] Spiritual Life, however, is an active reality which produces a new spiritual world. 'There thus arise whole fields such as science and art, law and morals, and they develop their own contents, their own motive forces, their own laws.'[16] Provided that he breaks with the natural-istic and egoistic point of view man can rise to a participation in this Spiritual Life. He then becomes 'more than a mere point; a universal Life becomes for him his own life'.[17]

Spiritual Life, therefore, is an active reality which operates in and through man. And it can be regarded as the move-ment of reality towards the full actualization of Spirit. It is, as it were, reality organizing itself from within into a spiritual unity. And as it is through participation in this Life that man achieves real personality, the Life which is the founda-tion of human personality can be regarded as being itself per-sonal. It is in fact God. 'The concept of God receives here the meaning of an absolute Spiritual Life,'[18] 'the Spiritual Life which attains to complete independence and at the same time to the embracing in itself of all reality.'[19]

Philosophy is or should be the expression of this Life. 'The synthesis of the manifold which philosophy undertakes must not be imposed on reality from without but should proceed out of reality itself and contribute to its development.'[20] That is to say, philosophy should be the conceptual expres-sion of the unifying activity of the Spiritual Life, and it should at the same time contribute to the development of this Life by enabling men to understand their relation to it.

The concept of *das Geistesleben* naturally recalls to mind the philosophy of Hegel. And from this point of view Euck-en's thought can be described as neo-idealism. But whereas Hegel emphasized the conceptual solution of problems, Eucken is inclined to say that the important problems of life are solved by action. A man attains to truth in so far as he overcomes the pull of his non-spiritual nature and partici-pates actively in the one Spiritual Life. Hence Eucken de-scribed his philosophy as 'activism'.[21] As for the affinities be-tween his own philosophy and pragmatism, Eucken was inclined to interpret pragmatism as involving the reduction of truth to an instrument in the service of 'mere man's' egoistic search for satisfaction and thus as favouring the very frag-mentation of philosophy which he wished to overcome. In his view truth is that towards which Spiritual Life actively strives.

In his own day Eucken had a considerable reputation. But

what he offers is obviously one more world-view, one more *Lebensanschauung*, rather than an effective overcoming of the conflict of systems. And his philosophy is one in which the element of precise statement and explanation is by no means always conspicuous. It is all very well, for example, to talk about problems being solved by action. But when it is a question of theoretical problems, the concept of solution through action requires much more careful analysis than is given it by Eucken.

7. Hegel, as we have seen, gave a powerful impetus to the study of the history of philosophy. But for him the history of philosophy was absolute idealism in the making or, to express the matter metaphysically, absolute Spirit's progressive understanding of itself. And the historian of philosophy who is thoroughly imbued with Hegelian principles sees in the development of philosophical thought a constant dialectical advance, later systems presupposing and subsuming in themselves earlier phases of thought. It is understandable, however, that there should be other philosophers who look back to past phases of thought as valuable sources of insights which have been later forgotten or overlooked rather than taken up and elevated in succeeding systems.

As an example of the philosophers who have emphasized the objective study of the past with a view to rethinking and reappropriating its perennially valuable elements we can mention Adolf Trendelenburg (1802–72) who occupied the chair of philosophy at Berlin for many years and exercised a considerable influence on the development of historical studies. He applied himself especially to the study of Aristotle, though his historical writings dealt also with Spinoza, Kant, Hegel and Herbart. A vigorous opponent both of Hegel and Herbart, he contributed to the decline of the former's prestige in the middle of the century. And he directed men's attention to the perennially valuable sources of European philosophy in Greek thought, though he was convinced that the insights of Greek philosophy needed to be rethought and appropriated in the light of the modern scientific conception of the world.

Trendelenburg's own philosophy, described by him as the 'organic world-view' (*organische Weltanschauung*) was de-

veloped in his two-volume *Logical Inquiries* (*Logische Untersuchungen*, 1840). It owed much to Aristotle, and, as in
Aristotelianism, the idea of finality was fundamental. At the
same time Trendelenburg endeavoured to reconcile Aristotle
and Kant by depicting space, time and the categories as forms
both of being and of thought. He also attempted to give a
moral foundation to the ideas of right and law in his works
on *the Moral Idea of Right* (*Die sittliche Idee des Rechts*,
1849) and *Natural Right on the Foundation of Ethics*
(*Naturrecht auf dem Grunde der Ethik*, 1860).

Aristotelian studies were also pursued by Gustav Teichmüller (1832–88) who came under Trendelenburg's influence at Berlin. But Teichmüller subsequently developed a
philosophy inspired by Leibniz and Lotze, especially by the
former.

Among Trendelenburg's pupils was Otto Willmann
(1839–1920) whose mind moved from the thought of Aristotle through criticism of both idealism and materialism to
Thomist philosophy. And some allusion can be made here
to the reappropriation of mediaeval philosophy, in particular
of the thought of St. Thomas Aquinas. It is indeed rather
difficult to treat this subject simply within the context of
German philosophy in the nineteenth century. For the rise
of Thomism was a phenomenon within the intellectual life
of the Catholic Church in general, and it can hardly be
claimed that the German contribution was the most important. At the same time the subject cannot be simply passed
over in silence.

In the seventeenth, eighteenth and early part of the nineteenth centuries philosophy in ecclesiastical seminaries and
teaching institutions generally tended to take the form of
an uninspired Scholastic Aristotelianism amalgamated with
ideas taken from other currents of thought, notably Cartesian-
ism and, later, the philosophy of Wolff. And it lacked the intrinsic vigour which was required to make its presence felt in
the intellectual world at large. Further, in the first half of
the nineteenth century there were a number of Catholic
thinkers in France, Italy and Germany whose ideas, developed either in dialogue with or under the influence of contemporary thought, seemed to the ecclesiastical authorities to

compromise, whether directly or indirectly, the integrity of the Catholic faith. Thus in Germany Georg Hermes (1775–1831), professor of theology first at Münster and then at Bonn, was judged by the Church to have adopted far too much from the philosophers whom he tried to oppose, such as Kant and Fichte, and to have thrown Catholic dogma into the melting-pot of philosophical speculation. Again, in his enthusiasm for the revivification of theology Anton Günther (1783–1863) attempted to make use of the Hegelian dialectic to explain and prove the doctrine of the Trinity,[22] while Jakob Froschhammer (1821–93), a priest and a professor of philosophy at Munich, was judged to have subordinated supernatural faith and revelation to idealist philosophy.[23]

In the course of the nineteenth century, however, a number of Catholic thinkers raised the call for a reappropriation of mediaeval thought, and especially of the theological-philosophical synthesis developed in the thirteenth century by St. Thomas Aquinas. As far as Germany was concerned, the revival of interest in Scholasticism in general and Thomism in particular owed much to the writings of men such as Joseph Kleutgen (1811–83), Albert Stöckl (1832–95) and Konstantin Gutberlet (1837–1928). Most of Gutberlet's works appeared after the publication in 1879 of Pope Leo XIII's encyclical letter *Aeterni Patris* in which the Pope asserted the permanent value of Thomism and urged Catholic philosophers to draw their inspiration from it while at the same time developing it to meet modern needs. But Stöckl's *Textbook of Philosophy* (*Lehrbuch der Philosophie*) had appeared in 1868, and the first editions of Kleutgen's *The Theology of Early Times Defended* (*Die Theologie der Vorzeit verteidigt*) and *The Philosophy of Early Times Defended* (*Die Philosophie der Vorzeit verteidigt*) had appeared respectively in 1853–60 and 1860–3. Hence it is not quite accurate to say that Leo XIII inaugurated the revival of Thomism. What he did was to give a powerful impetus to an already existing movement.

The revival of Thomism naturally demanded a real knowledge and understanding not only of the thought of Aquinas in particular but also of mediaeval philosophy in general.

And it is natural that the first phase of the revival should have been succeeded by specialist studies in the sphere, such as we associate with the names of Clemens Baeumker (1853–1924) and Martin Grabmann (1875–1949) in Germany, of Maurice De Wulf (1867–1947) in Belgium, and of Pierre Mandonnet (1858–1936) and Étienne Gilson (b. 1884) in France.

At the same time, if Thomism was to be presented as a living system of thought and not as possessing a purely historical interest, it had to be shown, first that it was not entangled with antiquated physics and discarded scientific hypotheses, and secondly that it was capable of development and of throwing light on philosophical problems as they present themselves to the modern mind. In the fulfilment of the first task much was accomplished by the work of Cardinal Mercier (1851–1926) and his collaborators and successors at the university of Louvain.[24] In regard to the fulfilment of the second task we can mention the names of Joseph Geyser (1869–1948) in Germany and of Jacques Maritain (b. 1882) in France.

Having established itself as, so to speak, a respectable system of thought, Thomism had then to show that it was capable of assimilating the valuable elements in other philosophies without self-destruction. But this is a theme which belongs to the history of Thomist thought in the present century.

Chapter Twenty-one

NIETZSCHE (1)

Life and writings – The phases of Nietzsche's thought as 'masks' – Nietzsche's early writings and the critique of contemporary culture – The critique of morals – Atheism and its consequences.

1. As we have already strayed into the twentieth century, it may seem inappropriate to reserve to this stage of the volume two chapters on a philosopher who died physically in 1900 and, as far as writing was concerned, some ten years previously. But though this procedure is questionable from the chronological point of view, one can also argue in favour of closing a volume on nineteenth-century German philosophy with a thinker who died in 1900 but whose influence was not fully felt until the present century. Whatever one may think about Nietzsche's ideas, one cannot question his vast reputation and the power of his ideas to act like a potent wine in the minds of a good many people. And this is something which can hardly be said about the materialists, Neo-Kantians and the inductive metaphysicians whom we have been considering in the foregoing chapters.

Friedrich Wilhelm Nietzsche was born on October 15th, 1844, at Röcken in Prussian Saxony. His father, a Lutheran pastor, died in 1849, and the boy was brought up at Naumburg in the feminine and pious society of his mother, his sister, a grandmother and two aunts. From 1854 to 1858 he studied at the local *Gymnasium*, and from 1858 to 1864 he was a pupil at the celebrated boarding-school at Pforta. His admiration for the Greek genius was awakened during his schooldays, his favourite classical authors being Plato and Aeschylus. He also tried his hand at poetry and music.

In October 1864 Nietzsche went to the university of Bonn in company with his school friend Paul Deussen, the future orientalist and philosopher. But in the autumn of the following year he moved to Leipzig to continue his philological studies under Ritschl. He formed an intimate friendship with Erwin Rohde, then a fellow student, later a university professor and author of *Psyche*. By this time Nietzsche had abandoned Christianity, and when at Leipzig he made the acquaintance of Schopenhauer's main work one of the features which attracted him was, as he himself said, the author's atheism.

Nietzsche had published some papers in the *Rheinisches Museum*, and when the university of Basel asked Ritschl whether their author was a suitable person to occupy the chair of philosophy at Basel, Ritschl had no hesitation in giving an unqualified testimonial on behalf of his favourite pupil. The result was that Nietzsche found himself appointed a university professor before he had even taken the doctorate.[1] And in May 1869 he delivered his inaugural lecture on *Homer and Classical Philology*. On the outbreak of the Franco-Prussian war Nietzsche joined the ambulance corps of the German army; but illness forced him to abandon this work, and after an insufficient period of convalescence he resumed his professional duties at Basel.

Nietzsche's great consolation at Basel lay in his visits to Richard Wagner's villa on the lake of Lucerne. He had already been seized with admiration for Wagner's music while he was still a student at Leipzig, and his friendship with the composer had a possibly unfortunate effect on his writing. In *The Birth of Tragedy from the Spirit of Music* (*Die Geburt der Tragödie aus dem Geiste der Musik*) which appeared in 1872, he first drew a contrast between Greek culture before and after Socrates, to the disadvantage of the latter, and then argued that contemporary German culture bore a strong resemblance to Greek culture after Socrates and that it could be saved only if it were permeated with the spirit of Wagner. Not unnaturally, the work met with an enthusiastic reception from Wagner, but the philologists reacted somewhat differently to Nietzsche's views about the origins of Greek tragedy. Wilamowitz-Moellendorff in particular, then a young man, launched a devastating attack against the book. And not even Rohde's loyal defence of his friend could save Nietzsche from losing credit in the world of classical scholarship. Not that this matters much to us today. For it is Nietzsche as philosopher, moralist and psychologist who interests us, not as professor of philology at Basel.

In the period 1873–6 Nietzsche published four essays with the common title *Untimely Meditations* or *Considerations* (*Unzeitgemässe Betrachtungen*) which is rendered as *Thoughts out of Season* in the English translation of his works. In the first he vehemently attacked the unfortunate David Strauss as a representative of German culture-philistinism, while in the second he attacked the idolization of historical learning as a substitute for a living culture. The third essay was devoted to extolling Schopenhauer as an educator, to the disadvantage of the university professors of philosophy, while the fourth depicted Wagner as originating a rebirth of the Greek genius.

By 1876, the date of publication of the fourth essay, entitled *Richard Wagner in Bayreuth*, Nietzsche and Wagner had already begun to drift apart.[2] And his break with the composer represented the end of the first phase or period in Nietzsche's development. If in the first period he decries Socrates, the rationalist, in the second he tends to exalt him. In the first period culture, and indeed human life in general, is depicted as finding its justification in the production of the genius, the creative artist, poet and musician: in the second Nietzsche prefers science to poetry, questions all accepted beliefs and pretty well plays the part of a rationalistic philosopher of the French Enlightenment.

Characteristic of this second period is *Human, All-too-Human* (*Menschliches, Allzumenschliches*) which was originally published in three parts, 1878–9. In a sense the work is positivistic in outlook. Nietzsche attacks metaphysics in an indirect manner, trying to show that the features of human experience and knowledge which had been supposed to necessitate metaphysical explanations or to justify a metaphysical superstructure are capable of explanation on materialistic lines. For instance, the moral distinction between good and bad had its origin in the experience of some actions as beneficial to society and of others as detrimental to it, though in the course of time the utilitarian origin of the distinction was lost sight of. Again, conscience originates in a belief in authority: it is the voice not of God but of parents and educators.

A combination of bad health and dissatisfaction, amounting to disgust, with his professional duties led Nietzsche to resign from his chair at Basel in the spring of 1879. And for the next ten years he led a wandering life, seeking health in various places in Switzerland and Italy, with occasional visits to Germany.

In 1881 Nietzsche published *The Dawn of Day* (*Morgenröte*) in which, as he declared, he opened his campaign against the morality of self-renunciation. And this was followed in 1882[3] by *Joyful Wisdom* (*Die fröhliche Wissenschaft*) in which we find the idea of Christianity as hostile to life. The report that God is dead, as Nietzsche puts it, opens up vast horizons to free spirits. Neither book was successful. Nietzsche sent a copy of *The Dawn of Day* to Rohde, but his former friend did not even acknowledge it. And the indifference with which his writings were met in Germany was not calculated to increase Nietzsche's fondness for his fellow countrymen.

In 1881 the idea of the eternal recurrence came to Nietzsche while he was at Sils-Maria in the Engadine. In infinite time there are periodic cycles in which all that has been is repeated over again. This somewhat depressing idea was scarcely new, but it came to Nietzsche with the force of an inspiration. And he conceived the plan of presenting the ideas which were fermenting in his mind through the lips of the Persian sage Zarathustra. The result was his most famous work, *Thus Spake Zarathustra* (*Also sprach Zarathustra*). The first two parts were published separately in 1883. The third, in which the doctrine of the eternal recurrence was proclaimed, appeared at the beginning of 1884, and the fourth part was published early in 1885.

Zarathustra, with its ideas of Superman and the transvaluation of values, expresses the third phase of Nietzsche's thought. But its poetic and prophetical style gives it the appearance of being the work of a visionary.[4] Calmer expositions of Nietzsche's ideas are to be found in *Beyond Good and Evil* (*Jenseits von Gut und Böse*, 1886) and *A Genealogy of Morals* (*Zur Genealogie der Moral*, 1887), which, together with *Zarathustra*, are probably Nietzsche's most important writings. *Beyond Good and Evil* elicited an appreciative letter from Hippolyte Taine, and after the publication of *A Genealogy of Morals*, Nietzsche received a similar letter from Georg Brandes, the Danish critic, who later delivered a course of lectures on Nietzsche's ideas at Copenhagen.

Beyond Good and Evil had as its subtitle *Prelude to a Philosophy of the Future*. Nietzsche planned a systematic exposition of his philosophy, for which he made copious notes. His idea of the appropriate title underwent several changes. At first it was to be *The Will to Power, a New Interpretation of Nature* or *The Will to Power, an Essay towards a New Interpretation of the Universe*. In other words, just as Schopenhauer had based a philosophy on the concept of the will to life, so would Nietzsche base a philosophy on the idea of the will to power. Later the emphasis changed, and the proposed title was *The Will to Power, an Essay towards the Transvaluation of all Values* (*Der Wille zur Macht: Versuch einer Umwerthung aller Werthe*). But in point of fact the projected *magnum opus* was never completed, though *The Antichrist* (*Der Antichrist*) was meant to be the first part of it. Nietzsche's notes for the work which he planned have been published posthumously.

Nietzsche turned aside from his projected work to write a ferocious attack on Wagner, *The Case of Wagner* (*Der Fall Wagner*, 1888), and followed it up with *Nietzsche contra Wagner*. This second essay was published only after Nietzsche's breakdown, as were also other writings of 1888, *The Twilight of the Idols* (*Die Götzendämmerung*), *The Antichrist* and *Ecce Homo*, a kind of autobiography. The works of this year show evident signs of extreme tension and mental instability, and *Ecce Homo* in particular, with its exalted spirit of self-assertion, gives a marked impression of psychical disturbance. At the end of the year definite signs of madness began to show themselves, and in January 1889 Nietzsche was taken from Turin, where he then was, to a clinic at Basel. He never really recovered, but after treatment at Basel and then at Jena he was able to go to his mother's home at Naumburg.[5] After her death he lived with his sister at Weimar. By that time he had become a famous man, though he was hardly in a position to appreciate the fact. He died on August 25th, 1900.

2. In the foregoing section reference has been made to periods or phases in the development of Nietzsche's thought. The philosopher himself, as he looked back, described these phases as so many masks. For example, he asserted that the attitude of a free spirit, that is, of a critical, rationalistic and sceptical observer of life, which he adopted in his second period, was an 'eccentric pose', a second nature, as it were, which was assumed as a means whereby he might win through to his first or true nature. It had to be discarded as the snake sloughs its old skin. Further, Nietzsche was accustomed to speak of particular doctrines or theories as though they were artifices of self-preservation or self-administered tonics. For instance, the theory of the eternal recurrence was a test of strength, of Nietzsche's power to say 'yes' to life instead of the Schopenhauerian 'no'. Could he face the thought that his whole life, every moment of it, every suffering, every agony, every humiliation, would be repeated countless times throughout endless time? Could he face this thought and embrace it not only with stoical resignation but also with joy? If so, it was a sign of inner strength, of the triumph in Nietzsche himself of the yea-saying attitude of life.

Obviously, Nietzsche did not say to himself one fine day: 'I shall now pose for a time as a positivist and a coolly critical and scientific observer, because I think that it would be good for my mental health.' It is rather that he seriously attempted to play such a part until, having grown out of it, he recognized it in retrospect as a self-administered tonic and as a mask under which the real direction of his thought could develop unseen. But what was the real direction of his thought? In view of what Nietzsche says about winning through to his true nature, one is inclined, of course, to assume that the doctrine of his later works and of the posthumously-published notes for *The Will to Power* represents his real thought. Yet if we press the theory of masks, we must apply it also, I think, to his third period. As already mentioned, he spoke of the theory of the eternal recurrence as a trial of strength; and this theory belongs to his third period. Further, it was in the third period that Nietzsche explicitly stated his relativistic and pragmatist view of truth. His general theory of truth was indeed social rather than personal, in the sense that those theories were said to be true which are biologically useful for a given species or for a certain kind of man. Thus the theory of Superman would be a myth which possessed truth in so far as it enabled the higher type of man to develop his potentialities. But if we press the idea of masks, we must take such a statement as 'the criterion of truth lies in the intensification of the feeling of power'[6] in a personal sense and apply it to the thought of Nietzsche's third period no less than to that of the first and second periods.

In this case, of course, there remains no 'real thought' of Nietzsche which is statable in terms of definite philosophical theories. For the whole of his expressed thought becomes an instrument whereby Nietzsche as an existing individual, to use Kierkegaard's phrase, seeks to realize his own possibilities. His ideas represent a medium through which we have to try to discern the significance of an existence. We then have the sort of interpretation of Nietzsche's life and work of which Karl Jaspers has given us a fine example.[7]

The present writer has no intention of questioning the value of the existential interpretation of Nietzsche's life and thought. But in a book such as this the reader has a right to expect a summary account of what Nietzsche said, of his public face or appearance, so to speak. After all, when a philosopher commits ideas to paper and publishes them, they take on, as it were, a life of their own and exercise a greater or lesser influence, as the case may be. It is true that his philosophy lacks the impressiveness of systems such as those of Spinoza and Hegel, a fact of which Nietzsche was well aware. And if one wishes to find in it German 'profundity', one has to look beneath the surface. But though Nietzsche himself drew attention to the personal aspects of his thinking and to the need for probing beneath the surface, the fact remains that he held certain convictions very strongly and that he came to think of himself as a prophet, as a reforming force, and of his ideas as 'dynamite'. Even if on his own view of truth his theories necessarily assume the character of myth, these myths were intimately associated with value-judgments which Nietzsche asserted with passion. And it is perhaps these value-judgments more than anything else which have been the source of his great influence.

3. We have already referred to Nietzsche's discovery, when he was a student at Leipzig, of Schopenhauer's *World as Will and Idea*. But though Nietzsche received a powerful stimulus from the great pessimist, he was at no time a disciple of Schopenhauer. In *The Birth of Tragedy*, for example, he does indeed follow Schopenhauer to the extent of postulating what he calls a 'Primordial Unity' which manifests itself in the world and in human life. And, like Schopenhauer, he depicts life as terrible and tragic and speaks of its transmutation through art, the work of the creative genius. At the same time even in his early works, when the inspiration derived from Schopenhauer's philosophy is evident, the general direction of Nietzsche's thought is towards the affirmation of life rather than towards its negation. And when in 1888 he looked back on *The Birth of Tragedy* and asserted that it expressed an attitude to life which was the antithesis of Schopenhauer's, the assertion was not without foundation.

The Greeks, according to Nietzsche in *The Birth of Tragedy*, knew very well that life is terrible, inexplicable, dangerous. But though they were alive to the real character of the world and of human life, they did not surrender to pessimism by turning their backs on life. What they did was to transmute the world and human life through the medium of art. And they were then able to say 'yes' to the world as an aesthetic phenomenon. There were, however, two ways of doing this, corresponding respectively to the Dionysian and Apollonian attitudes or mentalities.

Dionysus is for Nietzsche the symbol of the stream of life itself, breaking down all barriers and ignoring all restraints. In the Dionysian or Bacchic rites we can see the intoxicated votaries becoming, as it were, one with life. The barriers set up by the principle of individuation tend to break down; the veil of Maya is turned aside; and men and women are plunged into the stream of life, manifesting the Primordial Unity. Apollo, however, is the symbol of light, of measure, of restraint. He represents the principle of individuation. And the

Apollonian attitude is expressed in the shining dream-world of the Olympic deities.

But we can, of course, get away from metaphysical theories about the Primordial Unity and Schopenhauer's talk about the principle of individuation, and express the matter in a psychological form. Beneath the moderation so often ascribed to the Greeks, beneath their devotion to art and beauty and form, Nietzsche sees the dark, turgid and formless torrent of instinct and impulse and passion which tends to sweep away everything in its path.

Now, if we assume that life is in itself an object of horror and terror and that pessimism, in the sense of the no-saying attitude to life, can be avoided only by the aesthetic transmutation of reality, there are two ways of doing this. One is to draw an aesthetic veil over reality, creating an ideal world of form and beauty. This is the Apollonian way. And it found expression in the Olympic mythology, in the epic and in the plastic arts. The other possibility is that of triumphantly affirming and embracing existence in all its darkness and horror. This is the Dionysian attitude, and its typical art forms are tragedy and music. Tragedy does indeed transmute existence into an aesthetic phenomenon, but it does not draw a veil over existence as it is. Rather does it exhibit existence in aesthetic form and affirm it.

In *The Birth of Tragedy*, as its title indicates, Nietzsche is concerned immediately with the origins and development of Greek tragedy. But we cannot discuss the matter here. Nor does it matter for our present purposes how far Nietzsche's account of the origins of tragedy is acceptable from the point of view of classical scholarship. The important point is that the supreme achievement of Greek culture, before it was spoiled by the spirit of Socratic nationalism, lay for Nietzsche in a fusion of Dionysian and Apollonian elements.[8] And in this fusion he saw the foundation for a cultural standard. True culture is a unity of the forces of life, the Dionysian element, with the love of form and beauty which is characteristic of the Apollonian attitude.

If existence is justified as an aesthetic phenomenon, the fine flower of humanity will be constituted by those who transmute existence into such a phenomenon and enable men to see existence in this way and affirm it. In other words, the creative genius will be the highest cultural product. Indeed, in the period which we are considering Nietzsche speaks as though the production of genius were the aim and end of culture, its justification. He makes this quite clear in, for instance, his essay on *The Greek State* (*Der griechische Staat*, 1871). Here and elsewhere he insists that the toil and labour of the majority in the struggle of life are justified by forming the substructure on which the genius, whether in art, music or philosophy, can arise. For the genius is the organ whereby existence is, as it were, redeemed.

On the basis of these ideas Nietzsche proceeds to give a highly critical evaluation of contemporary German culture. He contrasts, for example, historical knowledge about past cultures with culture itself, described as 'unity of artistic style in all the expressions of the life of a people'.[9] But his critique of the German culture of his time need not detain us here. Instead we can note two or three general ideas which also look forward to Nietzsche's later thought.

Nietzsche varies the question whether life should dominate knowledge or knowledge life. 'Which of the two is the higher and decisive power? Nobody will doubt that life is the higher and dominating power. . . .'[10] This means that the nineteenth-century culture, characterized by the domination of knowledge and science, is exposed to the revenge, as it were, of the vital forces, the explosion of which will produce a new barbarism. Beneath the surface of modern life Nietzsche sees vital forces which are 'wild, primitive and completely merciless. One looks at them with a fearful expectancy as though at the cauldron in a witch's kitchen . . . for a century we have been ready for world-shaking convulsions.'[11] In nineteenth-century society we can see both a complacency in the condition which man has already reached and a widespread tendency, fostered by the national State and manifested in the movements towards democracy and socialism, to promote a uniform mediocrity, hostile to genius. But there is no reason to suppose that the development of man's potentialities has reached its term. And the emergence of the latent destructive forces will pave the way for the rise of higher specimens of humanity in the form of outstanding individuals.

Obviously, this view involves a supra-historical outlook, as

Nietzsche puts it. It involves, that is to say, a rejection of the Hegelian canonization of the actual in the name of a necessary self-manifestation of the *Logos* or Idea, and a vision of values which transcend the historical situation. The human being is plastic; he is capable of transcending himself, of realizing fresh possibilities; and he needs a vision, a goal, a sense of direction. Empirical science cannot provide this vision. And though Nietzsche does not say much about Christianity in his early writings, it is clear that he does not look to the Christian religion as the source of the requisite vision.[12] There remains philosophy, not indeed as represented by learned university professors, but in the guise of the lonely thinker who has a clear vision of the possibilities of man's self-transcendence and who is not afraid to be 'dangerous'. Once it has been decided how far things are alterable, philosophy should set itself 'with ruthless courage to the task of *improving that aspect of the world which has been recognized as susceptible to being changed'*.[13] When in later years Nietzsche looks back on these early essays, he sees in this ideal of the philosopher as judge of life and creator of values Zarathustra or himself. It comes to the same thing.

4. A criticism of the ethical attitude in so far as this involves the assertion of a universal moral law and of absolute moral values is implicit in Nietzsche's early writings. We have seen that according to his own statement only aesthetic values were recognized in *The Birth of Tragedy*. And in his essay on David Strauss Nietzsche refers to Strauss's contention that the sum and substance of morality consists in looking on all other human beings as having the same needs, claims and rights as oneself and then asks where this imperative comes from. Strauss seems to take it for granted that the imperative has its basis in the Darwinian theory of evolution. But evolution provides no such basis. The class *Man* comprises a multitude of different types, and it is absurd to claim that we are required to behave as though individual differences and distinctions were non-existent or unimportant. And we have seen that Nietzsche lays stress on outstanding individuals rather than on the race or species.

However, it is in *Human, All-too-Human* that Nietzsche begins to treat of morality in some detail. The work is indeed composed of aphorisms; it is not a systematic treatise. But if we compare the remarks relating to morality, a more or less coherent theory emerges.

It is the first sign that the animal has become man when its notions are no longer directed simply to the satisfaction of the moment but to what is recognized as useful in an enduring manner.[14] But we can hardly talk about morality until utility is understood in the sense of usefulness for the existence, survival and welfare of the community. For 'morality is primarily a means of preserving the community in general and warding off destruction from it'.[15] Compulsion has first to be employed to make the individual conform his conduct to the interests of society. But compulsion is succeeded by the force of custom, and in time the authoritative voice of the community takes the form of what we call conscience. Obedience can become a second nature, as it were, and be associated with pleasure. At the same time moral epithets come to be extended from actions to the intentions of the agents. And the concepts of virtue and of the virtuous man arise. In other words, morality is interiorized through a process of progressive refinement.

So far Nietzsche speaks like a utilitarian. And his concept of morality bears some resemblance to what Bergson calls closed morality. But once we look at the historical development of morality we see a 'twofold early history of good and evil'.[16] And it is the development of this idea of two moral outlooks which is really characteristic of Nietzsche. But the idea is best discussed in relation to his later writings.

In *Beyond Good and Evil* Nietzsche says that he has discovered two primary types of morality, 'master-morality and slave-morality'.[17] In all higher civilizations they are mixed, and elements of both can be found even in the same man. But it is important to distinguish them. In the master-morality or aristocratic morality 'good' and 'bad' are equivalent to 'noble' and 'despicable', and the epithets are applied to men rather than to actions. In the slave-morality the standard is that which is useful or beneficial to the society of the weak and powerless. Qualities such as sympathy, kindness and humility are extolled as virtues, and the strong and independent individuals are regarded as dangerous, and therefore as 'evil'. By the standards of the slave-morality the 'good' man of the master-morality tends to be accounted as

'evil'. Slave-morality is thus herd-morality. Its moral valua
tions are expressions of the needs of a herd.

This point of view is expounded more systematically in *The*
Genealogy of Morals where Nietzsche makes use of the con
cept of resentment. The higher type of man creates his own
values out of the abundance of his life and strength. The
meek and powerless, however, fear the strong and powerful
and they attempt to curb and tame them by asserting as
absolute the values of the herd. 'The revolt of the slaves in
morals begins with resentment becoming creative and giving
birth to values.'[18] This resentment is not, of course, openly
acknowledged by the herd, and it can work by devious and
indirect paths. But the psychologist of the moral life can de
tect and bring to light its presence and complex modes of
operation.

What we see, therefore, in the history of morals is the con
flict of two moral attitudes or outlooks. From the point of
view of the higher man there can in a sense be coexistence.
That is to say, there could be coexistence if the herd, in
capable of anything higher, was content to keep its values to
itself. But, of course, it is not content to do this. It endeav
ours to impose its own values universally. And according to
Nietzsche it succeeded in doing this, at least in the West, in
Christianity. He does not indeed deny all value to Christian
morality. He admits, for instance, that it has contributed to
the refinement of man. At the same time he sees in it an ex
pression of the resentment which is characteristic of the herd-
instinct or slave-morality. And the same resentment is at
tributed to the democratic and socialist movements which
Nietzsche interprets as derivatives of Christianity.

Nietzsche maintains, therefore, that the concept of a uni
form, universal and absolute moral system is to be rejected.
For it is the fruit of resentment and represents inferior life,
descending life, degeneracy, whereas the aristocratic morality
represents the movement of ascending life.[19] And in place
of the concept of one universal and absolute moral system
(or indeed of different sets of values, relative to different so
cieties, if each set is regarded as binding all the members of
the society) we must put the concept of a gradation of rank
among different types of morality. The herd is welcome to its

own set of values, provided that it is deprived of the power of imposing them on the higher type of man who is called upon to create his own values which will enable man to transcend his present condition.

When, therefore, Nietzsche speaks of standing beyond good and evil, what he has in mind is rising above the so-called herd-morality which in his opinion reduces everyone to a common level, favours mediocrity and prevents the development of a higher type of man. He does not mean to imply that all respect for values should be abandoned and all self-restraint thrown overboard. The man who rejects the binding force of what is customarily called morality may be himself so weak and degenerate that he destroys himself morally. It is only the higher type of man who can safely go beyond good and evil in the sense which these terms bear in the morality of resentment. And he does so in order to create values which will be at once an expression of ascending life and a means of enabling man to transcend himself in the direction of Superman, a higher level of human existence.

When it comes to describing the content of the new values, Nietzsche does not indeed afford us very much light. Some of the virtues on which he insists look suspiciously like old virtues, though he maintains that they are 'transvalued', that is, made different by reason of the different motives, attitudes and valuations which they express. However, one can say in general that what Nietzsche looks for is the highest possible integration of all aspects of human nature. He accuses Christianity of depreciating the body, impulse, instinct, passion, the free and untrammelled exercise of the mind, aesthetic values, and so on. But he obviously does not call for the disintegration of the human personality into a bundle of warring impulses and unbridled passions. It is a question of integration as an expression of strength, not of extirpation or mortification out of a motive of fear which is based on a consciousness of weakness. Needless to say, Nietzsche gives a very one-sided account of the Christian doctrine of man and of values. But it is essential for him to insist on this one-sided view. Otherwise he would find it difficult to assert that he had anything new to offer, unless it were the type of ideal for man which some of the Nazis liked to attribute to him.

5. In *Joyful Wisdom* Nietzsche remarks that 'the greatest event of recent times—that "God is dead", that belief in the Christian God has become unworthy of belief—already begins to cast its first shadows over Europe. . . . At last the horizon lies free before us, even granted that it is not bright; at least the sea, *our* sea, lies open before us. Perhaps there has never been so open a sea.'[20] In other words, decay of belief in God opens the way for man's creative energies to develop fully; the Christian God, with his commands and prohibitions, no longer stands in the path; and man's eyes are no longer turned towards an unreal supernatural realm, towards the other world rather than towards this world.

This point of view obviously implies that the concept of God is hostile to life. And this is precisely Nietzsche's contention, which he expresses with increasing vehemence as time goes on. 'The concept God', he says in *The Twilight of the Idols*, 'was up to now the greatest *objection* against existence.'[21] And in *The Antichrist* we read that 'with God war is declared on life, Nature and the will to live! God is the formula for every calumny against this world and for every lie concerning a beyond!'[22] But it is unnecessary to multiply quotations. Nietzsche is willing to admit that religion in some of its phases has expressed the will to life, or rather to power; but his general attitude is that belief in God, especially in the God of the Christian religion, is hostile to life, and that when it expresses the will to power, the will in question is that of the lower types of man.

Given this attitude, it is understandable that Nietzsche tends to make the choice between theism, especially Christian theism, and atheism a matter of taste or instinct. He recognizes that there have been great men who were believers, but he maintains that nowadays at least, when the existence of God is no longer taken for granted, strength, intellectual freedom, independence and concern for the future of man demand atheism. Belief is a sign of weakness, cowardice, decadence, a no-saying attitude to life. True, Nietzsche attempts a sketch of the origins of the idea of God. And he cheerfully commits the genetic fallacy, maintaining that when it has been shown how the idea of God could have originated, any disproof of God's existence becomes superfluous. He also occasionally alludes to theoretical objections against belief in God. But, generally speaking, the illusory character of this belief is assumed. And the decisive motive for its rejection is that man (or Nietzsche himself) may take the place of God as legislator and creator of values. Considered as a purely theoretical attack, Nietzsche's condemnation of theism in general and of Christianity in particular is worth very little. But it is not an aspect of the matter to which he attaches much importance. As far as theology is concerned, there is no need to bother about such fables. Nietzsche's hatred of Christianity proceeds principally from his view of its supposed effect on man, whom it renders weak, submissive, resigned, humble or tortured in conscience and unable to develop himself freely. It either prevents the growth of superior individuals or ruins them, as in the case of Pascal.[23]

It is indeed noticeable that in his attack on Christianity Nietzsche often speaks of the seductiveness and fascination of Christian beliefs and ideals. And it is clear that he himself felt the attraction and that he rejected it partly in order to prove to himself that 'apart from the fact that I am a *decadent*, I am also the opposite of such a being'.[24] His rejection of God proved to himself his inner strength, his ability to live without God. But from the purely philosophical point of view the conclusions which he draws from atheism are more important than the psychological factors bearing on his rejection of the Christian God.

Some people have imagined, Nietzsche maintains, that there is no necessary connection between belief in the Christian God and acceptance of Christian moral standards and values. That is to say, they have thought that the latter can be maintained more or less intact when the former has been discarded. We have thus witnessed the growth of secularized forms of Christianity, such as democracy and socialism, which have tried to maintain a considerable part of the Christian moral system without its theological foundations. But such attempts are, in Nietzsche's opinion, vain. The 'death of God' will inevitably be followed, sooner or later, by the rejection of absolute values and of the idea of an objective and universal moral law.

The European man, however, has been brought up to recognize certain moral values which have been associated with Christian belief and, Nietzsche maintains, in a certain sense depend on it. If, therefore, European man loses his faith in these values, he loses his faith in all values. For he knows only 'morality', the morality which was canonized, as it were, by Christianity and given a theological foundation. And disbelief in all values, issuing in the sense of the purposelessness of the world of becoming, is one of the main elements in nihilism. 'Morality was the greatest *antidote (Gegenmittel)* against practical and theoretical *nihilism*.'[25] For it ascribed an absolute value to man and 'prevented man from despising himself as man, from turning against life and from despairing of the possibility of knowledge; it was a *means of preservation*'.[26] True, the man who was preserved in this way by the Christian morality was the lower type of man. But the point is that the Christian morality succeeded in imposing itself generally, whether directly or in the form of its derivatives. Hence the breakdown of belief in the Christian moral values exposes man to the danger of nihilism, not because there are no other possible values, but because most men, in the West at least, know no others.

Nihilism can take more than one form. There is, for instance, passive nihilism, a pessimistic acquiescence in the absence of values and in the purposelessness of existence. But there is also active nihilism which seeks to destroy that in which it no longer believes. And Nietzsche prophesies the advent of an active nihilism, showing itself in world-shaking ideological wars. 'There will be wars such as there have never been on earth before. Only from my time on will there be on earth *politics on the grand scale*.'[27]

The advent of nihilism is in Nietzsche's opinion inevitable. And it will mean the final overthrow of the decadent Christian civilization of Europe. At the same time it will clear the way for a new dawn, for the transvaluation of values, for the emergence of a higher type of man. For this reason 'this most gruesome of all guests',[28] who stands at the door, is to be welcomed.

Chapter Twenty-two

NIETZSCHE (2)

The hypothesis of the Will to Power – The Will to Power as manifested in knowledge; Nietzsche's view of truth – The Will to Power in Nature and man – Superman and the order of rank – The theory of the eternal recurrence – Comments on Nietzsche's philosophy.

1. 'This world', Nietzsche asserts, 'is the Will to Power—and nothing else! And you yourselves too are this Will to Power— and nothing else!'[1] These words are an adaptation of Schopenhauer's statements at the close of his *magnum opus*; and the way in which Nietzsche is accustomed to speak of 'the Will to Power' naturally gives the impression that he has transformed Schopenhauer's Will to Existence or Will to Live into the Will to Power. But though the impression is, of course, correct in a sense, we must not understand Nietzsche as meaning that the world is an appearance of a metaphysical unity which transcends the world. For he is never tired of attacking the distinction between this world, identified with merely phenomenal reality, and a transcendent reality which is 'really real'. The world is not an illusion. Nor does the Will to Power exist in a state of transcendence. The world, the universe, is a unity, a process of becoming; and it is the Will to Power in the sense that this Will is its intelligible character. Everywhere, in everything, we can see the Will to Power expressing itself. And though one can perhaps say that for Nietzsche the Will to Power is the inner reality of the universe, it exists only in its manifestations. Nietzsche's theory of the Will to Power is thus an interpretation of the universe, a way of looking at it and describing it, rather than a metaphysical doctrine about a reality which lies *behind* the visible world and transcends it.

Nietzsche had, of course, Schopenhauer at the back of his mind. But he did not jump straight from his reading of *The*

World as Will and Idea to a general theory of the universe.
Rather did he discern manifestations of the Will to Power in
human psychical processes and then extend this idea to organic life in general. In *Beyond Good and Evil* he remarks
that logical method compels us to inquire whether we can
find one principle of explanation, one fundamental form of
causal activity, through which we can unify vital phenomena.
And he finds this principle in the Will to Power. 'A living
thing seeks above all to *discharge* its force—life itself is Will
to Power: self-preservation is only one of the indirect and
most common *consequences* thereof.'[2] Nietzsche then proceeds to extend this principle of explanation to the world as
a whole. 'Granted that we succeed in explaining our whole
instinctive life as the development and ramification of *one*
fundamental form of will—namely the Will to Power, as *my*
thesis says; granted that one could refer all organic functions
to this Will to Power, . . . one would have thereby acquired
the right to define unequivocally *all* active force as *Will to
Power*. The world as seen from within, the world as defined
and characterized according to its "intelligible character",
would be precisely "Will to Power" and nothing else.'[3]

Thus Nietzsche's theory of the Will to Power is not so
much an *a priori* metaphysical thesis as a sweeping empirical
hypothesis. If, he says, we believe in the causality of the will,
a belief which is really belief in causality itself, 'we *must*
make the attempt to posit hypothetically the causality of the
will as the only form of causality'.[4] In Nietzsche's intention
at least the theory was an explanatory hypothesis, and in his
projected *magnum opus* he planned to apply it to different
classes of phenomena, showing how they could be unified in
terms of this hypothesis. The notes which he made for this
work indicate the lines of his thought, and in the next two
sections I propose to give some examples of his reflections.

2. 'Knowledge', Nietzsche insists, 'works as an instrument
of power. It is therefore obvious that it grows with every increase of power. . . .'[5] The desire of knowledge, the will to
know, depends on the will to power, that is, on a given kind
of being's impulse to master a certain field of reality and to
enlist it in its service. The aim of knowledge is not to know,
in the sense of grasping absolute truth for its own sake, but to

master. We desire to schematize, to impose order and form on the multiplicity of impressions and sensations to the extent required by our practical needs. Reality is Becoming: it is we who turn it into Being, imposing stable patterns on the flux of Becoming. And this activity is an expression of the Will to Power. Science can thus be defined or described as the 'transformation of Nature into concepts for the purpose of governing Nature'.[6]

Knowledge is, of course, a process of interpretation. But this process is grounded on vital needs and expresses the will to master the otherwise unintelligible flux of Becoming. And it is a question of reading an interpretation into reality rather than of reading it, so to speak, off or in reality. For instance, the concept of the ego or self as a permanent substance is an interpretation imposed upon the flux of Becoming: it is our creation for practical purposes. To be sure, the idea that 'we' interpret psychical states as similar and attribute them to a permanent subject involves Nietzsche in obvious and, in the opinion of the present writer, insoluble difficulties. His general contention is, however, that we cannot legitimately argue from the utility of an interpretation to its objectivity. For a useful fiction, an interpretation which was devoid of objectivity in the sense in which believers in absolute truth would understand objectivity, might be required and thereby justified by our needs.

But there is, according to Nietzsche, no absolute truth. The concept of absolute truth is an invention of philosophers who are dissatisfied with the world of Becoming and seek an abiding world of Being. '*Truth is that sort of error* without which a particular type of living being could not live. The value for *life* is ultimately decisive.'[7]

Some 'fictions', of course, prove to be so useful, and indeed practically necessary, to the human race that they tend to become unquestioned assumptions; for example, 'that there are enduring things, that there are equal things, that there are things, substances, bodies. . . .'[8] It was necessary for life that the concept of a thing or of substance should be imposed on the constant flux of phenomena. 'The beings which did not see correctly had an advantage over those who saw everything "in flux".'[9] Similarly, the law of causality has become so assimilated by human belief that 'not to believe in it would mean the ruin of our species'.[10] And the same can be said of the laws of logic.

The fictions which have shown themselves to be less useful than other fictions, or even positively harmful, are reputed as 'errors'. But those which have proved their utility to the species and have attained the rank of unquestioned 'truths' become embedded, as it were, in language. And here lies a danger. For we may be misled by language and imagine that our way of speaking about the world necessarily mirrors reality. 'We are still being constantly led astray by words and concepts into thinking things are simpler than they are, as separate from one another, indivisible and existing each on its own. A philosophical mythology lies hidden in *language*, and it breaks out again at every moment, however careful one may be.'[11]

All 'truths' are 'fictions'; all such fictions are interpretations; and all interpretations are perspectives. Even every instinct has its perspective, its point of view, which it endeavours to impose on other instincts. And the categories of reason are also logical fictions and perspectives, not necessary truths, nor *a priori* forms. But the perspectival view of truth admits, of course, of differences. Some perspectives, as we have seen, have proved to be practically necessary for the welfare of the race. But there are others which are by no means necessary. And here the influence of valuations becomes especially evident. For example, the philosopher who interprets the world as the appearance of an Absolute which transcends change and is alone 'really real' expounds a perspective based on a negative evaluation of the world of becoming. And this in turn shows what sort of a man he is.

The obvious comment on Nietzsche's general view of truth is that it presupposes the possibility of occupying an absolute standpoint from which the relativity of all truth or its fictional character can be asserted, and that this presupposition is at variance with the relativist interpretation of truth. Further, this comment by no means loses its point if Nietzsche is willing to say that his own view of the world, and even of truth, is perspectival and 'fictional'.[12] A few moments' reflection is sufficient to show this. Still, it is interesting to find Nietzsche anticipating John Dewey in applying a pragmatist or instrumentalist view of truth to such strong-holds of the absolute truth theory as logic. For him, even the fundamental principles of logic are simply expressions of the Will to Power, instruments to enable man to dominate the flux of Becoming.

3. If Nietzsche is prepared to apply his view of truth to alleged eternal truths, he must obviously apply it *a fortiori* to scientific hypotheses. The atomic theory, for example, is fictional in character; that is to say, it is a schema imposed on phenomena by the scientist with a view to mastery.[13] We cannot indeed help speaking as though there was a distinc-tion between the seat of force or energy and the force itself. But this should not blind us to the fact that the atom, con-sidered as an entity, a seat of force, is a symbol invented by the scientist, a mental projection.

However, if we presuppose the fictional character of the atomic theory, we can go on to say that every atom is a quan-tum of energy or, better, of the Will to Power. It seeks to discharge its energy, to radiate its force or power. And so-called physical laws represent relations of power between two or more forces. We need to unify, and we need mathemati-cal formulas for grasping, classifying, mastering. But this is no proof either that things obey laws in the sense of rules or that there are substantial things which exercise force or power. There are simply 'dynamic quanta in a relation of tension to all other dynamic quanta'.[14]

To turn to the organic world. 'A plurality of forces, united by a common nutritive process, we call *Life*.'[15] And life might be defined as 'a lasting form of processes of assertions of force, in which the various combatants on their side grow unequally'.[16] In other words, the organism is an intricate complexity of systems which strive after an increase in the feeling of power. And being itself an expression of the Will to Power, it looks for obstacles, for something to overcome. For example, appropriation and assimilation are interpreted by Nietzsche as manifestations of the Will to Power. And the same can be said of all organic functions.

When treating of biological evolution Nietzsche attacks Darwinism. He points out, for instance, that during most of the time taken up in the formation of a certain organ or quality, the inchoate organ is of no use to its possessor and cannot aid it in its struggle with external circumstances and foes. 'The influence of "external circumstances" is absurdly *overrated* by Darwin. The essential factor in the vital process is precisely the tremendous power to shape and create forms from within, a power which *uses* and *exploits* the environment.'[17] Again, the assumption that natural selection works in favour of the progress of the species and of its better-constituted and individually stronger specimens is unwarranted. It is precisely the better specimens which perish and the mediocre which survive. For the exceptions, the best specimens, are weak in comparison with the majority. Taken individually, the members of the majority may be inferior, but when grouped together under the influence of fear and the gregarious instincts they are powerful.

Hence if we based our moral values on the facts of evolution, we should have to conclude that 'the mediocre are more valuable than the exceptional specimens, and that the *decadent* are more valuable than the mediocre'.[18] For higher values we have to look to superior individuals who in their isolation are stimulated to set before themselves lofty aims.

In the field of human psychology Nietzsche finds ample opportunity for diagnosing the manifestations of the Will to Power. For example, he dismisses as quite unfounded the psychological theory presupposed by hedonism, namely the theory that pursuit of pleasure and avoidance of pain are the fundamental motives of human conduct. In Nietzsche's view pleasure and pain are concomitant phenomena in the striving after an increase of power. Pleasure can be described as the feeling of increased power, while pain results from a felt hindrance to the Will to Power. At the same time pain often provides a stimulus to this Will. For every triumph presupposes an obstacle, a hindrance, which is overcome. It is thus absurd to look on pain as an unmixed evil. Man is constantly in need of it as a stimulus to fresh effort and, for the matter of that, as a stimulus to obtaining new forms of pleasure as accompanying results of the triumphs to which pain urges him on.

Though we cannot enter in detail into Nietzsche's psychological analyses, it is worth noting the role played in these analyses by the concept of sublimation. For example, in his view self-mortification and asceticism can be sublimated forms of a primitive cruelty which is itself an expression of the Will to Power. And he raises the question, what instincts are sublimated in, say, the aesthetic view of the world? Everywhere Nietzsche sees the operation, often devious and hidden, of the Will to Power.

4. According to Nietzsche, rank is determined by power. 'It is quanta of power, and nothing else, which determine and distinguish rank.'[19] And one might well draw the conclusion that if the mediocre majority possesses greater power than individuals who are not mediocre, it also possesses greater value. But this, of course, is by no means Nietzsche's view. He understands power in the sense of an intrinsic quality of the individual. And he tells us, 'I distinguish between a type which represents ascending life and a type which represents decadence, decomposition, weakness'.[20] And even if the mediocre majority, united together, happens to be powerful, it does not, for Nietzsche, represent ascending life.

Yet the mediocre are necessary. For 'a high culture can exist only on a broad basis, on a strongly and soundly consolidated mediocrity'.[21] In fact, from this point of view Nietzsche welcomes the spread of democracy and socialism. For they help to create the requisite basis of mediocrity. In a famous passage in the first part of *Zarathustra* Nietzsche launches an attack against the national State, 'the coldest of all cold monsters'[22] and the new idol which sets itself up as an object of worship and endeavours to reduce all to a common state of mediocrity. But though he condemns the national State from this point of view, namely as preventing the development of outstanding individuals, he none the less insists that the mediocre masses are a necessary means to an end, the emergence of a higher type of man. It is not the mission of the new higher caste or type to lead the masses as a shepherd leads his flock. Rather is it the mission of the masses to form the foundation on which the new so-called lords of the earth can lead their own life and make possible the emergence of still higher types of man. But before this can happen there will come the new barbarians, as Nietzsche calls them, who will break the actual dominion of the masses and thus render possible the free development of outstanding individuals.

As a spur and goal to the potentially higher man Nietzsche offers the myth of Superman (*der Uebermensch*). 'Not "humanity" but *Superman* is the goal.'[23] 'Man is something which must be surpassed; man is a bridge and not a goal.'[24] But this must not be taken to mean that man will evolve into Superman by an inevitable process. Superman is a myth, a goal for the will. 'Superman is the meaning of the earth. Let your will say: Superman *is to be* the meaning of the earth.'[25] Nietzsche does indeed assert that 'man is a rope stretched between animal and Superman—a rope over an abyss'.[26] But it is not a question of man evolving into Superman by a process of natural selection. For the matter of that, the rope might fall into the abyss. Superman cannot come unless superior individuals have the courage to transvalue all values, to break the old table of values, especially the Christian tables, and create new values out of their superabundant life and power. The new values will give direction and a goal to the higher man, and Superman is, as it were, their personification.

If he were taxed with his failure to give a clear description of Superman, Nietzsche might reply that as Superman does not yet exist he can hardly be expected to supply a clear description. At the same time, if the idea of Superman is to act as a spur, stimulus and goal, it must possess some content. And we can say perhaps that it is the concept of the highest possible development and integration of intellectual power, strength of character and will, independence, passion, taste and physique. Nietzsche alludes in one place to 'the Roman Caesar with Christ's soul'.[27] Superman would be Goethe and Napoleon in one, Nietzsche hints, or the Epicurean god appearing on earth. He would be a highly-cultured man, we may say, skilful in all bodily accomplishments, tolerant out of strength, regarding nothing as forbidden unless it is weakness either under the form of 'virtue' or under that of 'vice', the man who has become fully free and independent and affirms life and the universe. In fine, Superman is all that ailing, lonely, tormented, neglected Herr Professor Dr. Friedrich Nietzsche would like to be.

5. The reader of *Zarathustra* may easily and not unnaturally assume that the idea of Superman, if taken in conjunction with that of the transvaluation of values, is the main idea of the book. And he may be inclined to conclude that Nietzsche hopes at least for a constant development of man's potentialities. But Zarathustra is not only the prophet of Superman but also the teacher of the doctrine of the eternal recurrence. Further, in *Ecce Homo* Nietzsche informs us that the fundamental idea of *Zarathustra* is that of the eternal recurrence as 'the highest formula of the yea-saying (attitude to life) which can ever be attained'.[28] He also tells us that this 'fundamental thought'[29] of the work was first presented in the last aphorism but one of *Joyful Wisdom*. If, therefore, the doctrine of the eternal recurrence is the fundamental thought of *Zarathustra*, it can hardly be dismissed as a strange excrescence in Nietzsche's philosophy.

To be sure, Nietzsche found the idea of the eternal recurrence somewhat dismaying and oppressive. But, as was remarked earlier, he used the idea as a test of his strength, of his ability to say 'yes' to life as it is. Thus in the relevant aphorism of *Joyful Wisdom* he imagines a spirit appearing to him and telling him that his life, even in all its smallest details, will recur again innumerable times; and he raises the question whether he would be prostrated by this thought and curse the speaker or whether he would welcome the message in a spirit of affirmation of life, inasmuch as the eternal recurrence sets the seal of eternity on the world of Becoming. Similarly, in *Beyond Good and Evil* Nietzsche speaks of the world-approving man who wishes to have the play all over again a countless number of times and who cries *encore* not only to the play but also to the players. And he sets this idea against the 'half-Christian, half-German narrowness and simplicity'[30] with which pessimism was presented in Schopenhauer's philosophy. Again, in the third part of *Zarathustra* Nietzsche speaks of feeling disgust at the thought that even the most inferior man will return and that he himself is to 'come again eternally to this self same life, in its greatest and smallest (events)'.[31] And he proceeds to welcome this return. 'Oh, how should I not be ardent for eternity and for the marriage-ring of rings—the ring of the return?'[32] Similarly, in the notes for his *magnum opus* he speaks several times of the theory of the eternal recurrence as a great disciplinary thought, at once oppressive and liberating.

At the same time the theory is presented as an empirical hypothesis, and not merely as a disciplinary thought or test of inner strength. Thus we read that 'the principle of conservation of energy demands the *eternal* recurrence'.[33] If the world can be looked at as a determinate quantum of force or energy and as a determinate number of centres of force, it follows that the world-process will take the form of successive combinations of these centres, the number of these combinations being in principle determinable, that is, finite. And 'in an infinite time every possible combination would have been realized at some point; further, it would be realized an infinite number of times. And as between each combination and its next recurrence all other possible combinations would have to occur, and as each of these combinations conditions the whole sequence of combinations in the same series, a cycle of absolutely identical series would be proved.'[34]

One main reason why Nietzsche lays stress on the theory of the eternal recurrence is that it seems to him to fill a gap in his philosophy. It confers on the flux of Becoming the semblance of Being, and it does so without introducing any Being which transcends the universe. Further, while the theory avoids the introduction of a transcendent Deity, it also avoids pantheism, the surreptitious reintroduction of the concept of God under the name of the universe. According to Nietzsche, if we say that the universe never repeats itself but is constantly creating new forms, this statement betrays a hankering after the idea of God. For the universe itself is assimilated to the concept of a creative Deity. And this assimilation is excluded by the theory of the eternal recurrence. The theory also excludes, of course, the idea of personal immortality in a 'beyond', though at the same time it provides a substitute for this idea, even if the notion of living one's life over again in all its details a countless number of times is unlikely to exercise a more than limited appeal. In other words, the theory of the eternal recurrence expresses Nietzsche's resolute will to this-worldliness, to *Diesseitigkeit*. The universe is shut in, as it were, on itself. Its significance is purely immanent. And the truly strong man, the truly Dionysian man, will affirm this universe with steadfastness, courage and even joy, shunning the escapism which is a manifestation of weakness.

It is sometimes said that the theory of the eternal recurrence and the theory of Superman are incompatible. But it can hardly be claimed, I think, that they are logically incompatible. For the theory of recurrent cycles does not exclude the recurrence of the will to Superman or, for the matter of that, of Superman himself. It is, of course, true that the theory of the eternal recurrence rules out the concept of Superman as the final end of a non-repeatable creative process. But Nietzsche does not admit this concept. On the contrary, he excludes it as being equivalent to a surreptitious reintroduction of a theological manner of interpreting the universe.

6. There have been disciples of Nietzsche who endeavoured to make his thought into a system which they then accepted as a kind of gospel and tried to propagate. But, generally speaking, his influence has taken the form of stimulating thought in this or that direction. And this stimulative influence has been widespread. But it certainly has not been uniform in character. Nietzsche has meant different things to different people. In the field of morals and values, for example, his importance for some people has lain primarily in his development of a naturalistic criticism of morality, while others would emphasize rather his work in the phenomenology of values. Others again, of a less academically philosophical turn of mind, have stressed his idea of the transvaluation of values. In the field of social and cultural philosophy some have portrayed him as attacking democracy and democratic socialism in favour of something like Nazism, while others have represented him as a great European, or as a great cosmopolitan, a man who was above any nationalistic outlook. To some he has been primarily the man who diagnosed the decadence and imminent collapse of western civilization, while others have seen in him and his philosophy the embodiment of the very nihilism for which he professed to supply a remedy. In the field of religion he has appeared to some as a radical atheist, intent on exposing the baneful influence of

religious belief, while others have seen in the very vehemence of his attack on Christianity evidence of his fundamental concern with the problem of God. Some have regarded him first and foremost from the literary point of view, as a man who developed the potentialities of the German language; others, such as Thomas Mann, have been influenced by his distinction between the Dionysian and Apollonian outlooks or attitudes; others again have emphasized his psychological analyses.

Obviously, Nietzsche's method of writing is partly responsible for the possibility of diverse interpretations. Many of his books consist of aphorisms. And we know that in some cases he jotted down thoughts which came to him on his solitary walks and later strung them together to form a book. The results are what might be expected. For instance, reflection on the tameness of bourgeois life and on the heroism and self-sacrifice occasioned by war might produce an aphorism or passage in praise of war and warriors, while on another occasion reflection on the way in which war leads to the waste and destruction of the best elements of a nation, and often for no appreciable gain to anyone except a few selfish individuals, might produce, and indeed did produce, a condemnation of war as stupid and suicidal for both victors and vanquished. It is then possible for the commentator to depict Nietzsche either as a lover of war or as almost a pacifist. A judicious selection of texts is all that is required.

The situation is complicated, of course, by the relation between the philosophizing of Nietzsche and his personal life and struggles. Thus while it is possible to confine one's attention to the written word, it is also possible to develop a psychological interpretation of his thought. And, as already noted, there is the possibility of giving an existentialist interpretation of the significance of the whole complex of his life and thought.

That Nietzsche was in some respects an acute and far-seeing thinker is hardly open to question. Take, for example, his excursions into psychology. It is not necessary to regard all his analyses as acceptable before one is prepared to admit that he divined, as it were, a number of important ideas which have become common coin in modern psychology. We have only to recall his notion of concealed operative ideals and motives or his concept of sublimation. As for his use of the concept of the Will to Power as a key to human psychology, an idea which found its classical expression in the psychological theory of Alfred Adler, we can say indeed that it was exaggerated and that the more widely the concept is applied the more indefinite does its content become.[35] At the same time Nietzsche's experimentation with the use of the concept as a key to man's psychical life helped to focus attention on the operation of a powerful drive, even if it is not the only one. Again, as we look back in the light of the events of the twentieth century on Nietzsche's anticipation of the coming of the 'new barbarism' and of world-wars we can hardly fail to recognize that he had a deeper insight into the situation than those of his contemporaries who showed a complacent optimistic belief in the inevitability of progress.

But though Nietzsche was clear-sighted in some respects, he was myopic in others. For instance, he certainly failed to give sufficient attention to the question whether his distinctions between ascending and descending life and between higher and lower types of men did not tacitly presuppose the very objectivity of values which he rejected. It would be open to him, of course, to make it a matter of taste and aesthetic preference, as he sometimes said that it was. But then a similar question can be raised about aesthetic values, unless perhaps the distinction between higher and lower is to become simply a matter of subjective feeling and no claim is made that one's own feelings should be accepted as a norm by anyone else. Again, as has already been hinted, Nietzsche failed to give the requisite prolonged consideration to the question how the subject can impose an intelligible structure on the flux of Becoming when the subject is itself resolved into the flux and exists as a subject only as part of the structure which it is said to impose.

As for Nietzsche's attitude to Christianity, his increasingly shrill attack on it is accompanied by an increasing inability to do justice to his foe. And it is arguable that the vehemence of his attack was partly an expression of an inner tension and uncertainty which he endeavoured to stifle.[36] As he himself put it, he had the blood of theologians in his veins. But if we abstract from the shrillness and one-sidedness of his attack on Christianity in particular, we can say that this attack forms part of his general campaign against all beliefs and philosophies, such as metaphysical idealism, which ascribe to the world and to human existence and history a meaning or purpose or goal other than the meaning freely imposed by man himself.[37] The rejection of the idea that the world has been created by God for a purpose or that it is the self-manifestation of the absolute Idea or Spirit sets man free to give to life the meaning which he wills to give it. And it has no other meaning.

The idea of God, whether theistically or pantheistically conceived, thus gives way to the concept of man as the being who confers intelligibility on the world and creates values. But are we to say that in the long run it is the world itself which has, so to speak, the last word, and that man, the moral legislator and conferer of meaning, is absorbed as an insignificant speck in the meaningless cycles of history? If so, man's effort to confer meaning and value on his life appear as a defiant 'No', a rejection of the meaningless universe, rather than as a yea-saying attitude.[38] Or are we to say that the interpretation of the world as without a given meaning or goal and as a series of endless cycles is a fiction which expresses man's Will to Power? If so, the question whether the world has or has not a given meaning or goal remains open.

A final remark. Professional philosophers who read Nietzsche may be interested principally in his critique of morality or in his phenomenological analyses or in his psychological theories. But it is probably true to say that the attention of the general reader is usually concentrated on the remedies which he offers for the overcoming of what he calls nihilism, the spiritual crisis of modern man. It is the idea of the transvaluation of values, the concept of the order of rank and the myth of Superman which strike their attention. It is arguable, however, that what is really significant in what one may call the non-academic Nietzsche is not his proposed antidotes to nihilism but rather his existence and thought considered precisely as a dramatic expression of a lived spiritual crisis from which there is no issue in terms of his own philosophy.

Chapter Twenty-three

RETROSPECT AND PROSPECT

Some questions arising out of nineteenth-century German philosophy – The positivist answer – The philosophy of existence – The rise of phenomenology; Brentano, Meinong, Husserl, the widespread use of phenomenological analysis – Return to ontology; N. Hartmann – The metaphysics of Being; Heidegger, the Thomists – Concluding reflections.

1. Kant endeavoured to overcome what he regarded as the scandal of conflicting metaphysical systems and to set philosophy on a secure basis. And at the beginning of the period covered in this volume we find Fichte insisting that philosophy is the fundamental science which grounds all other sciences. But when Fichte declared that philosophy was the fundamental science, he was referring, of course, to the *Wissenschaftslehre*, that is, to his own philosophy. And his system simply forms one member of the series of highly personal, though interesting and often fascinating, interpretations of reality which span the nineteenth century like a series of mountain peaks. Other examples are the speculative theism of Schelling, the absolute idealism of Hegel, Schopenhauer's philosophy of the world as presentation and will, Kierkegaard's vision of human history and Nietzsche's philosophy of the Will to Power. And it would need a bold man to maintain that the series provides empirical confirmation of the validity of Fichte's claim on behalf of the scientific character of philosophy.

It is indeed arguable that the differences between philosophies, even when these differences are very considerable, do not prove that philosophy has no cognitive value. For it may be that each philosophy expresses a truth, an apprehension of a real aspect of reality or of human life and history, and that these truths are mutually complementary. That is to say, the element of conflict does not arise from any incompatibility between the fundamental ideas which lie at the bases of the different systems, but rather from the fact that each philosopher exaggerates one aspect of the world or of human life and history, thus turning a part into the whole. For example, Marx undoubtedly draws attention to real aspects of man and of human history; and there is no fundamental incompatibility between these aspects and, say, the religious aspects of human existence which are emphasized by Schelling. The incompatibility arises when Marx turns one idea which expresses a partial aspect of man and his history into a key-idea to unlock all doors.

One trouble, however, with this way of looking at things is that it involves whittling down philosophical systems to what amounts practically to truisms, and that this process deprives the systems of most of their interest. It can be argued, for example, that Marx's philosophy is of interest precisely because of the element of exaggeration which sets the whole of human history in a certain perspective. If Marxism is whittled down to indubitable truths such as that without man's economic life there could be no philosophy or art or science, it loses a great deal of its interest and all of its provocative character. Similarly, if Nietzsche's philosophy is whittled down to the statement that the will to power or drive to power is one of the influential factors in human life, it becomes compatible with the reduced version of Marxism, but only at the cost of being itself reduced to a fairly obvious proposition.

A possible way of countering this line of argument is to say that the exaggerations in a philosophical system serve a useful purpose. For it is precisely the element of striking and arresting exaggeration which serves to draw attention in a forcible way to the basic truth which is contained in the system. And once we have digested this truth, we can forget about the exaggeration. It is not so much a question of whittling down the system as of using it as a source of insight and then forgetting the instrument by which we attained this insight, unless indeed we need to refer to it again as a means of recovering the insight in question.

But though this is in itself a not unreasonable line of thought, it is of very little use for supporting Fichte's con tention that philosophy is the science of sciences. For suppose that we reduce the philosophies of Schopenhauer, Marx and Nietzsche respectively to such statements as that there is a great deal of evil and suffering in the world, that we have to produce food and consume it before we can develop the sciences, and that the will to power can operate in devious and concealed forms. We then have three propositions of which the first two are for most people obviously true while the third, which is rather more interesting, is a psychological proposition. None of them would normally be called a specifically philosophical proposition. The philosophical propositions of Schopenhauer, Marx and Nietzsche would thus become instruments for drawing attention to propositions of some other type. And this is obviously not at all the sort of thing which Fichte had in mind when he claimed that philosophy was the basic science.

It may be objected that I have been concentrating simply on the outstanding original systems, on the mountain peaks, and neglecting the foothills, the general movements such as Neo-Kantianism. It may be suggested, that is to say, that while it is true that if we are looking for highly personal imaginative interpretations of the universe or of human life we must turn to the famous philosophers, it is also true that in those general movements in which the particular tends to be merged in the universal we can find more plebeian scientific work in philosophy, patient co-operative efforts at tackling separate problems.

But is it true? In Neo-Kantianism, for example, there are, of course, family-likenesses which justify our describing it as a definite movement, distinct from other movements. But once we start to inspect it at close hand we see not only somewhat different general tendencies within the movement as a whole but also a multitude of individual philosophies. Again, in the movement of inductive metaphysics this philosopher uses one idea as a key-idea for interpreting the world while that philosopher uses another. Wundt uses his voluntaristic interpretation of human psychology as a basis for a general philosophy, while Driesch uses his theory of entelechies, derived from reflection on biological processes. True, a sense of proportion and the requirements of mental economy suggest that in many cases individual systems are best forgotten or allowed to sink into the background of a general movement. But this does not alter the fact that the closer we look at the philosophy of the nineteenth century, the more do the massive groupings tend to break up into individual philosophies. Indeed, it is not altogether an exaggeration to say that as the century wears on each professor of philosophy seems to think it necessary to produce his own system.

Obviously, there can be different opinions within the framework of a common conviction about the nature and function of philosophy. Thus the Neo-Kantians were more or less agreed about what philosophy is incompetent to achieve. But though conflicting views about the nature and function of philosophy are not necessarily coextensive with different philosophical views or even systems, there were obviously in nineteenth-century German thought some very different concepts about what philosophy ought to be. For instance, when Fichte said that philosophy ought to be a science, he meant that it should be derived systematically from one fundamental principle. The inductive metaphysicians, however, had a different idea of philosophy. And when we turn to Nietzsche, we find him rejecting the concept of absolute truth and emphasizing the valuational foundations of different kinds of philosophy, the value-judgments themselves depending on the types of men who make them.[1]

Needless to say, the fact that two philosophers differ does not of itself prove that neither is right. And even if they are both wrong, some other philosopher may be right. At the same time the conflicting systems of the nineteenth century, and still more perhaps the conflicting views about the nature and competence of philosophy, show that Kant's attempt to settle once and for all the true nature and function of philosophy was from the historical point of view a failure. And the old questions present themselves to the mind with renewed force. Can philosophy be a science? If so, how? What sort of knowledge can we legitimately expect from it? Has philosophy been superseded by the growth and development of the particular sciences? Or has it still a field of its own? If so, what is it? And what is the appropriate method for investigating this field?

It is not indeed surprising that Kant's judgment about the nature and limits of scientific philosophy should have failed to win universal acceptance. For it was closely related to his own system. In other words, it was a philosophical judgment, just as the pronouncements of Fichte, Hegel, Marx, Nietzsche, Eucken and others were philosophical judgments. In fact, provided that one is not making a statement either about the current conventional use of terms or about the various uses of the word 'philosophy' in history, any pronouncement that one may make about the 'true' nature and function of philosophy is a philosophical statement, one which is made from within philosophy and commits one to or expresses a particular philosophical position.

It is obviously not the intention of the present writer to suggest that no definite philosophical position should be adopted or that it is improper to make philosophical judgments about the nature and function of philosophy. Nor is it his intention to suggest that no good reasons can be adduced in favour of accepting one judgment rather than another. At the same time he does not wish to make an abrupt transition at this moment from the role of historian to the role of one who speaks in the name of a definite philosophical system. He prefers instead to take a brief glance at some of the general lines of answer which have been offered in German thought during the first part of the twentieth century to the type of question mentioned above. This procedure will serve to provide some sort of bridge between past and present.

2. One possible line of answer to questions about the scope of philosophy is to maintain that the particular sciences are the only source of knowledge about the world and that philosophy has no field of its own in the sense that its function is to investigate a special level or type of being. It is indeed perfectly understandable that at one time men sought to acquire knowledge about the world through philosophical speculation. But in the course of their development the various sciences have taken over one part after another of the field of exploration which was once attributed to philosophy. There has thus been a gradual substitution of scientific knowledge for philosophical speculation. And it is no wonder if phi-

losophers who think that they can increase our knowledge of reality by other means than the employment of the scientific method of hypothesis, deduction and verification only succeed in producing conflicting systems which may possess some aesthetic value or emotive significance but which can no longer be seriously considered as possessing cognitive value. If philosophy is to be scientific and not a form of poetry masquerading as science, its function must be purely analytic in character. For example, it may be able to clarify some of the fundamental concepts employed in the sciences and to inquire into scientific methodology, but it cannot go beyond the sciences by adding to or supplementing our scientific knowledge of the world.

This general positivist attitude, the conviction that the empirical sciences are the only reliable source of knowledge about the world, is obviously widespread. In the nineteenth century it attained its classical expression in the philosophy of Auguste Comte, and we have seen that it also found expression, though on a less impressive scale, in the materialist and positivist current of thought in Germany. But we also noted how some of the German philosophers who represented this current of thought went well beyond the particular sciences by developing a general view of reality. Haeckel's monism was a case in point. And it was just this tendency of philosophy to develop into a *Weltanschauung* or world-view which the positivism of the twentieth century was concerned to exclude.

An obvious objection to the reduction of philosophy to the position of a handmaid of science is that there are questions and problems which are not raised by any particular science, which demand answers and which have been traditionally and properly regarded as belonging to the field of philosophical inquiry. The positivist is convinced, of course, that questions about ultimate reality or the Absolute, about the origin of finite existents, and so on have not in fact been answered by the metaphysical philosophers, such as Schelling for instance. But even if one agreed that the questions had not in fact been definitely answered, or even that we were not in a position to answer them, one might still wish to say that the raising and discussion of such questions has a great value.

for it helps to show the limits of scientific knowledge and reminds us of the mysteries of finite existence. Hence an effective exclusion of metaphysical philosophy requires the establishment of two complementary theses. It must be shown that metaphysical problems are unanswerable in principle and not merely in the sense that we are not in a position to answer them here and now. And it must further be shown that problems which are unanswerable in principle are pseudo-problems in the sense that they are not real questions at all but verbal expressions which lack any clear meaning.

This is precisely what the neopositivists of the Vienna Circle and their associates set out to show in the twenties of the present century by developing a criterion of meaning, the so-called principle of verifiability, which would effectively exclude metaphysical problems and statements from the class of meaningful problems and statements. Apart from the purely formal propositions of logic and pure mathematics, meaningful propositions were interpreted as empirical hypotheses, the meaning of which was coincident with the thinkable, though not necessarily practically realizable, mode of verification in sense-experience. And as, for instance, we can conceive no empirical verification in sense-experience of the statement of Parmenides that all things are really one changeless being, this statement could not be accepted as meaningful.[2]

As stated in this form, however, the neopositivist criterion of meaning was unable to stand up to criticism, whether from outside or inside the neopositivist movement, and it either came to be interpreted as a purely methodological principle for the purpose of delimiting the range of what could properly be called scientific hypotheses or was so whittled down and explained away that it became quite ineffective for excluding speculative philosophy.

The fact of the matter is, I think, that neopositivism as a philosophy was an attempt to provide a theoretical justification of positivism as a mentality or attitude. And the neopositivist criterion of meaning was heavily loaded with the implicit philosophical presuppositions of this attitude. Further, its effectiveness as a weapon against metaphysical philosophy depended on these presuppositions not being made explicit. For once they have been made explicit, neopositivism stands revealed as one more questionable philosophy. This obviously does not entail the disappearance of positivism as a mentality or attitude. But the whole episode of the rise and criticism (partly autocriticism) of neopositivism had the great advantage of dragging concealed presuppositions into the light of day. It was a question of the positivist mentality, which had become widespread in the nineteenth century, becoming reflectively conscious of itself and seeing its own presuppositions. True, this self-consciousness was attained within the philosophical field and left untouched great areas of the positivist mentality or attitude. But this simply helps to illustrate the need of philosophy, one of the functions of which is precisely to render explicit and subject to critical examination the concealed implicit presuppositions of non-reflective philosophical attitudes.[3]

3. According to the neopositivists, philosophy can become scientific, but only at the cost of becoming purely analytic and relinquishing any claim to increase our factual knowledge of reality. Another possible way of describing the function and nature of philosophy is to say that it has a field of its own, inasmuch as it is concerned with Being, and at the same time to deny that it is or can be a science, whether a universal science or a special science alongside the particular empirical sciences. In one sense philosophy is what it always has been, namely concerned with Being (das Sein) as distinct from die Seienden. But it was a mistake to suppose that there can be a science of Being. For Being is unobjectifiable; it cannot be turned into an object of scientific investigation. The primary function of philosophy is to awaken man to an awareness of Being as transcending beings and grounding them. But as there can be no science of Being, no metaphysical system can possess universal validity. The different systems are so many personal decipherings of unobjectifiable Being. This does not mean, however, that they are valueless. For any great metaphysical system can serve to push open, as it were, the door which positivism would keep shut. Thus to speak of the scandal of conflicting systems betrays a misconception of the true nature of philosophy. For the objection is valid only if philosophy, to be justified at all, should be a

science. And this is not the case. True, by claiming that philosophy is a science, the metaphysicians of the past have themselves provided the ground for talk about the scandal of different and incompatible systems. But once this claim is relinquished and we understand the true function of metaphysics as being that of awakening man to an awareness of the enveloping Being in which he and all other finite existents are grounded, the ground for scandal disappears. For that there should be different personal decipherings of transcendent Being is only what one ought to expect. The important thing is to see them for what they are and not to take the extravagant claims of their authors at their face value.

This point of view represents one aspect of the philosophy of Professor Karl Jaspers (b. 1883). But he combines acceptance of the Kantian contention that speculative metaphysics cannot provide us with theoretical knowledge with a theory of 'existence' which shows the influence of Kierkegaard. The human being can be objectified and studied scientifically by, say, the physiologist and the psychologist. The individual is then exhibited as classifiable in this or that way. But when looked at from the point of view of the free agent himself, from within the life of free choice, the individual is seen as this unique existent, the being who freely transcends what he already is and creates himself, as it were, through the exercise of his freedom. Indeed, from this point of view man is always in the making, his own making: *Existenz* is always possible existence, *mögliche Existenz*. Of man regarded under this aspect there can be no scientific study. But philosophy can draw attention to or illuminate 'existence' in such a way as to enable the existing individual to understand what is meant in terms of his own experience. It can also draw attention to the movement by which, especially in certain situations, the individual becomes aware both of his finitude and of the enveloping presence of Being as the Transcendent in which he and all other beings are grounded. But as transcendent Being can be neither objectified nor reduced to the conclusion of a demonstration or proof, the man who becomes aware of it as the unobjectifiable complement and ground of finite beings is free either to affirm it with

Kierkegaard, through what Jaspers calls 'philosophical faith', or to reject it with Nietzsche.

We cannot enter into further descriptions of the philosophy of Karl Jaspers,[4] as it has been mentioned less for its own sake than as one of the ways of depicting the nature and functions of philosophy which have been exemplified in German thought during the first half of the twentieth century. It should be noted, however, that Jaspers, like Kant before him, endeavours to place belief in human freedom and in God beyond the reach of scientific criticism. Indeed, we can see an evident recurrence of Kantian themes. For example, Jaspers' distinction between man as seen from the external scientific point of view and man as seen from the internal point of view of 'existence' corresponds in some way to the Kantian distinction between the phenomenal and noumenal levels. At the same time there are also evident differences between Kant and Jaspers. For instance, Kant's emphasis on the moral law, on which practical faith in God is grounded, disappears, and the Kierkegaardian concept of the existing individual comes to the fore. Besides, Jaspers' 'philosophical faith', which is a more academic version of Kierkegaard's leap of faith, is directed towards God as Being, not, as with Kant, to the idea of God as an instrument for synthesizing virtue and happiness.

An obvious objection to Jaspers' way of setting metaphysics beyond the reach of scientific criticism is that in speaking at all about freedom and, still more, about Being he is inevitably objectifying what according to him cannot be objectified. If Being is really unobjectifiable, it cannot be mentioned. We can only remain silent. But one might, of course, employ Wittgenstein's distinction and say that for Jaspers philosophy tries to 'show' what cannot be 'said'. Indeed, Jaspers' emphasis on the 'illuminating' function of philosophy points in precisely this direction.

4. For the neopositivists, philosophy can be scientific, but by the very fact of becoming scientific it is not a science in the sense of having a field peculiar to itself. For Jaspers philosophy has in a sense a field of its own,[5] but it is not a science and moves on a different plane from those of the sciences. The phenomenologists, however, have tried both to

assign to philosophy a field or fields and to vindicate its scientific character.

(i) In a few notes on the rise of phenomenology there is no need to go back beyond Franz Brentano (1838–1917). After studying with Trendelenburg Brentano became a Catholic priest. In 1872 he was appointed to a chair at Würzburg, and in 1874 at Vienna. But in 1873 he had abandoned the Church, and his status as a married ex-priest did not make his life as a university professor in the Austrian capital an easy one. In 1895 he retired from teaching and took up residence at Florence, moving to Switzerland on the outbreak of the First World War.

In 1874 Brentano published a book bearing the title *Psychology from the Empirical Standpoint* (*Psychologie vom empirischen Standpunkt*).⁶ Empirical psychology, he insists, is not a science of the soul, a term which has metaphysical implications, but of psychical phenomena. Further, when Brentano talks about empirical psychology, it is descriptive rather than genetic psychology which he has in mind. And descriptive psychology is for him an inquiry into psychical acts or acts of consciousness as concerned with 'inexistent' objects, that is, with objects as contained within the acts themselves. All consciousness is consciousness *of*. To think is to think of something, and to desire is to desire something. Thus every act of consciousness is 'intentional': it 'intends' an object. And we can consider the object precisely as intended and as inexistent, without raising questions about its extramental nature and status.

This theory of the intentionality of consciousness, which goes back to Aristotelian-Scholastic thought, is not in itself a subjectivist theory. The descriptive psychologist, as Brentano interprets his function, does not say that the objects of consciousness have no existence apart from consciousness. But he considers them only as inexistent, for the good reason that he is concerned with psychical acts or acts of consciousness and not with ontological questions about extramental reality.

Now, it is clear that in considering consciousness one can concentrate either on the inexistent objects of consciousness or on the intentional reference as such. And Brentano tends to concentrate on the second aspect of consciousness, distinguishing three main types of intentional reference. First there is simple presentation, in which there is no question of truth or falsity. Secondly there is judgment which involves recognition (*Anerkennen*) or rejection (*Verwerfen*), in other words affirmation or denial. Thirdly there are the movements of the will and of feelings (*Gemütsbewegungen*), where the fundamental attitudes or structures of consciousness are love and hate or, as Brentano also says, of pleasure and displeasure.

We may add that just as Brentano believed that there are logical judgments which are evidently true, so did he believe that there are moral sentiments which are evidently correct or right. That is to say, there are goods, objects of moral approval or pleasure, which are evidently and always preferable. But from the point of view of the rise of phenomenology the important feature of Brentano's thought is the doctrine of the intentionality of consciousness.

(ii) Brentano's reflections exercised an influence on a number of philosophers who are sometimes grouped together as the Austrian School, such as Anton Marty (1847–1914), a professor at Prague, Oskar Kraus (1872–1942), a pupil of Marty and himself a professor at Prague, and Carl Stumpf (1848–1936), who was a noted psychologist and had Edmund Husserl among his pupils.

Special mention, however, must be made of Alexius Meinong (1853–1920) who studied under Brentano at Vienna and subsequently became professor of philosophy at Graz. In his theory of objects (*Gegenstandstheorie*) Meinong distinguished different types of objects. In ordinary life we generally understand by the term 'objects' particular existing things such as trees, stones, tables, and so on. But if we consider 'objects' as objects of consciousness, we can easily see that there are other types as well. For example, there are ideal objects, such as values and numbers, which can be said to possess reality though they do not exist in the sense in which trees and cows exist. Again, there are imaginary objects such as a golden mountain or the king of France. There is no existing golden mountain and there has been no king of France for many years. But if we can talk about golden mountains, we must be talking about something. For to talk about nothing is not to talk. There is an object present to consciousness, even if there is no corresponding extramentally existent thing.

Bertrand Russell's theory of descriptions was designed to circumvent Meinong's line of argument and to depopulate, as it were, the world of objects which are in some sense real but do not exist. However, this is irrelevant to our present purpose. The main point is that Meinong's theory helped to concentrate attention on objects considered precisely as objects of consciousness, as, to use Brentano's term, inexistent.

(iii) The effective founder of the phenomenological movement was, however, neither Brentano nor Meinong but Edmund Husserl (1859–1938). After having taken his doctorate in mathematics Husserl attended Brentano's lectures at Vienna (1884–6) and it was Brentano's influence which led him to devote himself to philosophy. He became professor of philosophy at Göttingen and subsequently at Freiburg-im-Breisgau where Martin Heidegger was one of his pupils.

In 1891 Husserl published a *Philosophy of Arithmetic* (*Philosophie der Arithmetik*) in which he showed a certain tendency to psychologism, that is, to grounding logic on psychology. For example, the concept of multiplicity, which is essential for the concept of number, is grounded on the psychical act of binding together diverse contents of consciousness in one representation. This view was subjected to criticism by the celebrated mathematician and logician Gottlob Frege (1848–1925) and in his *Logical Investigations* (*Logische Untersuchungen*, 1900–1) Husserl maintained clearly that logic is not reducible to psychology.[7] Logic is concerned with the sphere of meaning, that is, with what is meant (*gemeint*) or intended, not with the succession of real psychical acts. In other words, we must distinguish between consciousness as a complex of psychical facts, events or experiences (*Erlebnisse*) and the objects of consciousness which are meant or intended. The latter 'appear' to or for consciousness: in this sense they are phenomena. The former, however, do not appear: they are lived through (*erlebt*) or experienced. Obviously, this does not mean that psychical acts cannot themselves be reduced to phenomena by reflection; but then, considered precisely as appearing to consciousness, they are no longer real psychical acts.

This involves a distinction between meanings and things, a distinction which is of considerable importance. For failure to make this distinction was one of the main reasons why the empiricists found it necessary to deny the existence of universal concepts or ideas. Things, including real psychical acts, are all individual or particular, whereas meanings can be universal. And as such they are 'essences'.

In the work which in its English translation bears the title *Ideas: General Introduction to Pure Phenomenology* (*Ideen zu einer reinen Phänomenologie und phänomenologischen Philosophie*, 1913) Husserl calls the act of consciousness *noesis* and its correlative object, which is meant or intended, *noema*. Further, he speaks of the intuition of essences (*Wesensschau*). In pure mathematics, for example, there is an intuition of essences which gives rise to propositions which are not empirical generalizations but belong to a different type, that of *a priori* propositions. And phenomenology in general is the descriptive analysis of essences or ideal structures. There could thus be, for example, a phenomenology of values. But there could also be a phenomenological analysis of the fundamental structures of consciousness, provided, of course, that these structures are 'reduced' to essences or *eidē*.

A point insisted on by Husserl is the suspension of judgment (the so-called *epoche*) in regard to the ontological or existential status or reference of the objects of consciousness. By means of this suspension existence is said to be 'bracketed'. Suppose, for example, that I wished to develop a phenomenological analysis of the aesthetic experience of beauty. I suspend all judgment about the subjectivity or objectivity of beauty in an ontological sense and direct my attention simply to the essential structure of aesthetic experience as 'appearing' to consciousness.

The reason why Husserl insists on this suspension of judgment can be seen by considering the implications of the title of one of his writings, *Philosophy as Strict Science* (*Philosophie als strenge Wissenschaft*, 1910–11). Like Descartes before him, Husserl wished to put philosophy on a firm basis. And in his opinion this meant going behind all presuppositions to that which one cannot doubt or question. Now, in ordinary life we make all sorts of existential assumptions, about, for instance, the existence of physical objects independently of consciousness. We must therefore prescind from or bracket this 'natural attitude' (*natürliche Einstellung*). It is not a question of saying that the natural attitude is wrong and its assumptions unjustified. It is a question of methodologically prescinding from such assumptions and going behind them to consciousness itself which it is impossible either to doubt or to prescind from. Further, we cannot, for example, profitably discuss the ontological status of values until we are quite clear what we are talking about, what value 'means'. And this is revealed by phenomenological analysis. Hence phenomenology is fundamental philosophy: it must precede and ground any ontological philosophy, any metaphysics.

As already hinted, Husserl's employment of the *epoche* bears a resemblance to Descartes' use of methodological doubt. And in point of fact Husserl saw in Descartes' philosophy a certain measure of anticipation of phenomenology. At the same time he insisted that the existence of a self in the sense of a spiritual substance or, as Descartes put it, a 'thinking thing' (*res cogitans*) must itself be bracketed. True, the ego cannot be simply eliminated. But the subject which is required as correlative to the object of consciousness is simply the pure or transcendental ego, the pure subject as such, not a spiritual substance or soul. The existence of such a substance is something about which we must suspend judgment, so far as pure phenomenology is concerned.

The methodological use of the *epoche* does not by itself commit Husserl to idealism. To say that the existence of consciousness is the only undeniable or indubitable existence is not necessarily to say that consciousness is the only existent. But in point of fact Husserl proceeds to make the transition to idealism by trying to deduce consciousness from the transcendental ego and by making the reality of the world relative to consciousness. Nothing can be conceived except as an object of consciousness. Hence the object must be constituted by consciousness.[8]

Already discernible in *Ideas*, this idealistic orientation of Husserl's thought became more marked in *Formal and Transcendental Logic* (*Formale und transzendentale Logik*, 1929) where logic and ontology tend to coincide, and in *Cartesian Meditations* (*Méditations cartésiennes*, 1931). It is understandable that this transition to idealism did not favour the acceptance by other phenomenologists of Husserl's original insistence on the *epoche*. Martin Heidegger, for example, decisively rejected the demand for the *epoche* and attempted to use the phenomenological method in the development of a non-idealistic philosophy of Being.

(iv) Phenomenological analysis is capable of fruitful application in a variety of fields. Alexander Pfänder (1870–1941) applied it in the field of psychology, Oskar Becker (b. 1889), a disciple of Husserl, in the philosophy of mathematics, Adolf Reinach (1883–1917) in the philosophy of law, Max Scheler (1874–1928) in the field of values, while others have applied it in the fields of aesthetics and the religious consciousness. But the use of the method does not necessarily mean that the user can be called a 'disciple' of Husserl. Scheler, for example, was an eminent philosopher in his own right. And phenomenological analysis has been practised by thinkers whose general philosophical position is markedly different from Husserl's. One has only to mention the French existentialists Jean-Paul Sartre (b. 1905) and Maurice Merleau-Ponty (b. 1908) or indeed the contemporary Thomists.

It is not unreasonable to argue that this widespread use of phenomenological analysis not only constitutes an eloquent testimony to its value but also shows that it is a unifying factor. At the same time it is also arguable that the fact that Husserl's demand for the *epoche* has generally been disregarded or rejected and that phenomenology has been used within the frameworks of different philosophies rather than as a foundation for a philosophy to put an end to conflicting systems shows that it has not fulfilled Husserl's original hopes. Besides, the nature of what is called phenomenological analysis can itself be called in question. For example, though the relations between continental phenomenology and the conceptual or 'linguistic' analysis practised in England is one of the main themes which permit a fruitful dialogue between groups of philosophers who in other respects may find it difficult to understand one another, one of the principal issues in such a dialogue is precisely the nature of what is called phenomenological analysis. Is it legitimate to speak of a phenomenological analysis of 'essences'? If so, in what precise sense? Is phenomenological analysis a specifically philosophical activity? Or does it fall apart into psychology on the one hand and so-called linguistic analysis on the other? We cannot discuss such questions here. But the fact that they can be raised suggests that Husserl was as over-optimistic as Descartes, Kant and Fichte before him in thinking that he had at last overcome the fragmentation of philosophy.

5. We have seen that at the turn of the century Neo-Kantianism was the dominant academic philosophy or *Schulphilosophie* in the German universities. And one obviously associates with this tradition a concern with the forms of thought and of the judgment rather than with objective categories of things. Yet it was a pupil of Cohen and Natorp at Marburg, namely Nicolai Hartmann (1882–1950), who expressed in his philosophy what we may call a return to things and developed an impressive realist ontology. And though it would be out of place to dwell here at any length on the ideas of a philosopher who belonged so definitely to the twentieth century, some general indication of his line of thought will serve to illustrate an important view of the nature and function of philosophy.

In his *Principles of a Metaphysics of Knowledge* (*Grundzüge einer Metaphysik der Erkenntnis*, 1921) Nicolai Hartmann passed from Neo-Kantianism to a realist theory of knowledge, and in subsequent publications he developed an ontology which took the form of an analysis of the categories of different modes or levels of being. Thus in his *Ethics* (*Ethik*, 1926) he devoted himself to a phenomenological study of values, which possess ideal being, while in *The Problem of Spiritual Being* (*Das Problem des geistigen Seins*, 1933) he considered the life of the human spirit both in its personal form and in its objectification. A *Contribution to the Foundation of Ontology* (*Zur Grundlegung der Ontologie*, 1935), *Possibility and Actuality* (*Möglichkeit und Wirklichkeit*, 1938), *The Construction of the Real World. Outline of the General Doctrine of Categories* (*Der Aufbau der realen Welt. Grundriss der allgemeinen Kategorienlehre*, 1940) and *New Ways in Ontology* (*Neue Wege der Ontologie*, 1941) represent general ontology, while in *Philosophy of Nature* (*Philosophie der Natur*, 1950) special attention is paid to the categories of the inorganic and organic levels.[9]

In general, therefore, Hartmann's thought moves from a study of the universal structural principles or categories of being, such as unity and multiplicity, persistence and becoming or change, to regional ontologies, that is, to the analysis of the specific categories of inorganic being, organic being and so on. And to this extent he distinguishes between being-there (*Dasein*) and being-thus-or-thus (*Sosein*). But his ontology takes throughout the form of a phenomenological analysis of the categories exemplified in the beings given in experience. The idea of subsistent being, in the sense of the infinite act of existence, *ipsum esse subsistens*, is entirely foreign to his thought. And any metaphysics of transcendent being, in the sense in which God is transcendent, is excluded. Indeed, metaphysics for Hartmann deals with insoluble problems, whereas ontology in his sense is perfectly capable of attaining definite results.

Hartmann's ontology, therefore, is an overcoming of Neo-Kantianism inasmuch as it involves a study of the objective categories of real being. It is an overcoming of positivism inasmuch as it assigns to philosophy a definite field of its own, namely the different levels or types of being considered precisely as such. And though Hartmann employs the method of phenomenological analysis, he is not involved in that restriction to a subjective sphere to which an observance of Husserl's *epoche* would have condemned him. At the same time his ontology is a doctrine of categories, not a metaphysics of Being (*das Sein*) as grounding beings (*die Seienden*). In his view scientific philosophy has no place for an inquiry into Being which goes beyond a study of beings as beings. There is indeed the ideal being of values which are recognized in varying degrees by the human mind. But though these values possess ideal reality, they do not, as such, exist. And existent beings are those which form the world.

6. (i) The recall of philosophy to the thought of Being (*das Sein*) is principally represented in contemporary German thought by that enigmatic thinker, Martin Heidegger (b. 1889). According to Heidegger the whole of western phi-

losophy has forgotten Being and immersed itself in the study of beings.[10] And the idea of Being has meant either an empty and indeterminate concept, obtained by thinking away all the determinate characteristics of beings, or the supreme being in the hierarchy of beings, namely God. Being as the Being of beings, as that which is veiled by beings and as that which grounds the duality of subject and object that is presupposed by the study of beings, is passed over and forgotten: it remains hidden, veiled. Heidegger asks, therefore, what is the meaning of Being? For him this is not a grammatical question. It is to ask for an unveiling of the Being of beings.

The very fact that man can ask this question shows, for Heidegger, that he has a pre-reflective sense of Being. And in the first part of *Being and Time* (*Sein und Zeit*, 1927) Heidegger sets out to give a phenomenological-ontological analysis of man as the being who is able to raise the question and who is thus open to Being. What he calls fundamental ontology thus becomes an existential analysis of man as 'existence' (*Dasein*). But though Heidegger's aim is in this way to bring Being to show itself, as it were, he never really gets further than man. And inasmuch as man's finitude and temporality are brought clearly to light, the work not unnaturally tends to give the impression, even if incorrect, that Being is for the author essentially finite and temporal. The second part of *Being and Time* has never been published.

In Heidegger's later writings we hear a great deal about man's openness to Being and of the need for keeping it alive, but it can hardly be said that he has succeeded in unveiling Being. Nor indeed would he claim to have done so. In fact, though Heidegger proclaims that the world in general and philosophers in particular have forgotten Being, he seems unable to explain clearly what they have forgotten or why this forgetfulness should be as disastrous as he says it is.

(ii) Heidegger's pronouncements about Being, as distinct from his existential analysis of man, are so oracular that they cannot be said to amount to a science of Being. The idea of metaphysics as a science of Being is most clearly maintained by the modern Thomists, especially by those who employ what they call the transcendental method. Inspired by Kant and, more particularly (inasmuch as Kant is concerned only with the transcendental deduction of the forms of thought) by German idealists such as Fichte, the transcendental method contains two main phases. To establish metaphysics as a science it is necessary to work backwards, as it were, to a foundation which cannot itself be called in question; and this is the reductive phase or moment.[11] The other phase consists in the systematic deduction of metaphysics from the ultimate starting-point.

In effect the transcendental method is used by the philosophers in question to establish Thomist metaphysics on a secure foundation and deduce it systematically, not to produce a new system of metaphysics as far as content is concerned, still less to discover startling new truths about the world. Hence to the outsider at least it seems to be a question of putting the same old wine into a new bottle. At the same time it is obvious that the question of scientific method inevitably tends to loom large and to grow in importance in proportion as emphasis is placed, as with the Thomists under discussion, on the task of converting man's unreflective and implicit apprehension of Being into systematically-grounded explicit knowledge.

7. This admittedly sketchy outline of some currents in thought in German philosophy during the first half of the twentieth century does not afford much ground for saying that the divergencies of systems and tendencies has been at last overcome. At the same time it suggests that in order to justify its claim to be more than a mere handmaid of the sciences philosophy must be metaphysical. If we assume that the aspects of the world under which it is considered by the particular sciences are the only aspects under which it can properly be considered, philosophy, if it is to continue to exist at all, must concern itself either with the logic and methodology of the sciences or with the analysis of ordinary language. For it obviously cannot compete with the sciences on their own ground. To have a field of its own other than analysis of the language of the sciences or of ordinary language, it must consider beings simply as beings. But if it confines itself, as with Nicolai Hartmann, to an inquiry into the categories of the different levels of finite being as revealed in experience, the crucial question of the being or existence of beings is

simply passed over. And unless this question is ruled out as meaningless, there can be no justification for this neglect. If, however, the question is once admitted as a genuine philosophical question, the problem of the Absolute comes once more into the foreground. And in the long run Schelling will be shown to be justified in claiming that no more important philosophical problem can be conceived than that of the relation of finite existence to the unconditioned Absolute.

This reference to Schelling is not equivalent to a demand for a return to German idealism. What I have in mind is this. Man is spirit-in-the-world. He is in the world not only as locally present in it but also as, by nature, involved in it. He finds himself in the world as dependent on other things for his life, for the satisfaction of his needs, for the material of his knowledge, for his activity. At the same time, by the very fact that he conceives himself as a being in the world he stands out from the world: he is not, as it were, totally immersed in the world-process. He is an historical being, but in the sense that he can objectify history he is a suprahistorical being. It is not, of course, possible to make a complete separation between these two aspects of man. He is a being in the world, a 'worldly' being, as standing out from the world; and he stands out from the world as a being in the world. Considered as spirit, as standing out from the world, he is able, and indeed impelled, to raise metaphysical problems, to seek a unity behind or underlying the subject-object situation. Considered as a being involved in the world, he is naturally inclined to regard these problems as empty and profitless. In the development of philosophical thought these divergent attitudes or tendencies recur, assuming different historical, and historically explicable, forms. Thus German idealism was one historically-conditioned form assumed by the metaphysical tendency or drive. Inductive metaphysics was another. And we can see the same fundamental tendency reasserting itself in different ways in the philosophies of Jaspers and Heidegger.

On the plane of philosophy each tendency or attitude seeks to justify itself theoretically. But the dialectic continues. I do not mean to imply that there is no means of discriminating between the proffered justifications. For example, inasmuch as man can objectify himself and treat himself as an object of scientific investigation, he is inclined to regard talk about his standing out from the world or as having a spiritual aspect as so much nonsense. Yet the mere fact that it is he who objectifies himself shows, as Fichte well saw, that he cannot be completely objectified, and that a phenomenalistic reduction of the self is uncritical and naïve. And once reflective thought understands this, metaphysics begins to reassert itself. Yet the pull of the 'worldly' aspect of man also reasserts itself, and insights once gained are lost sight of, only to be regained once more.

Obviously, reference to two tendencies or attitudes based on the dual nature of man would be a gross over-simplification if it were taken to be a sufficient key to the history of philosophy. For in explaining the actual development of philosophy very many factors have to be taken into account. Yet even if there is no simple repetition in history, it is only to be expected that persistent tendencies should constantly tend to recur in varying historical shapes. For, as Dilthey remarked, he who understands history also made history. The dialectic of philosophy reflects the complex nature of man.

The conclusion may appear to be pessimistic, namely that there is no very good reason to suppose that we shall ever reach universal and lasting agreement even about the scope of philosophy. But if fundamental disagreements spring from the very nature of man himself, we can hardly expect anything else but a dialectical movement, a recurrence of certain fundamental tendencies and attitudes in different historical shapes. This is what we have had hitherto, in spite of well-intentioned efforts to bring the process to a close. And it can hardly be called undue pessimism if one expects the continuation of the process in the future.

APPENDIX

A SHORT BIBLIOGRAPHY

General Works

Abbagnano, N. *Storia della filosofia*: II, *parte seconda*. Turin, 1950.

Adamson, R. *The Development of Modern Philosophy, with other Lectures and Essays*. Edinburgh, 1908 (2nd edition).

Alexander, A. B. D. *A Short History of Philosophy*. Glasgow, 1922 (3rd edition).

Bosanquet, B. *A History of Aesthetic*. London, 1892.

Bréhier, E. *Histoire de la philosophie*: II, *deuxième partie*. Paris, 1944. (Bréhier's work is one of the best histories of philosophy, and it contains brief, but useful, bibliographies.)

Histoire de la philosophie allemande. Paris, 1933 (2nd edition).

Castell, A. *An Introduction to Modern Philosophy in Six Problems*. New York, 1943.

Catlin, G. *A History of the Political Philosophers*. London, 1950.

Collins, J. *A History of Modern European Philosophy*. Milwaukee, 1954. (This work by a Thomist can be highly recommended. It contains useful bibliographies.)

God in Modern Philosophy. London, 1960. (In the relevant period this work contains treatments of Hegel, Feuerbach, Marx and Kierkegaard.)

De Ruggiero, G. *Storia della filosofia*: IV, *la filosofia moderna. L'età del romanticismo*. Bari, 1943.

Hegel. Bari, 1948.

Deussen, P. *Allgemeine Geschichte der Philosophie*: II, 3, *Neuere Philosophie von Descartes bis Schopenhauer*. Leipzig, 1922 (3rd edition).

Devaux, P. *De Thalès à Bergson. Introduction historique à la philosophie*. Liège, 1948.

Erdmann, J. E. A *History of Philosophy*: II, *Modern Philosophy*, translated by W. S. Hough. London, 1889, and subsequent editions.

Falckenberg, R. *Geschichte der neuern Philosophie*. Berlin, 1921 (8th edition).

Fischer, K. *Geschichte der neuern Philosophie*. 10 vols. Heidelberg, 1897–1904. (This work includes separate volumes on Fichte, Schelling, Hegel and Schopenhauer, as listed under these names.)

Fischl, J. *Geschichte der Philosophie*. 5 vols. III, *Aufklärung und deutscher Idealismus*. IV, *Positivismus und Materialismus*. Vienna, 1950.

Fuller, B. A. G. *A History of Philosophy*. New York, 1945 (revised edition).

Hegel, G. W. F. *Lectures on the History of Philosophy*, translated by E. S. Haldane and F. H. Simson. Vol. III. London, 1895. (Hegel's history of philosophy forms part of his system.)

Heimsoeth, H. *Metaphysik der Neuzeit*. Munich, 1929.

Hirschberger, J. *The History of Philosophy*, translated by A. Fuerst, 2 vols. Milwaukee, 1959. (The second volume treats of modern philosophy.)

Höffding, H. *A History of Philosophy* (modern), translated by B. E. Meyer, 2 vols. London, 1900 (American reprint, 1924).

  A Brief History of Modern Philosophy, translated by C. F. Sanders, London, 1912.

Jones, W. T. *A History of Western Philosophy*: II, *The Modern Mind*. New York, 1952.

Klimke, F., S.J. and Colomer, E., S.J. *Historia de la filosofía*. Barcelona, 1961 (3rd edition).

Marías, J. *Historia de la filosofía*. Madrid, 1941.

Meyer, H. *Geschichte der abendländischen Weltanschauung*: IV, *Von der Renaissance zum deutschen Idealismus*: V, *Die Weltanschauung der Gegenwart*. Würzburg, 1950.

Oesterreich, T. K. *Die deutsche Philosophie des XIX Jahrhunderts*. Berlin, 1923 (reproduction, 1953). (This is the fourth volume of the new revised edition of Ueberweg's *Grundriss der Geschichte der Philosophie*. It contains extensive bibliographies and is useful as a work of reference.)

Randall, H., Jr. *The Making of the Modern Mind*. Boston, 1940 (revised edition).

Rogers, A. K. *A Student's History of Philosophy*. New York, 1954 (3rd edition reprinted). (A straightforward textbook.)

Russell, Bertrand. *History of Western Philosophy and its connection with Political and Social Circumstances from the Earliest Times to the Present Day*. London, 1946, and reprints.

Wisdom of the West. An Historical Survey of Western Philosophy in its Social and Political Setting. London, 1959. (For German philosophy in the nineteenth century the last-named work is to be preferred to the first.)

Sabine, G. H. *A History of Political Theory*. London, 1941. (A valuable study of the subject.)

Schilling, K. *Geschichte der Philosophie: II, Die Neuzeit*. Munich, 1953. (Contains useful bibliographies.)

Souilhé, J. *La philosophie chrétienne de Descartes à nos jours*. 2 vols. Paris, 1934.

Thilly, F. *A History of Philosophy*, revised by L. Wood. New York, 1951.

Thonnard, F. J. *Précis d'histoire de la philosophie*. Paris, 1941 (revised edition).

Turner, W. *History of Philosophy*. Boston and London, 1903.

Vorländer, K. *Geschichte der Philosophie: II, Philosophie der Neuzeit*. Leipzig, 1919 (5th edition).

Webb, C. C. J. *A History of Philosophy*. (Home University Library.) London, 1915 and reprints.

Windelband, W. *A History of Philosophy, with especial reference to the Formation and Development of its Problems and Conceptions*, translated by J. A. Tufts. New York and London, 1952 (reprint of 1901 edition). (This notable work treats the history of philosophy according to the development of problems.)

Lehrbuch der Geschichte der Philosophie, edited by H. Heimsoeth with a concluding chapter, *Die Philosophie im 20 Jahrhundert mit einer Uebersicht über den Stand der philosophie-geschichtlichen Forschung.* Tübingen, 1935.

Wright, W. K. *A History of Modern Philosophy.* New York, 1941.

Chapters XIII–XIV: Schopenhauer

Texts

Werke, edited by J. Frauenstädt. 6 vols. Leipzig, 1873–4 (and subsequent editions). New edition by A. Hübscher, Leipzig, 1937–41.

Sämmtliche Werke, edited by P. Deussen and A. Hübscher. 16 vols. Munich, 1911–42.

On the Fourfold Root of the Principle of Sufficient Reason, and On the Will in Nature, translated by K. Hillebrand. London, 1907 (revised edition).

The World as Will and Idea, translated by R. B. Haldane and J. Kemp. 3 vols. London, 1906 (5th edition).

The Basis of Morality, translated by A. B. Bullock. London, 1903.

Selected Essays, translated by E. B. Bax. London, 1891.

Studies

Beer, M. *Schopenhauer.* London, 1914.

Caldwell, W. *Schopenhauer's System in Its Philosophical Significance.* Edinburgh, 1896.

Copleston, F. C., S.J. *Arthur Schopenhauer, Philosopher of Pessimism.* London, 1946.

Costa, A. *Il pensiero religioso di Arturo Schopenhauer.* Rome, 1935.

Covotti, A. *La vita a il pensiero di A. Schopenhauer.* Turin, 1909.

Cresson, A. *Schopenhauer.* Paris, 1946.

Faggin, A. *Schopenhauer, il mistico senza Dio.* Florence, 1951.

Fauconnet, A. *L'ésthetique de Schopenhauer.* Paris, 1913.

Frauenstädt, J. *Schopenhauer-Lexikon.* 2 vols. Leipzig, 1871.

Grisebach, E. *Schopenhauer.* Berlin, 1897.

Hasse, H. *Schopenhauers Erkenntnislehre.* Leipzig, 1913.

Hübscher, A. *Arthur Schopenhauer. Ein Lebensbild.* Wiesbaden, 1949 (2nd edition).

Knox, I. *Aesthetic Theories of Kant, Hegel and Schopenhauer.* New York, 1936.

McGill, V. J. *Schopenhauer, Pessimist and Pagan.* New York, 1931.

Méry, M. *Essai sur la causalité phénoménale selon Schopenhauer.* Paris, 1948.

Neugebauer, P. *Schopenhauer in England, mit besonderer Berüktsichtigung seines Einflusses auf die englische Literatur.* Berlin, 1931.

Padovani, U. A. *Arturo Schopenhauer: L'ambiente, la vita, le opere.* Milan, 1934.

Robot, T. *La philosophie de Schopenhauer.* Paris, 1874.

Ruyssen, T. *Schopenhauer.* Paris, 1911.

Sartorelli, F. *Il pessimismo di Arturo Schopenhauer, con particolare riferimento alla dottrina del diritto e dello Stato.* Milan, 1951.

Schneider, W. *Schopenhauer.* Vienna, 1937.

Seillière, E. *Schopenhauer.* Paris, 1912.

Simmel, G. *Schopenhauer und Nietzsche.* Leipzig, 1907.

Siwek, P., S.J. *The Philosophy of Evil* (Ch. X). New York, 1951.

Volkelt, J. *Arthur Schopenhauer, seine Persönlichkeit, seine Lehre, seine Glaube.* Stuttgart, 1907 (3rd edition).

Wallace, W. *Schopenhauer.* London, 1891.

Whittaker, T. *Schopenhauer.* London, 1909.

Zimmern, H. *Schopenhauer: His Life and Philosophy.* London, 1932 (revised edition). (A short introduction.)

Zint, H. *Schopenhauer als Erlebnis.* Munich and Basel, 1954.

Chapter XV: Feuerbach

Texts

Sämmtliche Werke, edited by L. Feuerbach (the philosopher himself). 10 vols. Leipzig, 1846–66.

Sämmtliche Werke, edited by W. Bolin and F. Jodl. 10 vols. Stuttgart, 1903–11.

The Essence of Christianity, translated by G. Eliot. New

York, 1957. (London, 1881, 2nd edition, with translator's name given as M. Evans.)

Studies

Arvon, H. *Ludwig Feuerbach ou la transformation du sacré.* Paris, 1957.

Bolin, W. *Ludwig Feuerbach, sein Wirken und seine Zeitgenossen.* Stuttgart, 1891.

Chamberlin, W. B. *Heaven Wasn't His Destination: The Philosophy of Ludwig Feuerbach.* London, 1941.

Engels, F. *Ludwig Feuerbach and the Outcome of Classical German Philosophy.* (Contained in *Karl Marx, Selected Works,* edited by C. P. Dutt. See under Marx and Engels.)

Grégoire, F. *Aux Sources de la pensée de Marx, Hegel, Feuerbach.* Louvain, 1947.

Grün, K. *Ludwig Feuerbach in seinem Briefwechsel und Nachlass.* 2 vols. Leipzig, 1874.

Jodl, F. *Ludwig Feuerbach.* Stuttgart, 1904.

Lévy, A. *La philosophie de Feuerbach et son influence sur la littérature allemande.* Paris, 1904.

Lombardi, F. *Ludwig Feuerbach.* Florence, 1935.

Löwith, K. *Von Hegel bis Nietzsche.* Zürich, 1941.

Nüdling, G. *Ludwig Feuerbachs Religionsphilosophie.* Paderborn, 1936.

Rawidowicz, S. *Ludwig Feuerbachs Philosophie.* Berlin, 1931.

Schilling, W. *Feuerbach und die Religion.* Munich, 1957.

Secco, L. *L'etica nella filosofia di Feuerbach.* Padua, 1936.

Chapter XVI: Marx and Engels

Texts

Marx-Engels, Historisch-kritische Gesamtausgabe: Werke, Schriften, Briefe, edited by D. Ryazanov (from 1931 by V. Adoratsky). Moscow and Berlin. This critical edition, planned to contain some 42 vols., was undertaken by the Marx-Engels Institute in Moscow. It remains, however, sadly incomplete. Between 1926 and 1935 there appeared 7 vols. of the writings of Marx and Engels, with a special volume to commemorate the fortieth anniversary of Engels' death. And between 1929 and 1931 there appeared 4 vols. of correspondence between Marx and Engels.

Karl Marx–Friedrich Engels, Werke. 5 vols. Berlin, 1957–9. This edition, based on the one mentioned above, covers the writings of Marx and Engels up to November 1848. It is published by the Dietz Verlag. And a large number of the works of Marx and Engels have been reissued in this publisher's Library of Marxism-Leninism (*Bücherei des Marximus-Leninismus*).

Gesammelte Schriften von Karl Marx und Friedrich Engels, 1852–1862, edited by D. Ryazanov. 2 vols. Stuttgart, 1920 (2nd edition). (Four volumes were contemplated.)

Aus dem literarischen Nachlass von Karl Marx, Friedrich Engels und Friedrich Lassalle, 1841–1850, edited by F. Mehring. 4 vols. Berlin and Stuttgart, 1923 (4th edition).

Karl Marx. Die Frühschriften, edited by S. Landshut. Stuttgart, 1953.

Der Briefwechsel zwischen F. Engels und K. Marx, edited by A. Bebel and E. Bernstein. 4 vols. Stuttgart, 1913.

A number of the writings of Marx and Engels have been translated into English for the Foreign Languages Publishing House in Moscow and have been published in London (Lawrence and Wishart). For example: Marx's *The Poverty of Philosophy* (1956), Engels' *Anti-Dühring* (1959, 2nd edition) and *Dialectics of Nature* (1954), and *The Holy Family* (1957) by Marx and Engels.

Of older translations one can mention the following. Marx: *A Contribution to the Critique of Political Economy* (New York, 1904); *Selected Essays,* translated by H. J. Stenning (London and New York, 1926); *The Poverty of Philosophy* (New York, 1936). Engels: *The Origin of the Family, Private Property and the State* (Chicago, 1902); *Ludwig Feuerbach* (New York, 1934); *Herr Dühring's Revolution in Science,* i.e. *Anti-Dühring* (London, 1935). Marx and Engels: *The German Ideology* (London, 1938).

There are several English translations of *Capital*. For example: *Capital*, revised and amplified according to the 4th German edition by E. Untermann (New York, 1906), and the two-volume edition of *Capital* in the Everyman Library (London), introduced by G. D. H. Cole and translated from the 4th German edition by E. and C. Paul.

Of the English editions of *The Communist Manifesto* we can mention that by H. J. Laski: *Communist Manifesto: Socialist Landmark*, with an introduction (London, 1948).

Other Writings

Marx-Engels. Selected Correspondence. London, 1934.

Karl Marx. Selected Works, edited by C. P. Dutt. 2 vols. London and New York, 1936, and subsequent editions.

Karl Marx. Selected Writings in Sociology and Social Philosophy, edited by T. Bottomore and M. Rubel. London, 1956.

Three Essays by Karl Marx, translated by R. Stone. New York, 1947.

Karl Marx and Friedrich Engels. Basic Writings on Politics and Philosophy, edited by L. S. Feuer. New York, 1959.

Studies

Acton, H. B. *The Illusion of the Epoch, Marxism-Leninism as a Philosophical Creed*. London, 1955. (An excellent criticism.)

Adams, H. P. *Karl Marx in His Earlier Writings*. London, 1940.

Adler, M. *Marx als Denker*. Berlin, 1908.

   Engels als Denker. Berlin, 1921.

Aron, H. *Le marxisme*. Paris, 1955.

Aron, R., and Others. *De Marx au Marxisme*. Paris, 1948.

Baas, E. *L'humanisme marxiste*. Paris, 1947.

Barbu, Z. *Le développement de la pensée dialectique*. (By a Marxist.) Paris, 1947.

Bartoli, H. *La doctrine économique et sociale de Karl Marx*. Paris, 1950.

Beer, M. *Life and Teaching of Karl Marx*, translated by T. C.

Partington and H. J. Stenning. London, 1934 (reprint).

Bekker, K. *Marxs philosophische Entwicklung, sein Verhältnis zu Hegel.* Zürich, 1940.

Berdiaeff, N. *Christianity and Class War.* London, 1934.

The Origin of Russian Communism. London, 1937.

Berlin, I. *Karl Marx.* London, 1939 and subsequent editions. (A useful small biographical study.)

Bober, M. *Karl Marx's Interpretation of History.* Cambridge (U.S.A.), 1927.

Bohm-Bawerk, E. von. *Karl Marx and The Close of His System.* London, 1898.

Boudin, L. B. *Theoretical System of Karl Marx in the Light of Recent Criticism.* Chicago, 1907.

Bouquet, A. C. *Karl Marx and His Doctrine.* London and New York, 1950. (A small work published by the S.P.C.K.)

Calvez, J.-V. *La pensée de Karl Marx.* Paris, 1956. (An outstanding study of Marx's thought.)

Carr, H. *Karl Marx. A Study in Fanaticism.* London, 1934.

Cornu, A. *Karl Marx, sa vie et son œuvre.* Paris, 1934.

The Origins of Marxian Thought. Springfield (Illinois), 1957.

Cottier, G. M.-M. *L'athéisme du jeune Marx: ses origines hégéliennes.* Paris, 1959.

Croce, B. *Historical Materialism and the Economics of Karl Marx,* translated by C. M. Meredith. Chicago, 1914.

Desroches, H. C. *Signification du marxisme.* Paris, 1949.

Drahn, E. *Friedrich Engels.* Vienna and Berlin, 1920.

Gentile, G. *La filosofia di Marx.* Milan, 1955 (new edition).

Gignoux, C. J. *Karl Marx.* Paris, 1950.

Grégoire, F. *Aux sources de la pensée de Marx: Hegel, Feuerbach.* Louvain, 1947.

Haubtmann, P. *Marx et Proudhon: leurs rapports personels, 1844–47.* Paris, 1947.

Hook, S. *Towards the Understanding of Karl Marx.* New York, 1933.

From Hegel to Marx. New York, 1936.

Marx and the Marxists. Princeton, 1955.

Hyppolite, J. *Études sur Marx et Hegel.* Paris, 1955.

Joseph, H. W. B. *Marx's Theory of Value.* London, 1923.

Kamenka, E. *The Ethical Foundations of Marxism*. London, 1962.

Kautsky, K. *Die historische Leistung von Karl Marx*. Berlin, 1908.

Laski, H. J. *Karl Marx*. London, 1922.

Lefebvre, H. *Le matérialisme dialectique*. Paris, 1949 (3rd edition).
Le marxisme. Paris, 1958. (By a Marxist author.)

Leff, G. *The Tyranny of Concepts: A Critique of Marxism*. London, 1961.

Lenin, V. I. *The Teachings of Karl Marx*. New York, 1930.
Marx, Engels, Marxism. London, 1936.

Liebknecht, W. *Karl Marx, Biographical Memoirs*. Chicago, 1901.

Loria, A. *Karl Marx*. New York, 1920.

Löwith, K. *Von Hegel bis Nietzsche*. Zürich, 1947.

Lunau, H. *Karl Marx und die Wirklichkeit*. Brussels, 1937.

Marcuse, H. *Reason and Revolution*. London, 1941.

Mandolfo, R. *Il materialismo storico in Friedrich Engels*. Genoa, 1912.

Mascolo, D. *Le communisme*. Paris, 1953. (By a Marxist.)

Mayer, G. *Friedrich Engels*. 2 vols. The Hague, 1934 (2nd edition).

Mehring, F. *Karl Marx: the Story of His Life*, translated by E. Fitzgerald. London, 1936. (The standard biography.)

Meyer, A. G. *Marxism. The Unity of Theory and Practice. A Critical Essay*. Cambridge (U.S.A.) and Oxford, 1954.

Nicolaievsky, N. *Karl Marx*. Philadelphia, 1936.

Olgiati, F. *Carlo Marx*. Milan, 1953 (6th edition).

Pischel, G. *Marx giovane*. Milan, 1948.

Plenge, J. *Marx und Hegel*. Tübingen, 1911.

Robinson, J. *An Essay in Marxian Economics*. London, 1942.

Rubel, M. *Karl Marx. Essai de biographie intellectuelle*. Paris, 1957.

Ryazanov, D. *Karl Marx and Friedrich Engels*. New York, 1927.
Karl Marx, Man, Thinker and Revolutionist. London, 1927.

Schlesinger, R. *Marx: His Time and Ours*. London, 1950.

Schwarzschild, L. *Karl Marx*. Paris, 1950.

Seeger, R. *Friedrich Engels*. Halle, 1935.

Somerhausen, L. *L'humanisme agissant de Karl Marx*. Paris, 1946.

Spargo, J. *Karl Marx. His Life and Work*. New York, 1910.

Tönnies, F. *Marx. Leben und Lehre*. Jena, 1921.

Touilleux, P. *Introduction aux systèmes de Marx et Hegel*. Tournai, 1960.

Tucker, R. C. *Philosophy and Myth in Karl Marx*. Cambridge, 1961.

Turner, J. K. *Karl Marx*. New York, 1941.

Vancourt, R. *Marxisme et pensée chrétienne*. Paris, 1948.

Van Overbergh, C. *Karl Marx, sa vie et son œuvre. Bilan du marxisme*. Brussels, 1948 (2nd edition).

Vorländer, K. *Kant und Marx*. Tübingen, 1911.

　Marx Engels und Lassalle als Philosophen. Stuttgart, 1920.

Wetter, G. A. *Dialectical Materialism* (based on 4th German edition). London, 1959. (This outstanding work is devoted mainly to the development of Marxism-Leninism in the Soviet Union. But the author treats first of Marx and Engels.)

Chapter XVII: Kierkegaard

Texts

Samlede Vaerker, edited by A. B. Drachmann, J. L. Herberg and H. O. Lange. 14 vols. Copenhagen, 1901–6. A critical Danish edition of Kierkegaard's *Complete Works* is being edited by N. Thulstrup. Copenhagen, 1951 ff. A German translation of this edition is being published concurrently at Cologne and Olten. (There are, of course, previous German editions of Kierkegaard's writings.)

Papirer (*Journals*), edited by P. A. Heiberg, V. Kuhr and E. Torsting. 20 vols. (11 vols. in 20 parts). Copenhagen, 1909–48.

Breve (*Letters*), edited by N. Thulstrup. 2 vols. Copenhagen, 1954.

　There is a Danish *Anthology* of Kierkegaard's writings, S. *Kierkegaard's Vaerker i Udvalg*, edited by F. J. Billeskov-Jansen. 4 vols. Copenhagen, 1950 (2nd edition).

　English translations, mainly by D. F. Swenson and W.

Lowrie, of Kierkegaard's more important writings are published by the Oxford University Press and the Princeton University Press. Exclusive of the Journals (mentioned separately below) there are 12 vols. up to date, 1936–53. Further references to individual volumes are made in the footnotes to the chapter on Kierkegaard in this book.

Johannes Climacus, translated by T. H. Croxall. London, 1958.

Works of Love, translated by H. and E. Hong. London, 1962.

Journals (selections), translated by A. Dru. London and New York, 1938 (also obtainable in Fontana Paperbacks).

A *Kierkegaard Anthology*, edited by R. Bretall. London and Princeton, 1946.

Diario, with introduction and notes by C. Fabro (3 vols., Brescia, 1949–52), is a useful Italian edition of selections from Kierkegaard's *Journals* by an author who has also published an *Antologia Kierkegaardiana*, Turin, 1952.

Studies

Bense, M. *Hegel und Kierkegaard*. Cologne and Krefeld, 1948.

Bohlin, T. *Sören Kierkegaard, l'homme et l'œuvre*, translated by P. H. Tisseau. Bazoges-en-Pareds, 1941.

Brandes, G. *Sören Kierkegaard*. Copenhagen, 1879.

Cantoni, R. *La coscienza inquieta: S. Kierkegaard*. Milan, 1949.

Castelli, E. (editor). Various Authors. *Kierkegaard e Nietzsche*. Rome, 1953.

Chestov, L. *Kierkegaard et la philosophie existentielle*, translated from the Russian by T. Rageot and B. de Schoezer. Paris, 1948.

Collins, J. *The Mind of Kierkegaard*. Chicago, 1953.

Croxall, T. H. *Kierkegaard Commentary*. London, 1956.

Diem, H. *Die Existenzdialektik von S. Kierkegaard*. Zürich, 1950.

Fabro, C. *Tra Kierkegaard e Marx*. Florence, 1952.

Fabro, C., and Others. *Studi Kierkegaardiani*. Brescia, 1957.

Friedmann, K. *Kierkegaard, the Analysis of His Psychological Personality*. London, 1947.

Geismar, E. *Sören Kierkegaard. Seine Lebensentwicklung und seine Wirksamkeit als Schriftsteller.* Göttingen, 1927.

Lectures on the Religious Thought of Sören Kierkegaard. Minneapolis, 1937.

Haecker, T. *Sören Kierkegaard,* translated by A. Dru. London and New York, 1937.

Hirsch, E. *Kierkegaardstudien.* 2 vols. Gütersloh, 1930–3.

Höffding, H. *Sören Kierkegaard als Philosoph.* Stuttgart, 1896.

Hohlenberg, J. *Kierkegaard.* Basel, 1949.

Jolivet, R. *Introduction to Kierkegaard,* translated by W. H. Barber. New York, 1951.

Lombardi, F. *Sören Kierkegaard.* Florence, 1936.

Lowrie, W. *Kierkegaard.* London, 1938. (A very full bibliographical treatment.)

Short Life of Kierkegaard. London and Princeton, 1942.

Martin, H. V. *Kierkegaard the Melancholy Dane.* New York, 1950.

Masi, G. *La determinazione de la possibilità dell' esistenza in Kierkegaard.* Bologna, 1949.

Mesnard, P. *Le vrai visage de Kierkegaard.* Paris, 1948.

Kierkegaard, sa vie, son œuvre, avec un exposé de sa philosophie. Paris, 1954.

Patrick, D. *Pascal and Kierkegaard.* 2 vols. London, 1947.

Roos, H., S.J. *Kierkegaard et le catholicisme,* translated from the Danish by A. Renard, O.S.B. Louvain, 1955.

Schremf, C. *Kierkegaard.* 2 vols. Stockholm, 1935.

Sieber, F. *Der Begriff der Mitteilung bei Sören Kierkegaard.* Würzburg, 1939.

Thomte, R. *Kierkegaard's Philosophy of Religion.* London and Princeton, 1948.

Wahl, J. *Études kierkegaardiennes.* Paris, 1948 (2nd edition).

Chapters XXI–XXII: Nietzsche

Texts

A complete critical edition of Nietzsche's writings and correspondence, *Nietzsches Werke und Briefe, histo-*

risch-kritische Ausgabe, was begun at Munich in 1933 under the auspices of the Nietzsche-Archiv. Five volumes of the *Werke* (comprising the *juvenilia*) appeared between 1933 and 1940, and four volumes of the *Briefe* between 1938 and 1942. But the enterprise does not seem to be making much progress.

Gesammelte Werke, Grossoktav Ausgabe. 19 vols. Leipzig 1901–13. In 1926 R. Oehler's *Nietzsche-Register* was added as a 20th vol.

Gesammelte Werke, Musarionausgabe. 23 vols. Munich, 1920–9.

Werke, edited by K. Schlechta. 3 vols. Munich, 1954–6. (Obviously incomplete, but a handy edition of Nietzsche's main writings, with lengthy selections from the *Nachlass*.)

There are other German editions of Nietzsche's *Works*, such as the *Taschenausgabe* published at Leipzig.

Gesammelte Briefe. 5 vols. Berlin and Leipzig, 1901–9. A volume of correspondence with Overbeck was added in 1916. And some volumes, such as the correspondence with Rohde, have been published separately.

The Complete Works of Friedrich Nietzsche, translated under the general editorship of O. Levy. 18 vols. London, 1909–13. (This edition is not complete in the sense of containing the *juvenilia* and the whole *Nachlass*. Nor are the translations above criticism. But it is the only edition of comparable scope in the English language.)

Some of Nietzsche's writings are published in *The Modern Library Giant*, New York. And there is the *Portable Nietzsche*, translated by W. A. Kaufmann. New York, 1954.

Selected Letters of Friedrich Nietzsche, edited by O. Levy. London, 1921.

The Nietzsche-Wagner Correspondence, edited by E. Förster-Nietzsche. London, 1922.

Friedrich Nietzsche. Unpublished Letters. Translated and edited by K. F. Leidecker. New York, 1959.

Studies

Andler, C. *Nietzsche: sa vie et sa pensée.* 6 vols. Paris, 1920–31.

Banfi, A. *Nietzsche*. Milan, 1934.

Bataille, G. *Sur Nietzsche. Volonté de puissance*. Paris, 1945.

Bäumler, A. *Nietzsche der Philosoph und Politiker*. Berlin, 1931.

Benz, E. *Nietzsches Ideen zur Geschichte des Christentums*. Stuttgart, 1938.

Bertram, E. *Nietzsche. Versuch einer Mythologie*. Berlin, 1920 (3rd edition).

Bianquis, G. *Nietzsche en France*. Paris, 1929.

Bindschedler, M. *Nietzsche und die poetische Lüge*. Basel, 1954.

Brandes, G. *Friedrich Nietzsche*. London, 1914.

Brinton, C. *Nietzsche*. Cambridge (U.S.A.) and London, 1941.

Brock, W. *Nietzsches Idee der Kultur*. Bonn, 1930.

Chatterton Hill, G. *The Philosophy of Nietzsche*. London, 1912.

Copleston, F. C., S.J. *Friedrich Nietzsche, Philosopher of Culture*. London, 1942.

Cresson, A. *Nietzsche, sa vie, son œuvre, sa philosophie*. Paris, 1943.

Deussen, P. *Erinnerungen an Friedrich Nietzsche*. Leipzig, 1901.

Dolson, G. N. *The Philosophy of Friedrich Nietzsche*. New York, 1901.

Drews, A. *Nietzsches Philosophie*. Heidelberg, 1904.

Förster-Nietzsche, E. *Das Leben Friedrich Nietzsches*. 2 vols. in 3. Leipzig, 1895–1904.

Der junge Nietzsche. Leipzig, 1912.

Der einsame Nietzsche. Leipzig, 1913. (These books by Nietzsche's sister have to be used with care, as she had several axes to grind.)

Gawronsky, D. *Friedrich Nietzsche und das Dritte Reich*. Bern, 1935.

Goetz, K. A. *Nietzsche als Ausnahme. Zur Zerstörung des Willens zur Macht*. Freiburg, 1949.

Giusso, L. *Nietzsche*. Milan, 1943.

Halévy, D. *Life of Nietzsche*. London, 1911.

Heidegger, M. *Nietzsche*. 2 vols. Pfulligen, 1961.

Jaspers, K. *Nietzsche: Einführung in das Verständnis seines*

Philosophierens. Berlin, 1936. (The two last-mentioned books are profound studies in which, as one might expect, the respective philosophical positions of the writers govern the interpretations of Nietzsche.)

Joël, K. *Nietzsche und die Romantik.* Jena, 1905.

Kaufmann, W. A. *Nietzsche: Philosopher, Psychologist, Antichrist.* Princeton, 1950.

Klages, L. *Die psychologischen Errungenschaften Nietzsches.* Leipzig, 1930 (2nd edition).

Knight, A. H. J. *Some Aspects of the Life and Work of Nietzsche, and particularly of His Connection with Greek Literature and Thought.* Cambridge, 1933.

Lannoy, J. C. *Nietzsche ou l'histoire d'un égocentricisme athée.* Paris, 1952. (Contains a useful bibliography, pp. 365–92.)

Lavrin, J. *Nietzsche. An Approach.* London, 1948.

Lea, F. A. *The Tragic Philosopher. A Study of Friedrich Nietzsche.* London, 1957. (A sympathetic study by a believing Christian.)

Lefebvre, H. *Nietzsche.* Paris, 1939.

Lombardi, R. *Federico Nietzsche.* Rome, 1945.

Lotz, J. B., S.J. *Zwischen Seligkeit und Verdamnis. Ein Beitrag zu dem Thema: Nietzsche und das Christentum.* Frankfurt a. M., 1953.

Löwith, K. *Von Hegel bis Nietzsche.* Zürich, 1941.

Nietzsches Philosophie der ewigen Wiederkehr des Gleichen. Stuttgart, 1956.

Ludovici, A. M. *Nietzsche, His Life and Works.* London, 1910.

Nietzsche and Art. London, 1912.

Mencken, H. L. *The Philosophy of Friedrich Nietzsche.* London, 1909.

Mess, F. *Nietzsche als Gesetzgeber.* Leipzig, 1931.

Miéville, H. L. *Nietzsche et la volonté de puissance.* Lausanne, 1934.

Mittasch, A. *Friedrich Nietzsche als Naturphilosoph.* Stuttgart, 1952.

Molina, E. *Nietzsche, dionisiaco y asceta.* Santiago (Chile), 1944.

Morgan, G. A., Jr. *What Nietzsche Means*. Cambridge (U.S.A.), 1941. (An excellent study.)

Mügge, M. A. *Friedrich Nietzsche: His Life and Work*. London, 1909.

Oehler, R. *Nietzsches philosophisches Werden*. Munich, 1926.

Orestano, F. *Le idee fondamentali di Friedrich Nietzsche nel loro progressivo svolgimento*. Palermo, 1903.

Paci, E. *Federico Nietzsche*. Milan, 1940.

Podach, E. H. *The Madness of Nietzsche*. London, 1936.

Reininger, F. *Friedrich Nietzsches Kampf um den Sinn des Lebens*. Vienna, 1922.

Reyburn, H. A., with the collaboration of H. B. Hinderks and J. G. Taylor. *Nietzsche: The Story of a Human philosopher*. London, 1948. (A good psychological study of Nietzsche.)

Richter, R. *Friedrich Nietzsche*. Leipzig, 1903.

Riehl, A. *Friedrich Nietzsche, der Künstler und der Denker*. Stuttgart, 1920 (6th edition).

Römer, H. *Nietzsche*. 2 vols. Leipzig, 1921.

Siegmund, G. *Nietzsche, der 'Atheist' und 'Antichrist'*. Paderborn, 1946 (4th edition).

Simmel, G. *Schopenhauer und Nietzsche*. Leipzig, 1907.

Steinbüchel, T. *Friedrich Nietzsche*. Stuttgart, 1946.

Thibon, G. *Nietzsche ou le déclin de l'esprit*. Lyons, 1948.

Vaihinger, H. *Nietzsche als Philosoph*. Berlin, 1905 (3rd edition).

Wolff, P. *Nietzsche und das christliche Ethos*. Regensburg, 1940.

Wright, W. H. *What Nietzsche Taught*. New York, 1915. (Mainly excerpts.)

NOTES

CHAPTER TWELVE

1 Modern logicians rightly look with disfavour on the psychologizing of logic. But the tendency to do this was connected, however mistakenly, with the notion that it was the expression of a scientific attitude.

2 I am speaking, of course, simply of Bradley's view that our ordinary ways of conceiving and describing things give rise to contradictions, whereas reality itself is a harmonious whole without any contradiction. On the issue between pluralism and monism there is a great difference between Herbart and the British absolute idealist.

3 Given the psychology outlined above, Herbart does not accept the theory of liberty of indifference. Indeed, he regards the theory as incompatible with the idea of a stable and firm character, the development of which is one of the principal aims of education. But he recognizes, of course, a psychological difference between choosing in accordance with conviction or conscience and being led by impulse or desire to act in a manner contrary to one's conscience.

4 For instance, he blames Kant for introducing the term 'experience' at the beginning of the first *Critique* without any adequate and unambiguous explanation of the meaning which he attaches to it.

5 *Theory of Science* (2nd edition, Leipzig, 1929), p. 77.

CHAPTER THIRTEEN

1 W, I, p. 4. References to Schopenhauer's *Works* are given according to volume and page of the edition by J. Frauenstädt (1877).

2 W, I, p. 5.

3 Complete in the sense that such presentations comprise both the form and the matter of phenomena. In other words, it is not a question here of abstract concepts.

4 W, I, p. 34.

5 W, I, p. 105.

6 The implication of this is that Hegel's identification of logic with metaphysics, in the sense of the science of the Absolute, is absurd.

7 W, I, p. 105.

8 W, I, p. 130.

9 W, I, p. 131.

10 W, I, p. 133.

11 W, I, p. 140.

12 W, I, p. 145.

13 W, II, p. 3; HK, I, p. 3. In references to *The World as Will and Idea HK* signifies the English translation by R. B. Haldane and J. Kemp.

14 W, II, p. 7; HK, I, p. 7.

15 W, III, pp. 19–20; HK, II, p. 181.

16 Schopenhauer liked to regard his philosophy of the Will as a development of Kant's doctrine of the primacy of the practical reason or rational will. But the former's metaphysical voluntarism was really foreign to the latter's mind. It was Schopenhauer's original creation.

17 W, III, p. 89; *HK*, II, p. 258.

18 W, II, p. 66; *HK*, I, p. 72.

19 An obvious line of objection is that there is an element of putting the cart before the horse in all this. It might be claimed, that is to say, that it is precisely because man possesses the power of reasoning that he is able to extend the scope and number of his wants and desires.

20 W, III, p. 80; *HK*, II, p. 248.

21 W, VI, p. 96. From *Parerga und Paralipomena*.

22 W, III, p. 219; *HK*, II, p. 406.

23 W, II, p. 323; *HK*, I, p. 354.

24 W, II, p. 195; *HK*, I, p. 213.

25 W, III, p. 403; *HK*, III, p. 111.

26 W, II, p. 376; *HK*, I, pp. 411–12.

27 *Ibid.*

28 W, III, p. 663; *HK*, III, p. 388.

CHAPTER FOURTEEN

1 W, II, p. 199; *HK*, I, p. 219.

2 W, III, p. 417; *HK*, III, p. 123.

3 W, II, pp. 209–10; *HK*, I, p. 230.

4 Following Kant, Schopenhauer distinguishes between the dynamical and the mathematically sublime. The man in the boat is contemplating an example of the first type. The mathematically sublime is the statically immense, a great range of mountains, for instance.

5 For instance, Homer does not simply talk about the sea or the dawn but brings the ideas nearer to the level of perception by the use of epithets such as 'wine-dark' and 'rosy-fingered'.

6 W, II, p. 298; *HK*, I, p. 326.

7 It is for this reason that Schopenhauer condemns imitative music, mentioning Haydn's *Seasons* as an example.

8 W, VI, p. 230. From *Parerga und Paralipomena*.

9 W, II, p. 415; *HK*, I, p. 454.

10 W, II, p. 416; *HK*, I, p. 454.

11 W, II, p. 444; *HK*, I, p. 485.

12 W, II, p. 339; *HK*, I, p. 371.

13 W, II, p. 487; *HK*, I, p. 532.

14 W, II, p. 486; *HK*, I, p. 531.

15 Cp. W, II, p. 485 and III, pp. 221–2; *HK*, I, p. 530 and II, p. 408.

16 W, II, p. 486; *HK*, I, p. 531.

17 Nietzsche, during the halcyon days of their friendship, gave Wagner every encouragement to think this.

CHAPTER FIFTEEN

1 W, II, p. 180. References to Feuerbach's writings are given according to volume and page of the second edition of his *Works* by Friedrich Jodl (Stuttgart, 1959–60).

2 W, II, p. 175.

3 W, II, p. 231.

4 Feuerbach, like Schelling, assumes that Hegel deduces existent Nature from the logical Idea. If this is not assumed, the criticism loses its point.

[5] W, II, p. 239.
[6] W, II, p. 240.
[7] W, VII, p. 434.
[8] W, VII, p. 438.
[9] W, VI, p. 3.
[10] W, VI, p. 17.
[11] W, VI, p. 41.
[12] W, II, p. 244.
[13] Ibid.
[14] W, II, p. 239.
[15] Ibid.
[16] W, II, p. 245.
[17] W, VI, p. 40.
[18] W, II, p. 319.
[19] W, II, p. 321.
[20] W, II, p. 318.
[21] W, II, p. 220.
[22] W, II, p. 219.
[23] W, II, p. 244.
[24] W, II, p. 221.
[25] Stirner's obscure remarks about 'creative nothing' recall to mind certain aspects of Heidegger's thought.

CHAPTER SIXTEEN

[1] Das Kapital, I, p. xvii (Hamburg, 1922); Capital, II, p. 873 (London, Everyman).
[2] Ludwig Feuerbach, p. 44 (Stuttgart, 1888); Ludwig Feuerbach, edited by C. P. Dutt with an introduction by L. Rudas, p. 53 (London, no date).
[3] Ludwig Feuerbach, pp. 12–13 (p. 28). When a translated work is referred to more than once, on all occasions but the first I give the pagination of the translation in parentheses, without repeating the title.
[4] It is true that in the Science of Logic Hegel passes from the category of quality to that of quantity, but when dealing with measure he speaks of nodal points at which a series of quantitative variations is succeeded by an abrupt qualitative change, a leap. This is succeeded in turn by further quantitative variations until a new nodal point is reached.
[5] Zur Kritik der politischen Oekonomie, p. xi (Stuttgart, 1897); Marx-Engels: Selected Works, I, p. 363 (London, 1958).
[6] Ludwig Feuerbach, p. 45 (p. 54).
[7] Das Kapital, I, p. 140 (I, pp. 169–70).
[8] Deutsche Ideologie, W, III, p. 28; The German Ideology, p. 16 (Parts I and III, translated by W. Lough and C. P. Magill, London, 1942). In references W signifies the edition of the Works of Marx and Engels published by Dietz Verlag, Berlin, 1957 f.
[9] Anti-Dühring, p. xv (Stuttgart, 1919); Anti-Dühring, p. 17 (London, 1959, 2nd edition).
[10] Ibid.
[11] Dialektik der Natur, p. 53 (Berlin, 1952); Dialectics of Nature, p. 83 (London, 1954).
[12] Anti-Dühring, p. 138 (p. 187).
[13] Strictly speaking, there are for Engels three fields of application. 'Dialectics is nothing else but the science of the general laws of movement and development in Nature, human society and thought'; Anti-Dühring, p. 144 (p. 193).
[14] Ludwig Feuerbach, p. 4 (p. 21).
[15] Anti-Dühring, p. 81 (p. 122).
[16] Zur Kritik der politischen Oekonomie, p. x (I, p. 363).

[17] Cf. *Das Kapital*, i, p. 143 (i, pp. 172–3).

[18] *Deutsche Ideologie*, W, iii, p. 20 (p. 7).

[19] *Ibid.*, p. 30 (p. 18).

[20] In *The Poverty of Philosophy* Marx says explicitly that the revolutionary proletariat is the greatest of all productive forces. See below, p. 98.

[21] *Zur Kritik der politischen Oekonomie*, p. x (i, p. 363).

[22] *Ibid.*, p. xi (i, p. 363).

[23] *Ibid.*

[24] *Manifest der kommunistischen Partei*, W, iv, p. 462; *Communist Manifesto*, p. 125 (edit. H. J. Laski, London, 1948). Obviously, this refers to all known history after the passing of primitive communism.

[25] That is to say, the class war is looked on as more fundamental, and national wars are interpreted in economic terms.

[26] This is what Marx says in the *Communist Manifesto* which dates, it should be remembered, from the beginning of 1848.

[27] W, iv, p. 181; *The Poverty of Philosophy*, edited by C. P. Dutt and V. Chattopadhyaya, p. 146 (London, no date); p. 174 (London, 1956).

[28] *Anti-Dühring*, p. 144 (p. 193).

[29] *Dialektik der Natur*, p. 28 (p. 54).

[30] It is probably Engels, with his extension of the dialectic to Nature, who provides most ground for a mechanical interpretation.

[31] The lines of criticism suggested are not, of course, in any way new. They are familiar enough to 'bourgeois' philosophers, that is to say, to objective observers.

CHAPTER SEVENTEEN

[1] As a boy, Kierkegaard's father had tended sheep on a Jutland heath. One day, afflicted with hunger, cold and loneliness, he had cursed God. And this incident was indelibly printed on his memory.

[2] I do not mean to imply that Kierkegaard had ever led what would be generally understood by a thoroughly immoral life. It was more a question of a change of interior attitude from a rejection to an acceptance of ethical self-commitment.

[3] *The Point of View*, p. 114 (translated by W. Lowrie, London, 1939).

[4] *Ibid*, pp. 88–9, in Note.

[5] See, for example, *The Sickness unto Death*, pp. 73–4 (translated by W. Lowrie, Princeton and London, 1941).

[6] This is discussed, for instance, in the first volume of *Either-Or* and in the first part of *Stages on Life's Way*.

[7] *The Sickness unto Death*, p. 67.

[8] *Fear and Trembling*, p. 109 (translated by R. Payne, London, 1939).

[9] *The Sickness unto Death*, p. 216.

[10] *Fear and Trembling*, p. 171.

[11] *The Sickness unto Death*, p. 192.

[12] *Concluding Unscientific Postscript*, p. 213 (translated by D. F. Swenson, Princeton and London, 1941).

13 *The Sickness unto Death*, p. 151.

14 *Concluding Unscientific Postscript*, p. 182.

15 *Ibid.*

16 *Ibid.*

17 We have to remember that for Kierkegaard faith is a self-commitment to the absolute and transcendent Thou, the personal God, rather than to propositions.

18 *Concluding Unscientific Postscript*, p. 448.

19 *Ibid.*, p. 368.

20 *Ibid.*, p. 350.

21 *Ibid.*, p. 84.

22 *Ibid.*, p. 85.

23 The Germans speak of *Angst*, the French of *angoisse*. Some English writers have employed 'anguish' or even 'anxiety'. I have retained 'dread'. In any case 'fear' should be avoided, for a reason explained in the text.

24 *The Concept of Dread*, p. 38 (translated by W. Lowrie, Princeton and London, 1944).

25 *Ibid.*

26 *Ibid.*, p. 139.

27 *Ibid.*, p. 40.

28 'The opposite of sin is not virtue but faith'; *The Sickness unto Death*, p. 132.

29 *The Concept of Dread*, p. 141.

30 Some of these, it is true, have repudiated the label. But we cannot discuss this matter here. In any case, 'existentialism', unless it is confined to the philosophy of M. Sartre, is a portmanteau term.

31 Jaspers is a professional philosopher and a university professor, whereas it is difficult to imagine the eccentric and passionate Danish thinker as the occupant of any chair. But the life and thought of Kierkegaard (as of Nietzsche) has been for Jaspers a subject of prolonged meditation.

CHAPTER EIGHTEEN

1 *Die Welträtsel*, p. 10 (Leipzig, 1908 edition).

2 *Ibid.*, p. 239.

3 *Ibid.*

4 *Ibid.*, pp. 140, 217 and 240.

5 *Ibid.*, p. 218. If Haeckel were still alive, he would doubtless express appreciation of the ethical ideas of Professor Julian Huxley.

6 *Der Monismus*, p. 27 (Stuttgart, 1905 edition).

7 *Gott-Natur*, p. 38 (Leipzig, 1914).

8 *Ibid.*

9 The Society's guiding idea was that of science as providing a way of life.

10 Mach rejects the concept of the ego as a spiritual substance standing over against Nature and interprets the self as a complex of phenomena which are continuous with Nature. But he does not work out this theory in any thorough-going manner, and he admits that the ego is the bond which unites experience.

11 The neopositivist attempted to transform phenomenalism from an ontological into a linguistic theory by saying that the statement that physical objects are sense-data means that a sentence in which a physical object is mentioned can be translated into a sentence or sentences in which only sense-data are mentioned, in such a way

that if the original sentence is true (or false) the translation will be true (or false) and *vice versa*. But I do not think that this attempt proved to be successful.

CHAPTER NINETEEN

[1] In his *System of Philosophy* the idea of God is discussed in the second volume. Cf. also *The Concept of Religion in the System of Philosophy* (*Der Begriff der Religion im System der Philosophie*, Giessen, 1915). The idea of God is depicted as the unifying ideal of truth and perfection.

[2] *System der Philosophie*, I, p. 15 (Berlin, 1922, 3rd edition). The term *Geisteswissenschaften* will be discussed later.

[3] *Ibid.*, p. 9. Cohen is obviously referring to metaphysics in the sense in which Kant accepted metaphysics.

[4] *System der Philosophie*, II, p. 1 (Berlin, 1921, 3rd edition).

[5] *Ibid.*, p. 620.

[6] *System der Philosophie*, III, p. 4 (Berlin, 1922).

[7] *Philosophie*, p. 13 (Göttingen, 1921, 3rd edition).

[8] Windelband, the well-known historian of philosophy, occupied chairs successively at Zürich, Freiburg and Strasbourg. In 1903 he was nominated professor of philosophy at Heidelberg. He was the first major figure of the so-called Baden School.

[9] *Einleitung in die Philosophie*, p. 390 (Tübingen, 1914).

[10] In his *System of Philosophy* (*System der Philosophie*, 1921) Rickert attempts to classify values in six groups or spheres; the values of logic (truth values), aesthetics (values of beauty), mysticism (values of impersonal sanctity or holiness), ethics (moral values), erotics (values of happiness) and religion (values of personal sanctity).

[11] In his *History and Natural Science* (*Geschichte und Naturwissenschaft*, 1894).

[12] A science is not 'idiographic' by reason simply of the fact that it treats of human beings. Empirical psychology, for instance, treats of human beings, but it is none the less a 'nomothetic' science. In Scholastic language, the distinction is formal rather than material.

[13] To do Vaihinger justice, it must be added that he endeavours to sort out the different ways in which the concepts of 'as-if' and 'fiction' operate. He does not simply throw the principles of logic, scientific hypotheses and religious doctrines indiscriminately into the same basket.

[14] According to Riehl, a philosophy which deserves to be called scientific must confine itself to the critique of knowledge as realized in the natural sciences. He did not, of course, deny the importance of values in human life; but he insisted that recognition of them is not, properly speaking, a cognitive act and falls outside the scope of scientific philosophy.

[15] *Gesammelte Schiften*, VII, p. 79. This collection of Dilthey's Works will be referred to hereafter as GS.

[16] GS, VII, p. 70.

[17] In the science of physiol-

ogy man regards himself from an impersonal and external point of view as a physical object, as part of Nature.

[18] GS, VII, p. 161.

[19] Dilthey was influenced by Hegel's concept of 'objective spirit'. But his own use of the term is obviously somewhat different from that of Hegel who classified art and religion under the heading of 'absolute spirit'. Hegel's use of the term is connected, of course, with his idealist metaphysics, for which Dilthey had no use. Further, Dilthey rejected what he regarded as Hegel's *a priori* methods of interpreting history and human culture.

[20] *Auf dem Verhältnis von Erlebnis, Ausdruck und Verstehen; GS*, VII, p. 131.

[21] GS, VII, p. 232.

[22] *Ibid.*

[23] GS, VII, p. 233.

[24] *Ibid.*

[25] GS, VII, p. 278.

CHAPTER TWENTY

[1] As a youth Fechner went through an atheistic phase, but a book by Oken, one of Schelling's disciples, convinced him that materialism and atheism were by no means entailed by an acceptance of exact science.

[2] In 1848 Fechner published *Nanna, or the Soul-Life of Plants* (*Nanna, oder das Seelenleben der Pflanzen*).

[3] Happiness for Fechner does not mean simply sense-pleasure. It includes joy in the beautiful, the good and the true and in the religious feeling of union with God.

[4] Cf. *Die Tagesansicht gegenüber der Nachtansicht*, 1879.

[5] Some of his medico-psychological publications, such as his *Medical Psychology or Physiology of the Soul* (*Medizinische Psychologie oder Physiologie der Seele*, 1852) are of importance for his philosophy.

[6] *Mikrokosmus*, Bk. I, ch. 3, sect. 1 (in 5th German edition, Leipzig, 1896–1909, I, p. 58).

[7] *System der Philosophie*, II, p. 447 (Leipzig, 1912; Bk. 2, ch. 8, sect. 229).

[8] *Ibid.*, p. 481 (sect. 243).

[9] When discussing the traditional proofs of God's existence, Lotze remarks that the immediate moral conviction that that which is greatest, most beautiful and most worthy has reality lies at the foundation of the ontological argument, just as it is the factor which carries the teleological argument far beyond any conclusions which could be logically derived from its assumptions. *Mikrokosmus*, Bk. IX, ch. 4, sect. 2 (5th German edition, III, p. 561).

[10] *Mikrokosmus*, Bk. IX, ch. 4, sect. 3 (5th German edition, III, p. 569).

[11] An enlarged edition in 3 vols. appeared in 1919–21.

[12] A two-volume edition appeared in 1919.

[13] In epistemology Driesch was influenced by Kant, but he departed from Kantian doctrine by attributing an objective character to the categories, such as to render possible a metaphysics of reality.

[14] At school Eucken came under the influence of a certain Wilhelm Reuter who was a dis-

ciple of the philosopher Krause.

[15] *Einführung in eine Philosophie des Geisteslebens*, p. 9 (Leipzig, 1908).

[16] *Ibid.*, p. 8.

[17] *Grundlinien einer neuen Lebensanschauung*, p. 117 (Leipzig, 1907).

[18] *Der Wahrheitsgehalt der Religion*, p. 138 (Leipzig, 1905, 2nd edition).

[19] *Ibid.*, p. 150.

[20] *Einführung in eine Philosophie des Geisteslebens*, p. 10.

[21] *Ibid.*, p. 155.

[22] Accused by the Church of rationalism, Günther submitted to her judgment.

[23] Froschhammer, who refused to submit to ecclesiastical authority when his views were censured, was later one of the opponents of the dogma of papal infallibility.

[24] Mercier was not concerned simply with showing that Thomism did not conflict with the sciences. He envisaged the development of Thomism in close connection with the positive and purely objective study of the sciences. An eminent representative of the fulfilment of Mercier's project is the Louvain psychologist Albert Michotte (b. 1881).

CHAPTER TWENTY-ONE

[1] The university of Leipzig thereupon conferred the degree without examination.

[2] Nietzsche thought, no doubt rightly, that Wagner regarded him as a tool to promote the cause of Wagnerism. But he also came to feel that the real Wagner was not all that he had imagined him to be. The publication of *Parsifal* was for Nietzsche the last straw.

[3] The fifth part of *Joyful Wisdom* was not added until 1887.

[4] Rudolf Carnap remarks that when Nietzsche wished to take to metaphysics, he very properly had recourse to poetry. Carnap thus looks on *Zarathustra* as empirical confirmation of his own neopositivist interpretation of the nature of metaphysics.

[5] Nietzsche was indeed dogged by bad health and insomnia. And loneliness and neglect preyed on his mind. But it seems probable, in spite of his sister's attempts to deny it, that as a university student he contracted a syphilitic infection and that the disease, after running an atypical course, finally affected the brain.

[6] W, III, p. 919 (XV, p. 49). Unless otherwise stated, references are given according to volume and page of the three-volume (incomplete) edition of Nietzsche's *Works* by K. Schlechta (Munich, 1954–6). The references in parentheses are always to the English translation of Nietzsche's *Works* edited by Dr. Oscar Levy (see Bibliography). The critical German edition of Nietzsche's writings is still unfinished.

[7] In his *Nietzsche: Einführung in das Verständnis seines Philosophierens* (Berlin 1936). For Jaspers Nietzsche and Kierkegaard represent two 'exceptions', two embodiments of different possibilities of human existence.

[8] According to Nietzsche, the tragedies of Aeschylus were the

supreme artistic expression of this fusion.

9 W, I, p. 140 (I, p. 8).

10 W, I, p. 282 (II, p. 96).

11 W, I, p. 313 (II, p. 137).

12 In *Schopenhauer as Educator* Nietzsche remarks that 'Christianity is certainly one of the purest manifestations of that impulse towards culture and, precisely, towards the ever renewed production of the saint'; W, I, p. 332 (II, p. 161). But he goes on to argue that Christianity has been used to turn the mill-wheels of the State and that it has become hopelessly degenerate. It is clear that he regards the Christian religion as a spent force. Looking back later on *The Birth of Tragedy* he sees in its silence about Christianity a hostile silence. For the book in question recognized only aesthetic values, which, Nietzsche maintains, Christianity denies.

13 W, I, p. 379 (I, p. 120).

14 W, I, p. 502 (VII/1, p. 92).

15 W, I, p. 900 (VII/2, p. 221).

16 W, I, p. 483 (VII/1, p. 64).

17 W, II, p. 730 (V, p. 227).

18 W, II, p. 782 (XIII, p. 34).

19 The general philosophy of life which these judgments require as a background will be considered later.

20 W, II, pp. 205–6 (X, pp. 275–6).

21 W, II, p. 978 (XVI, p. 43).

22 W, II, p. 1178 (XVI, p. 146). Nietzsche is speaking specifically of the Christian concept of God.

23 Nietzsche does occasionally say something in favour of Christian values. But his admissions are by no means always calculated to afford consolation to Christians. For instance, while admitting that Christianity has developed the sense of truth and the ideal of love, he insists that the sense of truth ultimately turns against the Christian interpretation of reality and the ideal of love against the Christian idea of God.

24 W, II, p. 1072 (XVII, p. 12).

25 W, III, p. 852 (IX, p. 9).

26 *Ibid.*

27 W, II, p. 1153 (XVII, p. 132).

28 W, III, p. 881 (IX, p. 5).

CHAPTER TWENTY-TWO

1 W, III, p. 917 (XV, p. 432).

2 W, II, p. 578 (V, p. 20).

3 W, II, p. 601 (V, p. 52).

4 *Ibid.*

5 W, III, p. 751 (XV, p. 11).

6 W, III, p. 440 (XV, p. 105).

7 W, III, p. 844 (XV, p. 20).

8 W, II, p. 116 (X, p. 153).

9 W, II, p. 119 (X, p. 157).

10 W, III, p. 443 (XV, pp. 21–2).

11 W, I, pp. 878–9 (VII/2, p. 192).

12 No doubt, Nietzsche would admit this in principle, while insisting that his interpretation of the world was the expression of a higher form of the Will to Power. But what is the standard of higher and lower?

13 Mastery is not to be understood, of course, in a vulgarly utilitarian sense. Knowledge itself is mastery, an expression of the Will to Power.

14 W, III, p. 778 (xv, p. 120).

15 W, III, p. 874 (xv, p. 123).

16 W, III, p. 458 (xv, p. 124).

17 W, III, p. 889 (xv, p. 127).

18 W, III, pp. 748–9 (xv, p. 159).

19 W, x, p. 105 (xv, p. 295). The first reference here is not to the Schlechta edition but to the *Taschen-Ausgabe* published by A. Kroner of Stuttgart, the date of the volume in question being 1921.

20 W, III, p. 829 (xv, p. 296).

21 W, III, p. 709 (xv, pp. 302–3).

22 W, II, p. 313 (IV, p. 54).

23 W, III, p. 440 (xv, p. 387).

24 W, II, p. 445 (IV, p. 241).

25 W, II, p. 280 (IV, p. 7).

26 W, II, p. 281 (IV, p. 9).

27 W, III, p. 422 (xv, p. 380).

28 W, II, p. 1128 (XVII, p. 96).

29 *Ibid.*

30 W, II, p. 617 (v, p. 74).

31 W, II, p. 467 (IV, p. 270).

32 W, II, p. 474 (IV, p. 280).

33 W, III, p. 861 (xv, p. 427).

34 W, III, p. 704 (xv, p. 430).

35 Obviously, similar remarks can be made about Freud's concept of *libido*.

36 To claim that a professed atheist was 'really' a believer simply because he attacked theism persistently and vehemently would be extravagant and paradoxical. But Nietzsche, who as a boy was profoundly religious, was never indifferent to the problems of Being and of the meaning or purpose of existence. Further, his dialogue, as it were, with Christ, culminating in the final words of *Ecce Homo*, '*Dionysus versus the Crucified*', shows clearly enough that 'the Antichrist' had to do violence to himself, even if he thought of it as a case of transcending his own inclinations to weakness. In spite of his rejection of God he was very far from being what would generally be thought of as an 'irreligious man'.

37 Nietzsche insists indeed that his main objection against Christianity is against the system of morals and values. At the same time he joins Christianity with German idealism, which he regards as a derivative of Christianity or as a masked form of it, in his attack on the view that the world has a given meaning or goal.

38 Unless indeed we understand by a yea-saying attitude an acceptance of the fact of differences between the strong and the weak, as opposed to an attempt to set all on the same level. But in this case a yea-saying attitude should also involve acceptance of the fact that the majority sets limits to the activities of the independent rebels.

CHAPTER TWENTY-THREE

1 This view naturally brings to mind Fichte's statement that the kind of philosophy which a man chooses depends on the kind of man that he is. But even if we prescind from the fact that

Fichte did not intend this statement to be understood in a sense which would exclude the concept of philosophy as a science and see in it an anticipation of the tendency to subordinate the concept of truth to the concept of human life or existence, in tracing the concrete development of this tendency we find it splitting up into different conceptions of man and of human life and existence. One has only to mention the names of Kierkegaard and Nietzsche, for example.

2 That is to say, the statement might be expressive and evocative of emotive attitudes, thus possessing 'emotive' significance; but according to strict neopositivist principles it would be meaningless in the sense that it would be incapable of being either true or false.

3 A bibliography of neopositivism is provided in *Logical Positivism* (an anthology), edited by A. J. Ayer, Glencoe, Ill., and London, 1959. Some writings illustrating the discussion of the principle of verifiability, together with a selected bibliography, can be found in *A Modern Introduction to Philosophy* edited by P. Edwards and A. Pap, pp. 543–621, Glencoe, Ill. 1957. Cf. also *Contemporary Philosophy*, by F. C. Copleston, pp. 26–60, London, 1956, for a critical discussion of neopositivism.

4 As a sympathetic study one can recommend *Karl Jaspers et la philosophie de l'existence*, by M. Dufrenne and P. Ricoeur, Paris, 1947.

5 The term 'philosophy of existence' suggests that *Existenz* constitutes this field. But Jaspers insists more on Being, the illumination of 'existence' being the path to the awareness of Being. Being, however, is not a field for scientific investigation by philosophy, though the philosopher may be able to reawaken or keep alive the awareness of Being.

6 Among other writings we can mention *On the Origin of Moral Knowledge* (*Vom Ursprung der sittlichen Erkenntnis*, 1889), *On the Future of Philosophy* (*Ueber die Zukunft der Philosophie*, 1893) and *The Four Phases of Philosophy* (*Die vier Phasen der Philosophie*, 1895).

7 In his rejection of psychologism Husserl was probably influenced not only by Frege but also by Bolzano (see pp. 19–23).

8 Constituting an object can mean making it an object *for* consciousness. And this does not necessarily mean idealism. Or it can be taken to refer to a creative activity by which things are given the only reality they possess, namely as related to consciousness, as consciousness-dependent. It is the transition to this second meaning which involves idealism.

9 We can also mention the posthumously-published works, *Teleological Thought* (*Teleologisches Denken*, 1951) and *Aesthetics* (*Aesthetik*, 1953), a study of beauty and aesthetic values.

10 Obviously, Nicolai Hartmann is included in this judgment.

11 Some see the proper starting-point in an analysis of the judgment as an act of absolute affirmation. So, for example, J.

B. Lotz in *Das Urteil und das Sein. Eine Grundlegung der Metaphysik* (Pullach bei München, 1957) and *Metaphysica operationis humanae methodo transcendentali explicata* (Rome, 1958). Others go behind the judgment to the *question*, what is the ultimate foundation of all knowledge and judgment? So E. Coreth in *Metaphysik. Eine methodisch-systematische Grundlegung* (Innsbruck, Vienna and Munich, 1961).

INDEX

(Asterisked numbers refer to bibliographical information. References in ordinary type to a continuous series of pages, e.g. 195–98, do not necessarily indicate continuous treatment. References to two persons together are usually under the person criticized or influenced. Note abbreviations given in italics, e.g. *B*, are referred to the pages explaining them.)

OTHER IMAGE BOOKS

These prices subject to change without notice

OTHER IMAGE BOOKS

These prices subject to change without notice

OTHER IMAGE BOOKS

These prices subject to change without notice

OTHER IMAGE BOOKS

CHRISTIAN COMMUNITY: Response to Reality – Bernard J. Cooke (D315) – $1.45
THE JESUS MYTH – Andrew M. Greeley (D316) – $1.45
THE SURVIVAL OF DOGMA – Avery Dulles, S.J. (D317) – $1.75
CONTEMPLATION IN A WORLD OF ACTION – Thomas Merton (D321) – $2.45
AN AUGUSTINE READER (An Image Original) – Edited with an Intro. by John J. O'Meara (D322) – $2.45
HOPE IS THE REMEDY – Bernard Häring, C.Ss.R. (D323) – $1.25
SEX: THOUGHTS FOR CONTEMPORARY CHRISTIANS – Edited by Michael J. Taylor, S.J. (D324) – $1.45
WE ARE FUTURE – Ladislaus Boros, S.J. (D326) – $1.45
THE NEW SEXUALITY: Myths, Fables and Hang-ups – Eugene C. Kennedy (D328) – $1.45
CATHOLIC AMERICA – John Cogley (D332) – $1.75
PROTESTANTISM – Martin E. Marty (D334) – $2.45
OUR PRAYER – Louis Evely (D338) – $1.45
A RELIGION FOR OUR TIME – Louis Evely (D339) – $1.45
A THOMAS MERTON READER – Revised Edition – Ed. by Thomas P. McDonnell (D341) – $2.95
THE MYSTERY OF SUFFERING AND DEATH – Edited by Michael J. Taylor, S.J. (D342) – $1.75
THOMAS MERTON ON PRAYER – John J. Higgins (D345) – $1.75
IN THE CHRISTIAN SPIRIT – Louis Evely (D348) – $1.45
THE SINAI MYTH – Andrew M. Greeley (D350) – $1.75

These prices subject to change without notice